Same-Sex Marriage

Same-Sex Marriage

The Legal and Psychological Evolution in America

Donald J. Cantor,

Elizabeth Cantor,

James C. Black,

and Campbell D. Barrett

Wesleyan University Press | Middletown, Connecticut

Published by Wesleyan University Press, Middletown, CT 06459
www.wesleyan.edu/wespress

Printed in the United States of America

5   4   3   2   1

ISBN 0-8195-6812-0 cloth

Design by Chris Crochetière
Set in Minion type by BW&A Books, Inc., Durham, N.C.

Cataloging-in-Publication Data appear on the last
printed page of the book.

To Patricia Cantor,
who has shown me how much is lost
if marriage is unavailable.

—DJC

To Paul,
who shares with me the peace, joy,
and passion that marriage can bring.

—EC

To my wife, Monica McCabe-Black,
whose encouragement and steadfast patience
have made my contribution to this work possible.

—JCB

To Suzanna,
my wife and best friend,
for her enduring patience, support, and wit.

—CDB

Contents

Preface

American sexual law and the United States Constitution were barely acquainted forty years ago. What Americans were allowed to do sexually in the 1960s was the province of the state legislatures, and they were not lax in issuing proscriptions. Americans could not have sexual relations with a person to whom they were not wed—admitting to having a "significant other" would have been confessing to a crime. Statutes not only prohibited the ways in which homosexuals had sexual activity but often penalized these acts between heterosexuals, even, occasionally, if the heterosexuals were married to each other.

State legislatures attempted to exert control over American sexuality in a number of ways. Many state statutes made it unlawful for persons of different races to marry; persons in many states were barred from using birth control materials even if they were married and perused such materials in their homes; state statutes barred people from having in their homes reading matter deemed obscene; abortion was proscribed. The control that the states exercised over marriage included the means of terminating marriage, that is, the law of divorce, a body of precepts that embodied the philosophy that divorce was available not if the marriage had ceased to be viable but rather only to persons whose deportment during marriage had made them worthy of freedom. Those statutes had the effect of keeping marriages legally intact when one or often both parties desperately wanted them to end.

America has changed, and American law has changed, not with a big bang, but incrementally, so that today we stand at the door of constitutionally protected marriage between homosexual persons. How we got here and what should be done now that we are here are the twin subjects of this work. We know that the legal and philosophical evolution that has occurred over the last forty years involves more complex causes than the fields of law and psychology can explain, but these are the disciplines that we practice and understand and feel sufficient to present the issue. We believe that same-sex marriage is mandated by social justice, is consistent with the best interests of America's children, and is constitutionally consistent with antecedent rulings.

Chapter 1 traces the evolution in Supreme Court decisions over the past forty years toward leaving private, consensual, adult sexual decisions to the participants rather than the government. It explains the philosophical and constitutional reasons why same-sex marriage seems on the verge of becoming a constitutional right.

Chapter 2 illustrates the pronounced changes in sexual law that over the past forty years have originated not in the minds of "activist judges" but in the various state legislatures. These changes parallel, and are philosophically consistent with, the evolution described in chapter 1.

Chapter 3 reviews the history of theories of the origin of homosexuality and demonstrates how they have only recently been based in scientific evidence rather than religious doctrine or personal opinion. A detailed examination of the evolution of thinking within psychology and psychiatry reveals how important the role of psychologists and psychiatrists has been in first perpetuating myths about homosexuality and then helping shift public opinion by focusing efforts on sound empirical investigation.

Chapter 4 reviews the research on gay and lesbian families and illustrates that children raised by gay and lesbian parents are as well-adjusted as their peers raised in heterosexually parented homes, that gay and lesbian parents are no less capable parents than their heterosexual counterparts, and that homosexual couples function similarly to heterosexual couples. There is no empirically sound research that suggests that children born to, or raised by, gay or lesbian parents are at risk for social, emotional, academic, or sexual difficulties. In chapter 5, a psychiatrist, expert in the area of child placement in custody litigation, gives his opinion that children born to or raised by gay or lesbian parents will develop as healthfully as those raised by heterosexual parents.

Chapter 6 shows how the evolution in thought has affected the law of adoption, with the result that gays and lesbians desirous of adopting and raising children are now, on the whole, qualified to do so. Chapter 7 looks at the law defining marriage and explores the recent trend to expand the definition of marriage to include same-sex partners, both in the United States and abroad. Marriage carries with it an enormous number of both federal and state rights and benefits. Chapter 8 outlines the extent to which these benefits affect and assist those who marry and the losses and deprivations caused to those who cannot marry.

To those who believe in same-sex marriage by instinct alone, we invite you to learn what has transpired so that your opinion rests on fact. To those who oppose same-sex marriage by instinct alone, we invite you to test your conclusions by understanding what the last forty years have taught us all. And to those whose minds are open on this culturally divisive issue, we invite your attention to our efforts as you formulate your view.

A Note on Definitions

Many words and terms have been used to describe individuals who are sexually attracted to people of the same gender. The term *homosexual* was first used by sexologists in the nineteenth century, and the term refers to both men and women with a same-gender sexual orientation. Today, however, the terms *homosexual* and *homosexuality* are often used in scientific writing, but the terms *lesbian* (female homosexual) and *gay* (male homosexual) are preferred terms in the community. However, *gay* can refer to both men and women (e.g., the gay community). In this book, *gay* is used to refer to gay men, and *lesbian* is used for women. A person who is attracted to the opposite gender is referred to as *heterosexual*. A person who is attracted to both genders is referred to as *bisexual*. A person who has had surgery to change his or her gender is referred to as a *transsexual*, and it does not presuppose sexual attraction to either gender. The term *sexual preference* is not used, since it presumes choice; instead, the more accurate term *sexual orientation* is used to refer to the category of people one is sexually attracted to. Thus a person's sexual orientation can be heterosexual, homosexual, or bisexual. It is important to note that being gay or lesbian or heterosexual implies sexual attraction, but it also includes the drive toward a full loving relationship with someone of a specific gender. Although these terms also imply discrete categories, it is the case that they exist on a continuum, so that individuals may have, for example, a stronger or more primary heterosexual orientation while still experiencing some homosexual attraction, and vice versa.

1

The U.S. Supreme Court:
Five Cases and One Anomaly

Donald J. Cantor

Because life is a continuum and every event is the product of preceding events, it is always inaccurate to pick a single date or event and claim that a political or social movement started then. Some events, however, are so momentous that they can serve as appropriate starting points to trace the effects of the philosophies, or the changes in philosophies, that these events represent. Therefore when we set out to show how the United States Supreme Court has come to seem poised to find same-sex marriage a constitutional right, we are fortunate in having five major cases that illustrate and explain this journey.

The case that is our genesis, the one of momentous importance, is the matter of *Griswold et al. v. Connecticut.*[1] Estelle Griswold was the executive director of the Planned Parenthood League of Connecticut. Her coappellant, Dr. Lee Buxton, was a licensed physician who was a professor at Yale Medical School and also medical director for the Planned Parenthood League at its center in New Haven, Connecticut. The center had opened on November 1, 1961. On November 10, 1961, Mrs. Griswold and Dr. Buxton were arrested. Their alleged crime was giving information, instruction, and medical advice to *married* persons about the means of preventing conception. They did this by examining the wife and then presenting the best contraceptive device or material for her to use. The wives were generally charged fees, but some were assisted without charge.

The author gratefully acknowledges the assistance of Jonathan Cantor, J.D., for his prompt, professional, and essential legal research throughout the book.

I

Connecticut had at this time, and of course Mrs. Griswold and Dr. Buxton were aware of it, a statute that explicitly made it criminal for "any person" to use "any drug, medicinal article or instrument for the purpose of preventing conception."[2] An additional statute of general application made it criminal to assist another to commit any criminal offense.[3] They were convicted as accessories and fined $100 each. Their convictions were affirmed by the Appellate Division of the Circuit Court and then by the Connecticut Supreme Court. Key to this case was the fact that when the statute referred to "any person," it included any married person as well.

There were five opinions offered by the justices in *Griswold*. The court's opinion was authored by Justice Douglas; Justice Goldberg wrote a separate concurring opinion, as did Justice Harlan. Justices Stewart and Black dissented.

The court's judgment was that the Connecticut statute was unconstitutional. The court's reasoning can be summarized thus:

1. The First Amendment has been construed previously to include "the right to educate one's children as one chooses" and to include "the right to study the German language in a private school."[4] The right of freedom of speech and press includes the peripheral rights, not expressly enunciated in the First Amendment, to expand available knowledge, to inquire, to think, to teach, and to freely and privately associate.

2. These rights flow from the First Amendment, although they are not specifically articulated in it. They represent zones-of-privacy guarantees that emanate from the specific rights that *are* articulated in the First Amendment.

3. Similar rights of privacy are to be inferred from the penumbras of the Third, Fourth, Fifth, and Ninth Amendments. When the Fourth Amendment specifically grants "the right of the people to be secure in their persons, houses, papers and effects against unreasonable searches and seizures," the court reasoned that the right of privacy so created would also bar a police search of marital bedrooms for the purpose of discovering contraceptive use. The Third and Fifth Amendments similarly create areas of privacy that derive from the Third Amendment's proscription of the quartering of soldiers "in any house" during peacetime without the owner's consent and the Fifth Amendment's privilege against self-incrimination.

4. The Ninth Amendment is an additional source of penumbral privacy rights. When it says that "the enumeration in the Constitution, of certain rights, shall not be construed to deny or disparage others retained by the people," it is a caution to those who argue that a right cannot exist if it is

not specifically set forth in the Constitution. This amendment attests to the humility and wisdom of the framers, who knew that they could not possibly articulate every right that the coming ages would prove to be essential to a free people. They thus provided a repository in "the people" for such rights.

5. These penumbral rights of privacy inherent in the First, Third, Fourth, Fifth, and Ninth Amendments are applicable to state actions pursuant to the Fourteenth Amendment.[5]

6. There is a right of privacy inherent in the marriage relationship. The court said that "we deal with a right of privacy older than The Bill of Rights— older than our political parties, older than our school system. Marriage is a coming together for better or for worse, hopefully enduring, and intimate to the degree of being sacred. It is an association that promotes a way of life, not causes; a harmony in living, not political faiths; a bilateral loyalty, not commercial or social projects. Yet it is an association for as noble a purpose as any involved in our prior decisions."[6]

Two years and five days after *Griswold* was decided (June 7, 1965), the United States Supreme Court decided *Loving v. Virginia*.[7] In June 1958, Mildred Jeter, a black woman, and Richard Loving, a white man, committed what was then an audacious act. They married. Both were residents of Virginia, but they married in the District of Columbia, where it was legal to do so. After they married, they returned to Virginia, where they established residence. About four months after their marriage, a grand jury returned an indictment accusing Mr. and Mrs. Loving of violating Virginia's law disallowing interracial marriages. The statutory punishment pursuant to this law was confinement in the penitentiary "for not less than one nor more than five years."

On January 6, 1959, Mr. and Mrs. Loving pleaded guilty and were each sentenced to one year in jail. The sentence was suspended, however, on the condition that the pair leave Virginia and not return *together* for twenty-five years. The trial judge stated in his opinion, inter alia, that "Almighty God created the races white, black, yellow, and red, and he placed them on separate continents. And but for the interference with his arrangement there would be no cause for such marriages. The fact that he separated the races shows that he did not intend for the races to mix."[8]

The trial judge did not acknowledge that, but for the "interference" of white migration to "red" America, there would never have been a Virginia. Nor did he ponder how "Almighty God" could have been unaware of intercontinental travel and its upsetting effects on his racial master plan.

Not surprisingly, the Lovings left Virginia after their convictions and resided in the District of Columbia, where they initiated legal action in both the Virginia state courts (to vacate the criminal decision) and the Federal District Court (to declare the Virginia antimiscegenation statutes unconstitutional and enjoin state officials from enforcing the terms of their convictions). Again not surprisingly, the Virginia Supreme Court of Appeals upheld the constitutionality of that state's antimiscegenation statutes, and thus the issue arose before the United States Supreme Court.

In its decision upholding the conviction of the Lovings, the Supreme Court of Appeals of Virginia stated that the legitimate purpose that the antimiscegenation law served was "to preserve the racial integrity of its citizens" and to prevent "the corruption of blood," "a mongrel breed of citizens," and "the obliteration of racial pride." The court also opined that marriage had traditionally been a state province in accordance with the Tenth Amendment. Those representing the State of Virginia before the United States Supreme Court, in asserting that the states' police power under the Tenth Amendment was the proper source for laws concerning marriage, did not go so far as to claim that this power was unlimited by the dictates of the Fourteenth Amendment's Equal Protection Clause. Instead they argued that as long as whites and Negroes were equally punished by violation of the miscegenation statutes, there was no contravention of the Equal Protection Clause, even though racial classifications were the basis for the statutes. They then argued that because the races were punished equally, "the question of constitutionality would thus become whether there was any rational basis for a State to treat interracial marriages differently from other marriages," and they argued further that the scientific evidence was in doubt and therefore the Supreme Court should defer to the state legislature's policy of discouraging interracial marriages.

The Supreme Court concluded the obvious—that Virginia's antimiscegenation statutes rested solely on racial distinctions. Indeed, the statutes' purpose was only to preserve "the integrity" of the white race. Whites in Virginia were barred from marrying nonwhites (except for descendants of Pocahontas); all other races could intermarry at will.

The Court, however, did not stop by simply ruling the Virginia antimiscegenation statutes unconstitutional under the Equal Protection Clause of the Fourteenth Amendment. It went further by also deciding that these statutes deprived the Lovings of due process of law pursuant to the same amendment.

The Court's opinion characterized "the freedom to marry" as "one of the vital personal rights essential to the orderly pursuit of happiness" and called marriage one of the "basic civil rights of man, fundamental to our very existence and survival."[9] The Court's opinion began with this summation: "The Fourteenth Amendment requires that the freedom of choice to marry, or not marry, a person of another race resides with the individual and cannot be infringed by the state."[10]

Roughly two months short of two years later, on April 7, 1969, the Supreme Court rendered a decision in *Stanley v. Georgia*.[11] Law enforcement agents suspected that Mr. Stanley was engaged in bookmaking, and so obtained a search warrant for his home. While looking for evidence of bookmaking, the efficient searchers found films deemed obscene. Stanley was convicted of knowingly possessing obscene material in violation of Georgia law. His conviction was upheld by the Georgia Supreme Court.

On appeal the United States Supreme Court found the Georgia statute to be unconstitutional and did so with no dissenting opinion. Distinguishing Mr. Stanley's possession of obscenity solely for his private use in his home from cases involving the public use or distribution of obscenity, the Court held that "the mere private possession of obscene matter cannot constitutionally be made a crime."[12]

Three years and nine months after the decision in *Stanley*, on January 22, 1973, the Supreme Court decided *Roe et al. v. Wade*.[13] At the time the action commenced, the plaintiff was a pregnant single woman who was unable to obtain an abortion in Texas because of statutory prohibitions. Roe could only have obtained an abortion in Texas if the procedure had been medically advised as necessary to save her life. She initiated a class action challenging the constitutionality of the Texas criminal abortion laws.

The Court, in a seven-to-two decision, surveyed the history of the antiabortion statutes, noting that such proscriptions were not "of ancient or even of common-law origin" and stemmed for the most part from statutes passed in the "latter half of the 19th century." The Court also reviewed the distinctions in fetal growth between quickening, viability, and the state before quickening and even traced the stance of the American Medical Association on the subject. The Court's tripartite decision can be summarized as follows.

State criminal abortion laws, like those involved here, that except from criminality only a life-saving procedure on the mother's behalf without regard to the stage of her pregnancy and other interests involved violate the due process clause of the Fourteenth Amendment, which protects the right to privacy, including a woman's qualified right to terminate her pregnancy, against state action. Though the state cannot override that right, it has legitimate interests in protecting both the pregnant woman's health and the potentiality of human life, each of which interests grows and reaches a "compelling point at various stages of the woman's approach to term."

For the stage prior to approximately the end of the first trimester, the abortion decision and its effectuation must be left to the medical judgment of the pregnant woman's attending physician.

For the stage subsequent to approximately the end of the first trimester, the state in promoting its interest in the health of the mother, may, if it chooses, regulate the abortion procedure in ways that are reasonably related to maternal health.

For the stage subsequent to viability the state in promoting its interest in the potentiality of human life, may, if it chooses, regulate, and even proscribe, abortion except where necessary, in appropriate medical judgment, for the preservation of the life or health of the mother.[14]

The state may define the term "physician" to mean only a physician currently licensed by the state and may proscribe any abortion by a person who is not a physician as so defined.

The ruling rested squarely on the constitutional right of privacy that the Court found to be part of the Fourteenth Amendment's concept of personal liberty and corresponding restrictions on state action and broad enough "to encompass a woman's decision whether or not to terminate her pregnancy." It did, however, find that a "compelling state interest" could exist in the latter two trimesters of pregnancy and thus that the state did have limited scope to regulate abortion.

After *Roe v. Wade*, because of the *Griswold, Stanley, Loving,* and *Roe* cases, and as a result of other cases representing the expansion of the right of privacy,[15] it appeared logical to assume that sodomy laws were fated to unconstitutionality if for no other reason than that they often forbade certain forms of adult and private sexual expression not only between heterosexuals as well as homosexuals but also between married persons.

But evolution is not wholly predictable. It seldom follows a straight line. In the process of a basic social alteration of views held over time, which are of passionate importance to a segment of society, it is especially true that setbacks and snags will slow and threaten that evolution.

Bowers v. Hardwick et al., decided on June 30, 1986, was such a snag.[16] Mr. Hardwick was charged with violating Georgia's sodomy law with another adult male in the bedroom where he lived. Curiously, however, the district attorney did not present this case to a grand jury, concluding apparently that additional evidence was needed to prevail. Mr. Hardwick then initiated suit in the Federal District Court claiming that the Georgia sodomy law was unconstitutional. His position was upheld by the court of appeals, which held that Georgia's law violated his fundamental rights under the Ninth and Fourteenth Amendments. The United States Supreme Court ruled five to four that the Constitution did *not* confer any fundamental right to commit sodomy, consensual or not, even in the privacy of one's home.

The Georgia statute in question read: "A person commits the offense of sodomy when he performs or submits to any sexual act involving the sex organs of one person and the mouth or anus of another." Conviction under this statute carried a maximum sentence of twenty years.[17] The statute applied to *any* person and thus proscribed acts also between heterosexuals and proscribed them *wherever* they occurred.

The majority of the Court was plainly unwilling to expand the right of privacy and its concomitant liberty of sexual, adult private behavior to sodomitic acts. It found nothing in the Constitution that compelled it to constitutionalize private, consensual, adult homosexual or heterosexual sodomy and thus refused to do so, stating in its opinion that sodomy had been proscribed since ancient times and was proscribed here in Colonial times, reflecting the morality of Georgians.

One wonders whether any member of the majority deciding the case ever considered what would happen in Georgia if everyone—heterosexual and homosexual—who violated this law were apprehended, convicted, and jailed, if everyone guilty of cunnilingus, fellatio, and anal intercourse were no longer free. We suspect that the shopping malls would have been deserted and not many people would have shown up for Braves games.

The Hardwick case was an anomaly, a step backward after a march forward. But though it delayed that march, it did not stop it. The delay lasted until June 26, 2003, seventeen years less four days, when *Lawrence v. Texas* was decided.[18]

Consistent with the proposition that great events often have their genesis in commonplace occurrences, *Lawrence* began with a spurious report to the Houston police that there was a disturbance involving weapons in the apartment residence of Mr. Lawrence. When the police entered the apartment, they found Mr. Lawrence and Mr. Garner, both adult males, engaging in consensual, private (up to the time the police arrived) anal intercourse. Both men were arrested and convicted of deviate sexual intercourse. No weapons were found; no disturbance had occurred except, of course, the one inflicted on Lawrence and Garner by the police. The Texas statute in question made it a crime for two persons of the same gender to engage in this and other forms of sexual behavior.[19] The Court, by a vote of six to three, ruled the Texas statute unconstitutional.

Of *Bowers v. Hardwick et al.*, the majority opinion said that *Bowers* had not been correct when it was decided, and it was not correct today. It ought not to remain binding precedent. *Bowers v. Hardwick* should have been and now was overruled. The *Lawrence* case did not involve minors. It did not involve persons who might be injured or coerced or who were situated in relationships where consent might not easily be refused. It did not involve public conduct or prostitution. It did not involve whether the government must give formal recognition to any relationship that homosexual persons seek to enter. The case did involve two adults who, with full and mutual consent from each other, engaged in sexual practices common to a homosexual lifestyle. The petitioners were entitled to respect for their private lives. The state could not demean their existence or control their destiny by making their private sexual conduct a crime. Their right to liberty under the Due Process Clause gave them the full right to engage in their conduct without the intervention of the government.[20]

The Court went on to say: "Had those who drew and ratified the Due Process Clause of the Fifth Amendment or the Fourteenth Amendment known the components of liberty in its manifold possibilities, they might have been more specific. They did not presume to have this insight. They know times can blind us to certain truths and later generations can see that laws once thought necessary and proper in fact serve only to oppress. As the Constitution endures, persons in every generation can invoke its principles in their own search for greater freedom."[21]

A concurring opinion was filed by Justice O'Connor. While she agreed that the Texas statute was unconstitutional, she did not agree that the Fourteenth Amendment's Due Process Clause was the appropriate basis, nor did she join in the overruling of *Bowers v. Hardwick*. Her view was that because the Texas statute criminalized homosexual sodomy but not heterosexual sodomy, it was not a statute intended to express moral disapproval of sodomy (which would have been constitutional) but rather a statute embodying moral disapproval of only one group—homosexuals. This was "like a bare desire to harm the group . . . without any other asserted state interest" and thus unconstitutional under the Equal Protection Clause of the Fourteenth Amendment. The difference between the majority opinion and the opinion of Justice O'Connor is not simply technical; it is philosophically basic. The first says that private adult consensual sexual activity, whether heterosexual or homosexual, is a form of fundamental liberty entitled to constitutional protection against all governmental abridgment. The second says that a state can criminalize sodomitic relations as long as it equally punishes all persons who so indulge.

The dissenting opinion of Justice Scalia is noteworthy for several reasons. It is, first of all, an angry, disrespectful dissent. He calls the majority "manipulative" and accuses it of having "signed on to the so-called homosexual agenda" and of having "taken sides in the culture war." Secondly, what hides transparently behind these angry words is his personal dread that this decision will lead to same-sex marriage being deemed a constitutionally protected right. A reading of his dissent can easily lead one to believe that Scalia would criminalize homosexual sodomy for the reason alone that decriminalization paves the way for same-sex marriage. Thirdly, and ironically, Scalia's dissent contains an accusation that the majority opinion provides a clear basis for same-sex marriage. He says:

The Court says that the present case does not involve whether the government must give formal recognition to any relationship that homosexual persons seek to enter. Do not believe it. More illuminating than this bald unreasoned disclaimer is the progression of thought displayed by an earlier passage in the Court's opinion, which notes the constitutional protections afforded to personal decisions relating to marriage, procreation, contraception, family relationships, child rearing and education, and then declares that "persons in a homosexual relationship may seek autonomy for these purposes, just as heterosexual persons do. Ante, at 13. . . . Today's opinion dismantles the structure of constitutional law that has permitted a distinction to be made between heterosexual and homosexual unions, insofar as formal recognition in marriage is concerned. If moral disapprobation of homosexual conduct is no legitimate state interest for purposes of proscribing that conduct, ante, at 18; and if, as the Court coos (casting aside all pretense of neutrality), when sexuality finds overt expression in intimate conduct with another person, the conduct can be but one element in a personal bond that is more enduring, ante, at 6; what justification could there possibly be for denying the benefits of marriage to homosexual couples exercising "the liberty protected by the Constitution, ibid.? Surely not the encouragement of procreation, since the sterile and the elderly are allowed to marry. This case "does not involve" the issue of homosexual marriage only if one entertains the belief that principle and logic have nothing to do with the decisions of this Court. Many will hope that, as the Court comfortingly assures us, this is so.[22]

If Justice Scalia's angry words bespeak his belief, then how can he responsibly vote against giving same-sex marriage constitutional sanction if he is sitting when the question is presented to the Court? His reasoning, however ill-natured, is logical, but the Court *did* specifically leave the constitutionality of same-sex marriage open in its opinion, and only a fool would bet his life on how the issue will be treated when it comes to the Court. Will it carve out a special niche for marriage in constitutional theory? Will it decide that civil unions are a satisfactory substitute? Or, more likely, will the angry logic of Justice Scalia prevail, and same-sex marriage become a constitutional right?

We believe that what Justice Scalia finds ominous is in fact just and justice delayed far too long. But *Bowers v. Hardwick* was a surprise, and most importantly, the holding of *Lawrence v. Texas* was supported by only five justices, since Justice O'Connor would have joined the dissenters had Texas equally criminalized *heterosexual* sodomy. Will there be a majority on the Court that agrees with the holding in *Lawrence* when the constitutionality of prohibiting same-sex marriage comes on its docket? Who knows? We certainly do not.

What is clear, however, is that the evolutionary pattern of our sexual law exemplified by Supreme Court cases over the past four decades, culminating with *Lawrence v. Texas*, points philosophically to the acceptance of same-sex marriage as a right. The Supreme Court and the state legislatures have taken different steps, but in the same direction, to advance this evolution in American sexual thought. We turn to this state-originated evolution next.

The Evolution of State Law
toward Sexual Privacy

Donald J. Cantor

The striking evolution that has occurred in the United States over the past forty or so years in the realm of sexual law and philosophy cannot be dismissed as the work of "a few activist judges." It cannot even be accurately characterized as only the work of judges, whether activist or not. Of course, as chapter 1 indicated, the United States Supreme Court over this period decided cases that clearly galvanized this evolution and gave it constitutional basis, but it was not alone. Quite to the contrary, actions by state legislatures throughout America, in every part of the nation, not only sometimes complemented the decisions of the Supreme Court but also covered a broader scope, bringing this evolutionary process into areas the Supreme Court decisions did not cover.

Consider adultery. Adultery has been the criminal law's way of attempting to preserve marriage by making it a crime for anyone who is married to have sexual intercourse with someone not his or her spouse. In the mid-1960s, forty-four American states made adultery criminal. Thus it was a crime in 88 percent of American states. In six of the states in which adultery was a crime, only fines could be assessed as punishment. Prison was therefore possible for adultery, then, in 76 percent of our states. In five of the states in which adultery was a crime, imprisonment could have been for up to five years.[1]

Today the picture is markedly different. Only 44 percent of American states (twenty-two) have criminal adultery statutes. Of these twenty-two states, three (West Virginia, Maryland, and Rhode Island) provide only for fines in the event of conviction. In Maryland the fine must be $10, in Rhode Island the fine may not exceed $500, and in West Virginia it cannot "be less than twenty dollars." In six other states, adultery has a definition it had in no state forty years ago—it is a crime only if it occurs during cohabitation, or "openly," or is "habitual." (South Carolina law says "habitual"; North Carolina, "co-habit"; Mississippi, "cohabit"; Illinois, "open and notorious"; Florida, "open"; Alabama, "cohabitation.") Thus in these states adultery is not criminally punishable if it occurs secretly or sporadically, thus benefiting the sly, the effective liars, and the quiet.

Some states have provisions in their adultery laws concerning how prosecutions can be instituted, which was unheard of up to the 1960s—in Minnesota, Arizona, and North Dakota, prosecutions can be instituted only if the spouse of an adulterer files a complaint.[2]

So, of the 22 states that today have a legal basis for punishing adultery, only 16 can do so if the adultery has not been flagrant; and of these 16, only 13 can punish other than by fine; and of these 13, only 10 can do so without the need for a spousal complaint.

Consider fornication. In 1965 forty states punished it as a crime.[3] Today only ten states do so—a percentage drop from 80 percent to 20 percent,[4] although four other states do outlaw cohabitation (Arizona, Florida, Michigan, and New Mexico).[5] The evidence today that unmarried American heterosexuals are sexually very active is so overwhelming that it surely requires no citations or proof. And it follows ineluctably from this that such activity is occurring in the same volume in the states that outlaw it as in the states that criminalize it. In part this is because laws about fornication, like those about adultery, seek to ban activity between consenting adults in private. Thus there are no participants in these activities who are victims, and thus the participants are not likely to file complaints. But beyond that, I suggest, is a greater, more powerful reason—America has evolved to the point where the great majority do not think consensual sex between adults in private is wrong out of marriage, and even those who feel that it's wrong usually don't think it should be criminal; and where marriage is involved, though many more will think that it's wrong, not many believe that it should be criminal. More and more, we have evolved into a people who see sex as private, and though we may deplore some aspects and results of adultery and fornication, we do not see the government and its police as the remedy.

Consider the abortion statutes. *Roe v. Wade*, of course, made abortion a matter of constitutional definition in 1973, so there is no forty-year legal evolution to describe. But it is quite noteworthy to what extent popular feeling on this issue manifested itself and produced state legislative action in the five years before the *Roe* decision. The state legislatures during this period "had liberalized abortion laws in 16 states with 41 percent of the population."[6] Today, though *Roe v. Wade* is national law, seventeen states still have laws that ban abortion, while thirty-three do not. What the situation would be today if there were no *Roe v. Wade* is unknown, but what is clear is that the sexual evolution that began in the sixties militated against antiabortion sentiments and accomplished significant reform by the time *Roe v. Wade* became law.

Consider sodomy. When, in 2003, *Lawrence v. Texas* was decided by the U.S. Supreme Court and sodomy statutes thereby became unconstitutional, there were thirteen states that had such statutes.[7] In 1960, all our states punished sodomy as a felony. In 1961 Illinois repealed its statute, so that by the mid-sixties, forty-nine states retained sodomy proscriptions.[8] State legislatures therefore rid thirty-seven jurisdictions of these laws, an evolutionary attrition rate of 74 percent by the time *Lawrence v. Texas* became law.

These sodomy statutes have an importance and relevance that require additional examination. Although sodomy was defined by common law as the anal penetration of a man by a man, the sodomy statutes existent in America in the sixties "for the most part, however, included most acts of sexual connection with the exception of vaginal intercourse."[9] Every state prohibited consensual anal intercourse by 1964 except Illinois. Twenty-three states explicitly banned fellatio, and the states where the language was not explicit had general proscriptive language that obviously included it.

These statutes, moreover, were not only aimed at homosexuality. They included bestiality, and occasionally masturbation; and much more importantly, they made heterosexual contacts other than vaginal intercourse major felonies. The same penalties that threatened homosexuals threatened heterosexuals. Heterosexual fellation, anal intercourse, and often cunnilingus were activities barred by these sodomy statutes.

These statutes were noteworthy, if not remarkable, in ways other than the activities they criminalized. In seven states it was possible to be sentenced to life imprisonment, in thirteen states the maximum sentence was less than life but at least ten years, and in twenty-two states the maximum penalties were between ten and fifteen years. Of the eight remaining states, six had five-year maximums, with South Carolina's five-year sentence being mandatory. Delaware and Virginia had three-year maximum sentences. Illinois punished sodomy after 1961 only if force or fraud was involved. No other state except New

York varied punishment because of the presence of force or fraud. Thus in forty-eight states, the commission of a proscribed sexual act by adults, freely consenting, in private was a serious, life-destroying felony.[10]

These statutes had other characteristics that were unusual and today seem bizarre. The purpose of a criminal statute is to describe precisely what is forbidden and to set forth the penalty for doing it. But these sodomy statutes did more—they used adjectives to describe how loathsome the proscribed acts were. In 1964 the sodomy statutes of fourteen states referred to the offenses as "abominable" or as both "abominable" and "detestable." In seven states the offenses were termed "infamous." Ten other states used the phrases "crime against nature" or "against the order of nature." Three other states characterized the prohibited acts as "unnatural," "abnormal," and "perverted." Only sixteen states simply made sodomy a crime without statutes that also editorialized. Similar attitudes were evidenced in case reports and even in legal texts. To put the attitudes just described in perspective, it is helpful to remember that these are words and phrases aimed at consenting adults having sex in private who may be homosexual or heterosexual and who were not accused of force or being physically harmful. No such language appeared in any statute punishing assault, rape, or even murder. When one remembers that these statutes did not exempt married persons in the privacy of their bedrooms, it is truly difficult to avoid vertigo at the contemplation of the attitudes expressed.[11]

The sexual evolution that has occurred, as exemplified by the changes in sodomy laws, is evidenced in several ways. *Lawrence v. Texas* is the most dramatic and affecting event, without question, but other meaningful evolutionary changes have occurred over these forty years. Of the thirteen sodomy statutes that were alive until *Lawrence v. Texas* killed them, nine were directed only against same-sex sexuality, leaving only four that criminalized heterosexual behavior as well. The trend, therefore, among the few states that retained sodomy statutes was to aim these statutes only at homosexual behavior, not against all nonprocreative sexual acts, homosexual or heterosexual, as was the norm previously. This was a major philosophical change.

One final point—when Mr. Lawrence and his partner, Mr. Garner, were found guilty in the Texas trial court, after pleading nolo contendere, they were each fined $200 and assessed court costs of $141.25. Bearing in mind that Texas was in the sixties one of the states with a fifteen-year maximum prison sentence for sodomy, the punishment meted out to Mr. Lawrence and Mr. Garner may say more about the sexual evolution in America than all the other evidence combined.

Every Supreme Court case cited in the preceding chapter was a decision that invalidated a state criminal statute. Every area of state action examined in this chapter has also dealt with criminal behavior. The evolution in American sexual thought, however, is not confined to the question of what should or should not be criminal. There are two areas of law, noncriminal in nature, that embody this evolution as appropriately as the criminal areas cited. They are divorce and child custody.

Divorce in America through the 1960s was a pure travesty, making divorce extremely hard to get if contested, thus fostering blackmail by spouses against spouses, perpetuating many marriages long since devoid of personal or social value. I can best describe it today by drawing on the discussion of divorce in my earlier book *Escape from Marriage* (1971).

In a suit for divorce, the relief primarily sought is, quite obviously, the decree of the court dissolving the marriage. To qualify for divorce in the 1960s, however, the plaintiff, like other plaintiffs, had to allege injury; except under special statutes (to be discussed later), our law did not allow the relief of divorce without a showing of injury. It was not any type of injury, however, that sufficed. Here the state specified which precise types of injury did suffice, and these were called grounds. It was therefore mandatory that the plaintiff claim in the divorce complaint that the legal demands of at least one of the grounds allowable in the particular jurisdiction had been fulfilled by the acts of the defendant.

The grounds most widely recognized in the United States were adultery (49 states), desertion or abandonment (47 states), physical or mental cruelty (45 states), conviction of crime or imprisonment (44 states), alcoholism (41 states), nonsupport (32 states), and insanity (29 states). Since the great majority of divorces were granted on one of these grounds, contemplate the predicament of the spouse who, though thoroughly tired of the marriage, still wished not to besmirch the name of his or her partner. For any reason—mercy, kindness, sympathy, concern for the children—a wife may not have wished to allege in a public document that a husband was an alcoholic, or a husband may not have wished to allege adultery, or either may not have wished to allege anything even remotely injurious to the reputation of the other; but there was no choice. The law required allegations; fault was generally the key to freedom from a bad marriage, and it had to be alleged and proved. Thus the law imposed the role of adversary on both spouses and made what might have been a cease-fire assume at least the appearance of a duel.

Once a complaint was filed, and the defendant stood accused of adultery, cruelty, desertion, or some other ground, the next major move was up to the defendant. He or she had four choices.

First, the defendant could decide that it was all right with him if the plaintiff obtained the divorce, in which case he did nothing, the complaint went unanswered, and the matter was scheduled for trial as an uncontested divorce. At the hearing, the plaintiff and a given number of corroborating witnesses required by the particular jurisdiction (or judge within that jurisdiction) testified concerning the defendant's adultery, cruelty, desertion, or the like, to establish that the ground alleged was factually correct. The defendant did not testify, no witnesses appeared for him, and his lawyer did not cross-examine. Here the divorce trial differed markedly from other civil trials. In other types of cases, the failure of the defendant to answer the plaintiff's charges usually results in judgment being entered in favor of the plaintiff by default, and it is not necessary for the plaintiff to offer evidence to support the charge, though it may be to obtain the relief sought. An example of this would be a suit for personal injuries arising from an accident where a default judgment is entered but a hearing is still necessary to determine how much money should be awarded the plaintiff. In a divorce, however, the plaintiff always had to testify; no such thing as a divorce by default judgment existed. Thus the process of forced public disclosure, initiated by the complaint, was consummated by the hearing, where, before judge, clerk, stenographer, sheriff, lawyers, and all those awaiting their own hearings that day, the wife or husband to some extent had to detail the transgressions, weaknesses, and offenses of the other parent of his or her children.

The second course of action open to the defendant was to file an answer denying the allegations in the complaint charging him or her with acts constituting a ground for divorce. The filing of this denial raised as an issue of fact whether or not the defendant had behaved in such a manner as to warrant the plaintiff's request for a divorce. To determine this issue of fact, a trial had to be held. This set the stage for the contested divorce, but the only determination sought was as to the guilt of the defendant, and the only relief possible was for the plaintiff to receive a divorce from the defendant. If the defendant prevailed, establishing that he or she was accused of actions not actually perpetrated, then both the accused and the discredited accuser left the field of battle still locked in matrimony.

The third choice for a defendant was to deny the charges of the plaintiff, but, in addition, to file what the law calls a special defense. A special defense is a reason why, even if the allegations of the plaintiff are true, the plaintiff still cannot win. In the context of divorce in the 1960s, the important special defenses related directly to acts of the plaintiff that disqualified him or her for a divorce despite the culpability of the defendant. Thus the plaintiff could prove, for example, that the defendant had committed adultery, and still not obtain a divorce if one of the special defenses was established.

These special defenses were so indicative of the philosophy of fault that underlay divorce, being perhaps the most absurd aspect of an extremely absurd concept, that they merit detailed examination. There are four of these absurdities—condonation, collusion, connivance, and recrimination—to be considered.

Condonation is forgiveness conditioned on the nonrepetition of like offenses and the proper behavior thereafter of the party forgiven. Condonation was evidenced by a resumption of marital cohabitation, if such was interrupted as the result of the forgiving spouse having learned of the other spouse's offense, in the case of adultery, or having been victimized by it, in the event of acts of cruelty. Although sexual intercourse was not legally essential to the existence of condonation, it was difficult to disprove condonation if spouses mated and the "abused" spouse did so voluntarily, knowing of the offenses of the other spouse. In the 1960s, courts seldom believed that husbands and wives acted out of lust, and consequently inferred love from sexuality and forgiveness from love. Although a repetition of a matrimonial offense after a condonation could resurrect the original offense as a matter of law, the situation could easily become difficult to prove because of all the conflicting claims potentially raised by the parties. This is what could happen:

1. The plaintiff could file a complaint for divorce, alleging adultery as the ground.

2. The defendant, assuming that he or she had been caught flagrante delicto (in the act) and was unable to disprove the charge, admitted to the adultery but charged, as a special defense, that the plaintiff knew of the adultery but condoned it and thus could not assert it.

3. The plaintiff could either deny condonation, which could be difficult if he or she continued to live with the defendant after learning of the adultery,

or admit condonation but claim back that the adultery was revived because of offensive behavior by the defendant subsequent to the condonation.

4. The defendant could then deny any offenses subsequent to condonation or even admit their existence but claim that these too were condoned.

Collusion pertained when the acts that constituted the grounds for divorce were committed by agreement of the other spouse, or when such acts never took place but the spouses agreed to fabricate them, or when the parties agreed not to present evidence that would keep the plaintiff from procuring a divorce. Collusion is, by definition, agreement, and the adversarial nature of a divorce action demanded that the parties not agree and work together to achieve what the law required that they must at least seem to oppose. Consequently proof that the parties had colluded made divorce unobtainable even, of course, if one of the parties reneged on the collusion, admitted it, and raised it in court.

Connivance, the third special defense, was the consent of the plaintiff to the misconduct of the defendant that was alleged to be the ground for divorce. If, for example, a couple should, each with the other's permission, join a wife-swapping club, and either sought a divorce on the grounds of the resulting adultery, the other could raise as a special defense the fact that the adultery was committed with spousal consent, and this would suffice to establish the special defense of connivance, thus precluding the divorce.

Recrimination was somewhat more involved than condonation, collusion, and connivance and probably existed as at least a potential factor in many more divorces than the other three combined. "Divorce is a remedy for the innocent against the guilty," stated the court in an Idaho case, and where there was no innocent party, but rather two guilty parties, it followed—if you accept the dubious logic of the premise—that there could be no divorce. This is the philosophy that spawned and supported the special defense of recrimination. Hence if the plaintiff alleged and proved that the defendant had been guilty of acts constituting a ground for divorce, and the defendant raised as a defense, and proved, that the plaintiff had been similarly guilty, the divorce might not be granted. The guilt of the one nullified the guilt of the other, and those two wrongs (which had never been up to making a right) assumed sufficient stature to perpetuate a marriage.

The defendant's fourth choice was to deny the allegations of the plaintiff, allege a special defense to the claim of the plaintiff, and also file a cross-complaint (also called a "counterclaim," "cross bill," or "cross petition"), which was simply a complaint by the defendant that maintained that it was the defendant who deserved the divorce, not the plaintiff, and in which the defendant alleged what his or her grounds were. In such a case, each party defended against charges and also leveled them. Three results were possible: the plaintiff prevailed and obtained the divorce; the defendant prevailed and obtained the divorce; or neither prevailed, and another quarrelsome marriage was perpetuated.[12]

By the end of the 1960s, trends to ease the rigor of our fault-based divorce law were emerging. The ground of incompatibility had been adopted in New Mexico, Oklahoma, and Alaska. Ten additional states had adopted provisions whereby divorce could be granted simply because the parties had lived apart for a period varying from two to seven years.[13]

But evolutionary relief came from California, which enacted, effective January 1, 1970, America's first no-fault divorce law. This statute provided only two grounds for marital dissolution—"incurable insanity" and "irreconcilable differences, which have caused the irremediable breakdown of the marriage."[14] By 1975 divorce in America had changed in every state. Today incompatibility is available as a basis for divorce in five states.[15] Marital breakdown is available in twenty states,[16] marital breakdown plus two years' separation in four states,[17] irreconcilable differences in ten states,[18] separation alone in nine states,[19] and insupportability in one state.[20] New York is the only state that does not have a basis for divorce that will practically always provide an eventual divorce for a plaintiff spouse despite the defendant spouse's opposition to divorce, but it does have a basis for divorce based on a one-year separation where both parties agree. American divorce law today differs fundamentally with the law that preceded it, not just because it has become sensible enough to end marriages when they have ceased to function instead of doing so only if blame could be assigned, but because the changes have made divorce essentially available on demand to either spouse. It is therefore akin to all the other areas discussed in this and the preceding chapter where, because of Supreme Court decisions or state legislative action, the people involved now make the sexual decisions, not the government.

The ouster of the government from the arena of sexual decision making, whether it was caused by a constitutional right of privacy or a constitutional grant of liberty or a popular feeling that sexual choices should be personal, is the greatest single result of the sexual evolution in the past four decades. But it is not the only cultural trend that is relevant here. America's growing adherence to, and belief in, equality is also relevant, evident clearly in the abolition of miscegenation laws and the sodomy statutes by the Supreme Court and implicit in the actions of states in repealing statutes in these areas. Equality is a contagious doctrine; it spreads from area to area. A nation that concludes that blacks and whites should be treated equally will more easily treat men and women equally and will more readily treat heterosexuals and gays equally.

Consider, therefore, the law that pertains to the custody of children. Under common law, fathers were deemed the natural guardians of children. Though that was a presumption, not an automatic legal result, the presumption was a strong one, generally dispositive unless the father had been abusive to a large degree. An exception was the famous 1817 custody case involving the poet Percy Bysshe Shelley, who lost custody because "he blasphemously derided the truth of the Christian revelation and denied the existence of a God as creator of the universe," and because the judge felt Shelley would educate his children to so believe if he was awarded custody.[21]

This father presumption gave way to a "tender years doctrine" that favored maternal care for very young children, and then, as increasing industrialization put men to work outside the home, the law graduated to a maternal preference. This preference or legal presumption in favor of mothers came to thoroughly dominate American custodial decisions. In 1976 thirty-one states had specifically articulated support of the maternal preference by case law, in all instances but one in cases decided after 1960. In fact the maternal preference was by that time the controlling view throughout the United States.[22]

But then things changed again. The pendulum that had swung from the father preference to the mother preference slowed until it now approached the middle, where a new presumption called joint custody resides. This movement away from the maternal preference came with the clamor by women for equality outside the home, in the marketplace, fueled by the publication in 1963 of *The Feminine Mystique* by Betty Friedan. Women sought to define themselves as more than mothers, as being capable of having careers, not only nurturing children.

It is a curious fact that every group that is discriminated against and held to an inferior social position is credited with some superior abilities. Women were thus deemed superior nurturers by those who felt they belonged in the home and were not equal to men in the fields of business, and so forth. It therefore followed that as women sought cultural liberation, thronged into careers, and neared equality outside the home, they necessarily descended to equality as parents. Fathers in custody cases were not remiss in pointing this out, and custody evaluators and judges were not remiss in understanding it.

As a result, mothers and fathers stand in positions of substantial equality when custody decisions have to be made, with the present favored disposition being orders of joint custody, with as close to an equal division of the child's time with each parent as best serves the child's healthy development.

Moreover, this philosophy of gender equality has included the lessons learned about the parenting capabilities of gay and lesbian fathers and mothers, so that they often receive equal treatment under our custody law. However, this is not a transformation that has been completed. It is, rather, a transformation in process. Gay and lesbian parents are not equal everywhere, in all courts, to all custody evaluators, to all judges. But they are getting there. The fact that the Supreme Court has said that sodomy is lawful, that blacks and whites may marry, that women have a right to abortion, that pornography may be read and birth control used in the home, that Americans have rights based on privacy, liberty, and equality that allow these freedoms, does not mean that everyone accepts these decisions as right. But more and more do as time elapses. And perhaps more impressive, because more grassroots in nature, state legislative action over these past forty years indicates a quiet, growing belief in America that we all should have the right to be left alone by government when we make our sexual decisions.

3

The Evolution of Understanding Homosexuality within the Fields of Psychology and Psychiatry

Elizabeth Cantor

The current predominant theory that homosexuality in particular, and sexual orientation in general, is primarily biologically and genetically determined is the result of an accumulation of compelling scientific evidence. Countless theories of homosexuality articulated for centuries by philosophers, religious leaders, writers, doctors, sexologists, and others have ranged from the benign to the absurd. Historically, these theories of homosexuality have not been based on scientific evidence but instead have emerged out of fear and misunderstanding. This chapter will review the evolution of our understanding of homosexuality, from ancient times to today, and highlight how fear, religious doctrine, and random opinion have gradually given way to reasoned scientific investigation.

It is abundantly clear that homosexuality has existed for millennia, but it has generally been condemned, at least in the Western world. In fact, it is the religious view of homosexuality as sin and the psychiatric view of homosexuality as pathology that have contributed the most to the rejection that homosexuals have faced. Although current explanations of the origins of sexual orientation are still under investigation, scientists now believe that, under most circumstances, sexual orientation is likely a result of genetics and neurobiological factors that are established in utero. This, along with evidence that a range of interventions, such as aversion therapy and psychoanalysis, have been overwhelmingly unsuccessful at "reorienting" homosexual individuals, suggests that sexual orientation is basically unalterable. Scientific evidence also suggests that sexual orientation exists on a continuum, rather than as a dichotomous phenomenon. This means that an individual's orientation may be at one extreme or the other (i.e., exclusively heterosexual or exclusively homosexual), but that a wide range of other, bisexual, "orientations" exists in between.

Within the fields of psychology and psychiatry, there has been a slow but measurable shift in understanding the etiology of homosexuality and accepting it as a natural human variation. In 1952, when the first *Diagnostic and Statistical Manual of Mental Disorders* (*DSM-I*) was published by the American Psychiatric Association, homosexuality was listed among the Sociopathic Personality Disturbances. Today homosexuality is not listed at all. The fields of psychology and psychiatry have played a critical role in first perpetuating myths about homosexuality and then calling for empirical research to help answer the question of how sexual orientation is determined. It is our hope that this chapter will help the reader more fully appreciate the social and moral contexts that homosexuality has survived over the years, and the long road toward "understanding" that it has traveled. Given that we now have the capacity to examine sexual orientation from a scientific perspective and with scientific methods, it is our duty to do so. To continue to espouse theories of sexual orientation that lack a scientific foundation or, worse, are inconsistent with scientific evidence is irresponsible. As a look into the past will illustrate, it is also harmful.

Homosexuality as Sin

Over the course of the past two thousand years of Western civilization, homosexuality has been punished, by torture and death until the nineteenth century, and then by legal restrictions and discrimination into the present. Despite this overwhelming history of rejection and repulsion, some cultures throughout the ages have condoned and even celebrated homosexuality, including ancient Greece, China, and Japan. In his extensive history of homosexuality in different cultures across the ages, Crompton (2003) reports that, for the ancient Greeks, male homosexual relationships were fostered and considered valuable to their cultural survival: "Love between males was honored as a guarantee of military efficiency and civic freedom. It became a source of inspiration in poetry and art, was applauded in theaters and assemblies, and was enthusiastically commended by philosophers who thought it advantageous for young males to have lover-mentors" (p. 536). Japan also valued homosexual relationships for at least a thousand years (800–1868) and, "in its Samurai code, produced an ethos remarkably akin to that of classical Greece" (p. 539). According to Fone (2000), both Plato and Aristotle suggested that homosexuality is • "natural."

However, with the rise of Christianity in the West, homosexuality became more consistently rejected in Europe as a legitimate sexual option. And, in fact, the view of homosexual behavior as sin was accepted and promulgated for more than 1,400 years. During that time, homosexual behavior was considered one of the worst religious sins, along with heresy. In the book of Leviticus, male homosexual intercourse is condemned and referred to as an abomination punishable by death: "If a man has intercourse with a man as with a woman, they both commit an abomination. They shall be put to death; their blood shall be on their own heads" (Lev. 20:13). (Other acts of intercourse punishable by death—for both parties—mentioned in the same passage include a man and his neighbor's wife, a man and his father's wife, a man and his daughter-in-law, a man or a woman and a beast, and a man and his aunt.) Based on this brief biblical text, antihomosexual laws were adopted by Christianity and incorporated into Roman law and hence into European law. It is not completely clear why homosexuality was so vehemently reviled, but "the concern for procreation has been the most commonly suggested rationale for the anti-homosexual legislation of Leviticus" (Crompton, 2003, p. 35). One wonders whether this adequately explains the level of animosity and the severity of punishment that persisted for so many centuries.

In the Middle Ages, homosexuals "were blamed for such disasters as • plagues, earthquakes, floods, famines, and even defeat in battle" (Crompton, 2003, p. xii). In fact, homosexuals have been the scapegoats in many cultures throughout the centuries. In the Netherlands, after a period of economic growth in the seventeenth century, there was an economic downturn and a "steep decline in military and political prestige" following the Peace of Utrecht in 1713. Homosexuals were blamed: "Wealth, high living, and a failure to provide charity were perceived as promoting homosexual behavior. The remarkable prosperity that had itself been the sign of divine favor had, theologians argued, all too easily led to sodomy, which was in turn to blame for the country's economic decline" (p. 465).

In the Middle Ages and the Renaissance, Christian principles and biblical • law dominated, and attempts to *understand* why certain individuals engaged in homosexual relationships seem to have been limited to individual philosophers or religious thinkers who themselves were limited in their interest and ability to test their theories. Even some who believed that homosexuality was a "natural" phenomenon still believed that it should be punished. For example, in the thirteenth century, the philosopher and theologian Saint Thomas Aquinas viewed homosexuals as having a "defect of nature" in them (Fone, 2000, p. 137). Aquinas indicated that "the sodomite emerges as an infected and innately sinful creature, for whom there would be no salvation" (p. 138). Similarly, Saint Bernardino of Siena (1380–1444) believed that "the psychological mark of the sodomite—hatred of women—is not learned but is a part of his nature" (pp. 197–198), and he expected all sodomites to burn in hell.

Before the nineteenth century and the development of more systematic study of human behavior, theories regarding the origins of homosexual behavior were often fantastic and absurd. In sixteenth-century Peru, for example, legend had it that "sodomy had been introduced into the land by certain giants who had landed on the coast. . . . Lacking women, they consorted with each other and were destroyed by a fearful 'fire from heaven'" (Crompton, 2003, p. 318). Also in the sixteenth century, Juan Huarte de San Juan, a Basque physician, explained homosexuality as occurring in utero as a result of temperature changes. Specifically, male homosexuality would result when a fetus is female, the genitals are subjected to too much heat, and the genitals turn inside out. For female homosexuality to occur, the fetus is male, the genitals are subjected to too much cold, and the genitals turn inward, forming a baby that looks female but is really male, psychologically (p. 303).

During the Enlightenment, or the Age of Reason, in the eighteenth century, many prominent European intellectuals turned their attention to homosexuality and theories of its origin. These "rationalists" challenged religious doctrine and tried to apply reason and science, such as it was, to understand a range of social issues. For example, the French philosophers Montesquieu and Diderot both tried to explain homosexuality as a result of social and cultural influences. Montesquieu looked for "sociological causes for male homosexual behavior—causes that were mundane rather than demonic—and [found] different influences in different states at different times: naked athletics in ancient Greece, the scarcity of women in polygamous Asiatic societies, and the sequestering of young males in single-sex schools in France" (Crompton, 2003, pp. 501–502). Diderot theorized that there were many factors that caused homosexuality in Americans, which included the "heat of the climate," bodily proportions that were better between American men than between American men and women, and a lack of pleasure in having sex with women who were too tired (p. 519). Although these and other "rational" theories of the origin of homosexuality were still far from accurate, these thinkers moved the issue into the realm of debate and reason and thus set the stage for further scientific evaluation.

From Sin to Sickness: The Nineteenth and Twentieth Centuries

In the nineteenth century, following the Enlightenment and the increasing interest in science and medicine, the question of why some individuals have a predominantly homosexual orientation interested sexologists, psychologists, psychiatrists, and medical researchers. The terms "invert" and "third sex" were invented to try to describe homosexuals in a medical way. Karl Ulrichs, a German lawyer and a homosexual, published a pamphlet in 1864 explaining the concept of the "third sex," which applied to both female and male homosexuals (Miller, 1995). According to Ulrichs's theory, "a male homosexual was essentially a female soul in a male body; a lesbian was a male soul in a female body" (Miller, 1995, p. 14), and this occurred when the individual's brain did not fully develop, whereas his or her genitals did (Bayer, 1981). Although Ulrichs was gay and a defender of homosexuals, he believed that homosexuality was a "hereditary anomaly" (Bayer, 1981). These new terms ("invert" and "third sex") reflected "an evolution in nineteenth-century thought from a moral and religious attitude toward same-sex relations to a scientific one. As the century wore on, sodomy, the sin, was transformed into homosexuality, the medical category" (Miller, 1995, p. 13). There was a new perspective of homosexuality as a deviation, but one that should be tolerated, possibly treated, but not punished.

Some nineteenth-century medical writers and researchers considered "inverts" to be insane: "Benjamin Tarnovsky, a Russian researcher, insisted (1886) that homosexuality was 'incurable' and that homosexuals could not help being what they were, since the condition arose when parental genes were damaged by epilepsy, alcoholism, or a number of other psychological or physiological traumas" (Fone, 2000, pp. 274–275). Yet others subscribed to the belief that while homosexuality might be innate, it nonetheless represented degenerate behavior. At the beginning of his career, Richard von Krafft-Ebing, a psychiatry professor, wrote that any kind of nonprocreative sex is a "perversion with potentially disastrous personal and social consequences" (Bayer, 1981). By the end of his career, Krafft-Ebing no longer viewed homosexuality as degenerate but rather saw it as just a congenital anomaly. Cesar Lombroso, an Italian criminologist, believed that "homosexuals were at a lower stage of human development than heterosexuals" (Bayer, p. 20), but rather than being punished, they should be confined to asylums.

Toward the end of the nineteenth century, Havelock Ellis, a British sexologist, wrote that homosexuality was inborn and therefore natural, and he was interested in promoting acceptance. Ellis "was the first person to write a book [*Sexual Inversion*, published in 1897] in English that treated homosexuality neither as a disease nor a crime" (Miller, 1995, p. 16). By the turn of the century, many books and articles on inversion were published, and information was also presented in more popular publications, so that these ideas were transmitted into the population at large.

Sigmund Freud, the founder of psychoanalysis, brought scientific approaches to the understanding of homosexuality into the forefront of social theories, and he was one of the first prominent thinkers who gave a rational justification for *acceptance* of homosexuality. He believed that all humans are innately bisexual, and that "a very considerable measure of latent or unconscious homosexuality can be detected in all normal people." Therefore the idea "that nature in a freakish mood created a 'third sex' falls to the ground" (1920/1963, p. 159). For Freud, whether a man or woman would develop a primarily homosexual orientation was determined by both an innate predisposition and psychic factors based on personal experience. He wrote, for example, that male homosexuality is often a result of an unresolved Oedipal conflict whereby a boy identifies with his mother instead of his father and then chooses a male love object (1921/1957). In the end, Freud concluded, "it is not for psychoanalysis to solve the problem of homosexuality. It must rest content with disclosing the psychical mechanisms that resulted in determination of the object-choice, and with tracing the paths leading from them to the instinctual basis of the disposition. There its work ends, and it leaves the rest to biological research" (1920/1963, p. 158). Freud explicated many reasons why homosexuality often could not (or should not) be treated by psychoanalysis, including lack of client motivation (when other family members, but not the patient himself or herself, wanted the homosexuality cured), lack of clear impairment of daily functioning, and lack of subjective distress.

Despite Freud's prolific writing and global influence in the first half of the twentieth century, many psychoanalysts by midcentury rejected his call to try to understand homosexuality from a scientific or biological perspective. Instead, many promoted the notion that homosexuality was primarily a disorder resulting from dysfunctional family relationships that could, and should, be treated. Prominent psychoanalysts such as Sandor Rado (Columbia University) and Irving Bieber (New York Medical College) rejected Freud's view of innate bisexuality and disposition toward homosexuality. Their theories focused on the role of pathological family relationships and experiences, and the inevitable "morbid resolution of the Oedipus complex" (Bieber, 1967, p. 969). Rado posited that homosexuality is really an intense fear of the opposite sex (Miller, 1995), and it represents a "reparative" attempt to find a tolerable sexual outlet (Bayer, 1981). Bieber (1967) agreed that "the presence of anxiety and fear of heterosexuality is a central feature of the inversion" (p. 966). They also concluded from the chromosomal research of the day that "bisexuality is a fiction" and that there is no "existing evidence to support a genetic theory of homosexuality" (p. 968).

Other prominent psychoanalytic thinkers suggested variations on the Oedipal theme first described by Freud, but they regularly looked for causes within individual experience rather than biology. For example, Charles Socarides believed that male homosexuality was a learned behavior that had its roots in the pre-Oedipal period. It developed when a child had difficulty separating from the mother and a fear of merging with her (Bayer, 1981). Melanie Klein posited that homosexuality often developed when individuals had difficulty negotiating the oral phase of development, which created a "cannibalistic" fear of being devoured by the mother (Bieber, 1967, p. 969). Harry Stack Sullivan focused on adolescent experience. He claimed that male homosexual adolescents seek relationships with other males because of their interpersonal problems and fear of heterosexuality (Bieber, 1967, p. 970). Overall, the psychoanalytic school identified homosexuality as pathology, regardless of its specific developmental path. And it was this theoretical position that led to the listing of homosexuality as a personality disturbance in the *DSM-I* (1952).

The belief that male and female homosexuals inevitably emerge from households in which there is a domineering mother and a meek or detached father was pervasive in the field of psychoanalytic psychiatry, and much research was conducted to examine these relationships in detail (e.g., Bieber et al., 1962; Bene, 1965a, 1965b). Female homosexuality received much less theoretical and research attention than male homosexuality, but both were considered to be acquired as a result of childhood experiences. Irving Bieber and his colleagues conducted one of the most cited studies during the 1950s (published in 1962). Their goal was to identify the specific etiology of male homosexuality within family relationships. Their subjects were 106 homosexual patients receiving psychoanalysis from seventy-seven members of the Society of Medical Psychoanalysts in New York. The therapists completed a variety of questionnaires throughout their patients' treatment. Based on the therapists' reports, the researchers concluded:

> The "classical" homosexual triangular pattern is one where the mother is CBI [Close-Binding-Intimate] and is dominant and minimizing toward a husband who is a detached father, particularly a hostile-detached one. From our statistical analysis, the chances appear to be high that any son exposed to this parental combination will become homosexual or develop severe homosexual problems. (p. 172)

A full description of methodological problems in this study is well beyond the scope of this chapter, but a few obvious issues highlight the limits of this line of research. Researcher bias is one of the biggest concerns. Since the subjects were all in psychoanalysis and were all rated by their own psychoanalysts on these family dimensions, the theoretical assumptions of the analysts and of the researchers likely determined the nature of the findings, rather than the evidence guiding the development of their theory. In other words, the people who were "treating" the homosexuals were the ones to rate them on the dynamics that they had already determined were somehow at the root of the problem. Second, the subjects had a range of psychiatric diagnoses, including schizophrenia (27 subjects) and character disorders (42 subjects), and the role of this significant pathology (or of any parental pathology) in observed patterns was not considered. Third, the researchers assumed causation from association and casually dismissed the possibility that, in some cases, parents' behavior may represent a *response* to their children's behavior rather than a cause of it. This study thus seems to reflect the personal beliefs of the researchers rather than a systematic evaluation of the role of the family in the origin of homosexuality.

These and other methodological problems were pervasive in the research of the time. Eva Bene's work is another example. She was a British psychiatrist who also tried to evaluate the specific family relationship patterns associated with homosexuality (Bene, 1965a, 1965b). Her work is a methodological improvement over Bieber's work in that she used samples of homosexuals who did not have serious emotional disturbances, and her data derive from the homosexuals' own ratings of their family experiences. In addition, she conducted separate studies on homosexual men and women. Her conclusion from her data was that "the genesis" of both female and male homosexuality is a poor relationship with *father* rather than with mother and that the focus on mothers had been overstated. However, like Bieber, she equated association with causation, and she dismissed the possibility that homosexuals have different experiences with their parents, in part, *because* of their homosexuality. Gonsiorek (1991) provides a detailed review of the extensive methodological failings (e.g., sampling, interpretation of data) of these types of studies.

The strongly held belief in psychiatry that homosexuality was a pathological condition led to years of largely unsuccessful and, at times, painful "treatments." The most commonly used treatments included lengthy psychoanalysis focused on resolution of family conflicts, as well as aversion therapy, the purpose of which was to condition homosexuals to respond negatively to same-sex stimuli and respond positively to opposite-sex stimuli (for a comprehensive review of treatments and their outcomes, see Haldeman, 1991). In Bieber et al.'s study (1962), treatment outcome was also evaluated, and treatment "success" was defined as homosexuals who became exclusively heterosexual. Results are not compelling, but at the time, the fact that 19 percent of the patients who declared that they were exclusively homosexual at the beginning of treatment, then declared that they were exclusively heterosexual at the end of treatment, was considered a great success given the lack of "success" of other documented intervention efforts. In examining this work, though, it becomes clear that the treatment was really most successful at changing sexual behavior "where the homosexual adaptation was not deeply and thoroughly entrenched" in the first place (Bayer, 1981, p. 33). Many researchers claimed high change rates with aversion therapies as well. Yet these studies have been replete with ethically questionable practices such as disregard for possible mental and physical harm due to use of electric shocks or nausea-inducing drugs. In addition, results have been questionable (Haldeman, 1991). Although certain treatments have led to a reported increase in heterosexual behaviors and a decrease in homosexual behaviors for some patients, they have not generally led to a change in sexual orientation (Haldeman, 1991).

A recent study (Spitzer, 2003) has again raised the question of the appropriateness and effectiveness of reparative therapies, even though many professionals believed that the issue had been put to rest. In fact, leading professional mental health organizations (e.g., American Psychological Association, American Psychiatric Association, American Counseling Association) have already written position statements indicating that reparative therapies are not recommended and that they may cause harm to clients. In this study, Spitzer interviewed 200 men and women who claimed that they were able to change their sexual orientation from predominantly homosexual to predominantly heterosexual and have maintained this shift for at least five years. Ninety-three percent of the subjects reported being highly religious, and 76 percent of the men and 47 percent of the women were married at the time of the interview. This was a self-selected group, not a random sample of clients who sought reparative treatment, so the only conclusion that can be drawn (assuming that the data are accurate and not the product of self-deception) is that *some* people with homosexual tendencies may be able to shift to a predominantly heterosexual orientation, and strong religious motivation may be critical for its "success." Given the limitations of the study, especially regarding response bias and the lack of "objective" measures, these results are not so compelling as to suggest that previous findings should be dismissed or reinterpreted, or that positions regarding reparative treatments should be altered.

Twentieth-Century Pioneers: Evelyn Hooker and Alfred Kinsey

In the 1950s, Evelyn Hooker (UCLA) began to question the notion that homosexuals were, by definition, personality disordered and maladjusted. She raised the possibility that discrimination and stigmatization might play a role in maintaining some of the negative behaviors associated with homosexuality (e.g., lack of long-term relationships) (Bayer, 1981). She obtained a grant from the National Institute of Mental Health to study the question of adjustment in homosexuals, and unlike most other researchers, she used a nonclinical sample of male homosexual adults and compared them to a nonclinical sample of male heterosexual adults. At the time, the Rorschach inkblot test was widely used in psychology and psychiatry practice to assess personality structure and adjustment, and attempts had been made to identify specific kinds of responses that were more likely to occur in a homosexual record than a heterosexual record. With this in mind, and based on her personal hunches about homosexuality, Hooker designed a study to address two issues: (1) whether the two groups would differ in overall adjustment, based on judges' blind ratings, and (2) whether judges could accurately identify homosexuals' versus heterosexuals' profiles based on their responses. The subjects also completed two other projective measures, and expert judges rated adjustment based on those test results. Results from this study found no significant differences between the two groups on adjustment or on overall character style. Hooker concluded: "Homosexuality as a clinical entity does not exist. Its forms are as varied as are those of heterosexuality. . . . Even if one assumes that homosexuality represents a severe form of maladjustment to society in the sexual sector of behavior, this does not necessarily mean that the homosexual must be severely maladjusted in other sectors of his behavior" (Hooker, 1957, p. 30). Hooker recognized that "what is difficult to accept (for most clinicians) is that some homosexuals *may* be very ordinary individuals, indistinguishable, except in sexual pattern, from ordinary individuals who are heterosexual. Or . . . that some *may* be quite superior individuals, not only devoid of pathology . . . but also functioning at a superior level" (p. 29).

Hooker had also reviewed other research on homosexuals and pathology, and she noted that family pathology seemed to exist more often in families of those homosexuals who had greater psychopathology themselves, thus debunking the assumption that the oft-cited association between family psychopathology and maladjustment in homosexuals necessarily implied causation (Bayer, 1981). Hooker was eventually asked to lead the NIMH Task Force on Homosexuality, which produced a report in 1972 calling for homosexuals to be "relieved of discriminatory social practices" (Bayer, 1981, p. 53).

Hooker's research inspired many more studies in the 1960s and 1970s, and with improved methodologies and more objective measures (e.g., the MMPI and Cattell's Sixteen Personality Factor Questionnaire), her findings were replicated time and time again. As a group, homosexual subjects (male and female) did not score in the clinical range on psychometric measures, and researchers concluded that homosexuality was not related to significant psychopathology or maladjustment (see Gonsiorek, 1991, for a more detailed review of research results). In summary, "this line of research suggests that there are few differences between homosexual and heterosexual individuals related to psychiatric symptomatology and essentially no differences in areas related to performance in key areas of life functioning in the real world" (Gonsiorek, 1991, p. 135). By the end of the 1970s, this type of research was largely abandoned; at this point, "the question of inherent pathology in homosexuality has been answered from a scientific point of view and has not been seen as requiring more research" (p. 132).

Alfred Kinsey and his colleagues also presented evidence-based arguments against the prevailing view of homosexuality as pathology in their work on human sexual behavior. Kinsey's team conducted detailed interviews with over ten thousand men and women about their sexual behaviors and preferences, and the publication of this work (on males in 1948, and on females in 1953) caused a bit of a sensation. Interviews revealed that more than one in three adult males (37 percent) and more than 1 in 10 adult females (13 percent) had had some homosexual experience during adulthood. Results indicated that about 10 percent of males and about 2 to 3 percent of females reported "extensive" homosexual experiences (Gebhard & Johnson, 1998). In addition, about 8 percent of adult males reported that they were exclusively homosexual (Kinsey, 1948, pp. 623–651), while about 1 to 3 percent of women reported the same (Kinsey, 1953). Kinsey concluded:

> In view of the data which we now have on the incidence and frequency of the homosexual, and in particular on its co-existence with the hetero-sexual in the lives of a considerable portion of the male population, it is difficult to maintain the view that psychosexual reactions between individuals of the same sex are rare and therefore abnormal or unnatural, or that they constitute within themselves evidence of neuroses or even psychoses. (1948, p. 659)

Based on available data, Kinsey reasoned that humans are capable of a wide range of sexual expression and that there is a continuum of sexual behavior, rather than a dichotomy between homosexual and heterosexual practice. He concluded that "the homosexual has been a significant part of human sexual activity ever since the dawn of history, primarily because it is an expression of capacities that are basic in the human animal" (1948, p. 666).

Kinsey's interviews also included a question regarding the subjects' beliefs about the cause(s) of their homosexuality, and subjects endorsed a variety of the 15 offered explanations. However, they most commonly endorsed explanations that were pervasive in the field of psychiatry at the time. Besides "other" (33 percent), the most commonly endorsed items for "nondelinquent" (i.e., not in prison) white males (the sample size for nonwhite nondelinquent males was too small to draw conclusions; N = 59) were "poor relationship with mother"

(22 percent), "noncongruent gender development" (22 percent), and "early homosexual experience" (21 percent), while only 15 percent endorsed "born that way." For nondelinquent white females, the most commonly endorsed items were "poor relationship with father" (28 percent), "poor relationship with mother" (23 percent), and "other" (23 percent), while only 7 percent endorsed "born that way" (Gebhard & Johnson, 1998). Given differences between those data and the scientific findings that came later (after predominant psychoanalytic theories had fallen from favor), these responses suggest that many homosexuals had, to some degree, internalized the psychoanalytic model that was pervasive at the time.

At the same time that Kinsey and his colleagues were investigating Americans' sexual behaviors, Ford and Beach were investigating sexual behavior in societies around the globe. In their cross-cultural research on human sexual behavior in 190 societies, Ford and Beach (1951) found several cultures (49 out of the 76 for which information about homosexuality was available) in which homosexual behavior has been an accepted part of human sexual patterns, although they found less information regarding female homosexual behavior than male homosexual behavior. They concluded that there is a biological tendency toward homosexual behavior "in most if not all mammals including the human species" (p. 143), and that American society may be in the minority of societies that persistently condemns homosexual behavior.

From Evidence to Advocacy

In the 1950s and 1960s, the civil rights movement gained momentum, and the gay rights movement grew along with it. There was an increase in protest and writings that criticized psychiatry's continued insistence that homosexuality was a disease despite the growing evidence to the contrary (Bayer, 1981). In 1957 the British government asked Sir John Wolfenden, from Reading University, to head a committee whose purpose was to review the laws and research the issues related to both homosexuality and prostitution, and then advise the government. After two years of research, the Wolfenden Committee produced a report calling for the decriminalization of homosexuality in England. They reported that there was not sufficient evidence to indicate that homosexuality was a disease or indicative of pathology, or that it was detrimental to family life. They noted that "adultery, fornication and lesbian behavior" were not considered criminal offenses, so it was not valid to treat consensual male homosexual behavior as criminal (*Wolfenden Report*, 1963, p. 45). Although buggery (sodomy) was punishable by life in prison, they also noted great inconsistency with which male homosexuals were sentenced in the penal system, especially in Scotland. The position of the committee, to decriminalize private, consensual male homosexual behavior, was announced in 1957, but the law reform bill did not pass until 1965 (Miller, 1995). This report was published in the United States, and the well-known psychoanalyst Karl Menninger wrote the introduction. In it, he contradicts much of the content and conclusions of the report by referring to homosexuality as both an "evil" and a sickness.

In 1970 the American Psychiatric Association's yearly meeting was disrupted by protests and interruptions from gay rights activists calling for representation in discussion of this issue. The following year, a panel discussion was held on the topic, but even louder and better-planned disruptions by gay activists occurred at the convention. Finally, at the 1972 convention, there was a "fully institutionalized gay presence," and the disruptions decreased while more professional dialogue increased. According to Bayer (1981), who chronicles the details of the conventions over these important years, an anonymous, cloaked, gay psychiatrist announced that an underground gay psychiatry association met annually at the APA convention, and it included more than 200 members. Also in 1972, gay rights activists protested at the annual convention of the Association for the Advancement of Behavior Therapy, calling for an end to aversion therapies.

The field of psychiatry was polarized by this time, and some outspoken psychiatrists were sympathetic to the cause. Judd Marmor became a leading advocate for the use of psychiatry to help homosexuals adapt to, rather than change, their sexual orientation. He was also a leader in the fight to remove homosexuality from the *Diagnostic and Statistical Manual of Mental Disorders*. In 1972, Robert Spitzer, then head of the Nomenclature Committee for the American Psychiatric Association, agreed to hear arguments for removing homosexuality from *DSM-II*. In early 1973, a presentation was made to the committee, which included research findings as well as a claim that the psychoanalytic position on homosexuality was not only not scientifically founded but causing significant harm. Staunch objectors, such as Socarides and Bieber, formed a committee against removal of Homosexuality from *DSM-II*, and the arguments continued throughout the year.

The APA eventually voted to remove Homosexuality from *DSM-II* in 1973, and it was replaced with Sexual Orientation Disturbance. Part of the rationale for the change was that homosexuality, and other sexual disorders, were the only conditions labeled as psychiatric disorders that did not conform to the definitional requirement that a disorder necessarily causes subjective distress or functional impairment. The new "disorder" could be diagnosed only when the patient was significantly disturbed by his or her own sexual orientation. In addition, the APA board determined that there was sufficient scientific evidence to conclude that homosexuality itself was not a disorder. Despite the official change in nomenclature, the APA remained significantly divided around this issue. More than 10,000 psychiatrists participated in the vote to remove homosexuality from *DSM-II*, and while 58 percent of the votes were in favor of the change, 37 percent were not (Bayer, 1981). When the *DSM-III* was published in 1980, homosexuality was included only under Other Psychosexual Disorders with the label "Ego-Dystonic Homosexuality." The two diagnostic criteria were that the patient wants heterosexual relationships but cannot initiate or maintain them successfully, and that "there is a sustained pattern of homosexual arousal that the individual explicitly states has been unwanted and a persistent source of distress" (*DSM-III*, p. 282). In subsequent publications of the *DSM* (*DSM-III-R* in 1987 and the *DSM-IV*, published in 1994), the word "homosexuality" has been omitted completely. Now a person can be labeled with a Sexual Disorder Not Otherwise Specified if there is a "persistent and marked distress about sexual orientation." Note that it does not specify whether sexual orientation refers to homosexuality or heterosexuality.

There is now professional consensus that by pathologizing homosexuality without evidence to support doing so, the field of psychiatry is strongly implicated in perpetuating the stigmatization of homosexuals in this country. As Bayer (1981) points out, "In removing homosexuality from the *Diagnostic and Statistical Manual*, the Psychiatric Association symbolically deprived American society of its most important justification for refusing to grant legitimation to homosexuality" (p. 195). However, the role of science was critical as well. Gonsiorek (1991) notes that "the political pressure placed on the American Psychiatric Association in the early 1970s was a necessary but not sufficient condition for the depathologizing of homosexuality. The other condition that was also necessary but not sufficient was an empirical basis for discarding the illness model of homosexuality" (p. 116). The empirical data that the APA considered relevant for the argument to remove homosexuality from the *DSM-II* focused on two demonstrated findings: (1) homosexuals are often "satisfied" with their orientation and are not functionally or occupationally impaired, and (2) homosexuality does not appear to be "inherently" disadvantageous, since it is able to flourish in some cultures without detriment.

Although the field of psychiatry has made dramatic progress in the last 30 years, it is worth mentioning that there are still psychoanalytic thinkers who are strong proponents of an experience-based model of the origin of homosexuality despite growing scientific evidence to the contrary. Writing in the early 1990s, for example, Nicolosi (1995) posits that "homosexuality is a developmental problem that is almost always the result of problems in family relations, particularly between father and son. As a result of failure with father, the boy does not fully internalize male gender identity, and develops homosexually. This is the most commonly seen clinical model" (p. 51). At this point in the history of psychology and psychiatry, it is considered inappropriate for professionals to adhere to theories that not only have no apparent empirical support but exist in the context of empirical evidence that clearly refutes them. Gonsiorek (1991) warns:

> The diagnosis of homosexuality as an illness is bad science . . . [since] there is no basis for viewing homosexuality as a disease or as indicative of psychological disturbance. . . . [The] continuing attempt to pathologize homosexuality in the face of strong and consistent disconfirming evidence is unprofessional, irresponsible, and scientifically invalid. It is based on beliefs that have nothing to do with science, specifically dogmatic beliefs about religious, philosophical, and social concerns. (pp. 115–17)

It is also thus the job of professionals to educate the public about empirically based theories versus those that have no scientific basis. In the current American Psychological Association Resolution (adopted in 1975 and updated in 1987), homosexuality as pathology is clearly rejected. The resolution states: "Homosexuality, per se, implies no impairment in judgement, stability, reliability, or general social or vocational capabilities."

A Commitment to Understanding the Origins of Homosexuality: Biology and Genetics

Over the course of the past 30 years, research into the etiology of homosexuality has focused on biological and genetic explanations. Researchers now generally agree that the origin of sexual orientation is likely a complex constellation of factors, but psychosocial explanations alone, such as dysfunctional family relationships, are not generally implicated in the process. Further, there appears to be agreement that homosexuality is not a discrete entity, which is also what Kinsey argued in the 1950s. As Pillard (1991) writes: "There is no single 'type' or 'style' of homosexuality but rather many styles with many origins and outcomes. Homosexual behavior is simply too varied in its expression, too widely occurring in nature, to be the result of any simple, single 'cause'" (p. 42).

There is now evidence that sexual orientation is likely influenced by a range of biological and genetic processes. The exact process and the full range of specific areas of the brain that are implicated, however, are still being investigated. In addition, much of the research has focused on samples of gay men and not lesbians, so generalizability across genders is necessarily limited. In fact, some argue that women's and men's sexuality and sexual orientation are "very different phenomena" (Mustanski, Chivers, & Bailey, 2002), and that the "flexibility" observed in various aspects of female sexuality is not observed to the same degree in men. The biological research that has been conducted is complex and varied, but investigations primarily fall into three categories: neuroanatomy, prenatal hormones, and heritability. Although obviously connected, these three areas will be discussed separately and briefly summarized in the following sections (for more extensive reviews, see Rahman & Wilson, 2003; and Mustanski, Chivers, & Bailey, 2002).

Neuroanatomy

In 1991, Simon LeVay's article "A Difference in Hypothalamic Structure between Heterosexual and Homosexual Men" was published in *Science*. Although other neurobiological research had already been published identifying differences in brain anatomy between homosexual and heterosexual men (e.g., Swaab & Hofman, 1990), LeVay's article received a lot of media attention, and the evidence was used to support the simplistic notion of "a gay brain" (Allen, 1997). LeVay found differences between male homosexual and male heterosexual brains within one hypothalamic structure. He examined a series of nuclei within the hypothalamus (interstitial nuclei of the anterior hypothalamus, or INAH), since there was evidence that certain nuclei differed in size in men's and women's brains (INAH 2 and 3 were shown to be larger in men), and because lesions in the hypothalamus had been shown to "impair hetero-sexual behavior without eliminating sexual drive" (LeVay, 1991, p. 1034). LeVay examined forty-one autopsied brains of both homosexual and heterosexual men and heterosexual women and found that the size of one area, INAH 3, was significantly larger in heterosexual men than in both homosexual men and heterosexual women. LeVay cautioned against concluding that the size of INAH necessarily *causes* sexual orientation, since there is the possibility that sexual behavior causes brain changes, although he noted that the latter was not likely. Recent attempts to replicate LeVay's findings indicate "a nonsignificant trend toward INAH-3 occupying a smaller volume in gay men (N = 14) than in heterosexual men (N = 34)" (Byne et al., 2001, as cited in Mustanski, Chivers, & Bailey, 2002).

Evidence exists for gender differences (referred to as *sex dimorphism*) in other areas of neuroanatomy relevant to sexual behavior. Studies indicate some similar difference patterns, with male homosexuals demonstrating character-istics more similar to heterosexual women than to heterosexual men. Areas of difference within the hypothalamus include the anterior commisure (Allen & Gorski, 1992) and the suprachiasmatic nucleus (Swaab & Hofman, 1990). As with other research, it is important to consider whether conclusions regard-ing causation can reasonably be made based on these findings; while it is not possible to know for sure that neuroanatomical differences necessarily *cause* all adult sexual behavior, rather than vice versa, there appears to be a "trend" toward differences between heterosexual and homosexual men in certain neu-ral areas (Rahman & Wilson, 2003).

An extension of the research on neuroanatomical differences has been es-tablished in the area of neuropsychology. Since men and women have been shown to demonstrate group differences across global cognitive areas indicat-ing gender differences in the use of the two cerebral hemispheres (stronger verbal skills in women, stronger spatial skills in men), efforts have been made to determine whether homosexual men demonstrate cognitive profiles more similar to women than to men. Results suggest that there is a pattern con-sistent with this hypothesis in *some* areas measured; for example, stronger verbal fluency and weaker mental rotation skills (for reviews of this literature, see Rahman & Wilson, 2003; Mustanski, Chivers, & Bailey, 2002). Rahman and Wilson write that "for gay men at least, cognitive performance on mea-sures that typically elicit sex differences is shifted in a 'female-like' direction." In fact, data suggest that homosexual men may have a cerebral organization more similar to heterosexual women than to men; for instance, there is evidence that they have "a bilateral organization of linguistic function . . . that is female typical." While Mustanski, Chivers, and Bailey (2002) agree that the findings thus far suggest that there is "a different pattern" of functional cerebral asymmetry "dependent on sexual orientation in men," there exist only a few studies with small samples, and replication of results is necessary before conclusions can be drawn.

In addition to these cognitive differences, there also appear to be differences in other sexually dimorphic examples of functional cerebral asymmetry, including handedness, dichotic listening, and some motor skills. Handedness is a marker of early neurodevelopment, and it has been shown to be associated with sexual orientation (e.g., Mustanski, Bailey, & Kaspar, 2002; Pattatucci, Patterson, Benjamin, & Hamer, 1998). In their meta-analysis of 20 studies, Lalumiere, Blanchard, and Zucker (2000) found that "homosexual participants had 39% greater odds of being non-right-handed." Hand preference has also been shown to be related to transsexualism, with both male and female transsexuals demonstrating non-right-handedness more often than control subjects (Green & Young, 2001; Orlebeke, Boomsma, Gooren, Verschoor, & van den Bree, 1992). McCormick and Witelson (1994) used a linguistic dichotic listening task (i.e., stimuli presented to each ear separately) to assess functional cerebral asymmetry. All groups demonstrated greater accuracy with their right ear, which is expected given left-hemispheric dominance of language functions. However, heterosexual right-handers did better than heterosexual left-handers, while this pattern was not found in the gay and lesbian subjects. They found "different patterns of functional cerebral symmetry in gay men and lesbians compared with heterosexual people and, specifically, less association between motoric and linguistic components of cerebral symmetry." Using a task in which men and women were instructed to throw to a target, Hall and Kimura (1995) found expected sex differences in heterosexual subjects, with the men throwing more accurately than the women. They also found that "gay men threw less accurately and lesbians tended to throw more accurately than their heterosexual counterparts" and that "differences in sports history or hand strength did not account for these effects" (p. 395). These researchers also compared the groups on a fine-motor task, and they replicated the "female-typical superiority" but found no effect of sexual orientation.

Prenatal Hormones

In 1987, Ellis and Ames proposed a complex and influential theory of how sexual orientation (and not just homosexuality) is determined. They identified four factors, which in combination are likely to determine sexual orientation and behavior: genes, hormones, neuroanatomy, and environment. These interact in a complex way prenatally and affect the development of the hypothalamic-limbic region of the brain as well as those parts of the brain responsible for gender-typed behavior. Following their lead, researchers began to look carefully at the role of prenatal hormones on the development of sexual orientation, and, specifically, the role of prenatal androgen. Prenatal hormones are important in determining the sexual differentiation of the brain of the fetus, so it is reasonable to assume that they are implicated in the development of whatever brain systems are responsible for sexual orientation. Much research on the role of prenatal hormones has been conducted with animals, and results consistently show that animals develop gender-atypical sexual behavior when sex hormones are artificially introduced into their systems during gestation.

Mustanski, Chivers, and Bailey (2002) review a number of cases of prenatally normal males who had sexual reassignment surgeries soon after birth due to genital anomalies or circumcision accidents, and who were followed into adulthood: "The vast majority of patients rejected their assigned gender and reported sexual attraction toward females" (p. 94). The authors conclude: "The relatively consistent result across these various conditions, that prenatal androgen activity potentiates attraction to females and the absence of such activity potentiates attraction to males, is strongly suggestive of prenatal neurohormonal effects in determining sexual orientation" (p. 97).

Female patients with atypical sexual syndromes have also been studied, and results further support the notion that hormonal influences in utero are strongly related to sexual orientation. Congenital adrenal hyperplasia (CAH) is a condition where a female fetus is exposed to increased androgen levels and then develops masculinized genitals. If diagnosed accurately, the female infant receives genital reassignment surgery, and the child is raised as a female. Research with this small population has consistently shown that they have a greater incidence of homosexuality in adulthood (e.g., Meyer-Bahlburg, Gruen, New, & Bell, 1996; Zucker et al., 1996). There is also some evidence that exposure to prenatal estrogens is related to female homosexuality (Meyer-Bahlburg et al., 1995).

Genetics

In the field of genetic research, two main lines of study are used to help determine whether and how sexual orientation is heritable: twin and family studies, and investigations of DNA at the molecular level. To date, results suggest that homosexuality runs in families, and that there may be one or more specific genetic markers for some homosexuals.

Although results of family studies have varied, estimates are that about 9 percent of gay males have gay brothers, and that homosexual women have more homosexual sisters than do heterosexuals, although estimates for females vary more widely (Bailey & Pillard, 1995). There is also evidence of a greater incidence of "nonheterosexuality" (i.e., lesbian and bisexual women) in the daughters, nieces, and paternally related female cousins of lesbians (Pattatucci & Hamer, 1995). These data support the idea that homosexuality runs in families.

Many twin studies have been conducted to further investigate whether familiality is due to shared environmental effects or to genes. Results indicate that the familiality of homosexuality likely has a genetic basis, at least in large part (Hershberger, 1997; Kendler, Thornton, Gilman, & Kessler, 2000; Mustanski, Chivers, & Bailey, 2002; Rahman & Wilson, 2003). In 1952, Kallmann, a geneticist, examined 40 pairs of monozygotic twins and 45 pairs of dizygotic twins and found almost 100 percent concordance rates of homosexuality in the monozygotic pairs. The dizygotic twins had a 60 percent concordance rate, and non-twin controls had an 11 percent concordance rate. Although Kallmann's astonishing findings have never been replicated and his results have been called into question, he was nonetheless one of the first to claim that homosexuality is genetically determined. Since Kallmann's study, other research has consistently found approximately a 50 percent concordance rate for male and female homosexual monozygotic twins, and about 15 to 25 percent concordance for dizygotic twins (e.g., Bailey & Pillard, 1991; Bailey, Pillard, Neale, & Agyei, 1993). Even though rates vary within each study, a consistent finding has been that the incidence of monozygotic concordance is about twice that of dizygotic concordance (LeVay, 1996). In calculating heritability estimates, studies have usually found that heritability accounts for the most variance, followed by nonshared environmental influences, and then shared environmental influences (Mustanski, Chivers, & Bailey, 2002). That is, there is a genetic component to sexual orientation, and different environmental influences between siblings (which can include individual biological events) are more important than common environmental influences (such as growing up in the same family) in the development of homosexuality.

Dean Hamer, a leader in the search for the "gay gene," and his colleagues were the first to find a specific marker on the X chromosome that appears to be linked to male homosexuality (Xq28) (Hamer, S. Hu, Magnuson, N. Hu, & Pattatucci, 1993). Their article was published in *Science* and, as with LeVay's article on INAH 3, immediately caused a media sensation. Hamer and his team first examined the family trees of gay men and found increased incidence of homosexuality along the maternal line. Follow-up studies provided even more evidence that this genetic pathway was through the mother. Given these findings, Hamer logically looked for a DNA link on the X chromosome and found "an excess coinheritance of Xq28 markers by homosexual brothers" (Hamer et al., 1993). Hamer's results have been replicated (e.g., Hu et al., 1995), but not consistently (e.g., Rice, Anderson, Risch, & Ebers, 1999). Other efforts at finding alternative genetic explanations for male homosexuality have been less successful. For instance, a recent gene study was conducted on CYP19, which is the aromatase enzyme involved in converting androgens to estrogens, but the analysis did not differentiate between heterosexual and homosexual men. The authors conclude that the "variation in the gene for this subunit of the aromatase enzyme complex is not likely to be a major factor in the development of individual differences in male sexual orientation" (Dupree, Mustanski, Bocklandt, Nievergelt, & Hamer, 2004).

Hamer and Copeland (1994) note that finding a relevant genetic link for female homosexuality will be much more difficult than for male homosexuality, since "women display a wider diversity of sexual expressions . . . than do men" (p. 146), and because women inherit two X chromosomes, one from the mother and one from the father, while men inherit only one.

Where Are We Now?

Clearly, questions regarding the origin of sexual orientation remain, and more research is necessary to further our understanding of orientation variations, gender differences, and the critical biological, genetic, cultural, and environmental processes that determine sexual orientation. Contributions from behavioral geneticists, biologists, cultural and feminist psychologists, and others can inform this debate. Behavioral geneticists will need to continue to explore not only the genetic determinants of sexual orientation, but also the critical shared and individual environmental influences, and how these influences interact with genetics to determine sexual orientation (Pattatucci, 1998). Feminist scholars can help us understand how science, sexuality, and cultural values interact to influence our perceptions and definitions of sexual behavior (e.g., Fausto-Sterling, 2000; Terry, 1997).

For many years, the question that motivated researchers and practitioners was how homosexual orientation develops and whether or not evidence suggests that it is natural or immutable. This was true for the sexologists of the nineteenth century and the psychoanalysts of the twentieth. More recently, researchers have concluded that the rigid and dichotomous yes/no, immutable/changeable, innate/learned set of questions belies a more complex reality of human sexuality and sexual orientation. There are likely different pathways for different individuals, and there are more variations in sexual orientation than just exclusively heterosexual or exclusively homosexual. In addition, some argue that there is a stronger biological component for gay men than for lesbians, and that women's sexuality is more "fluid." It is true that attempts to answer these dichotomous questions can be a disservice to gays and lesbians, since such inquiries run the risk of promoting the idea that gays and lesbians are "different" and belong in a separate category rather than existing on the "normal" human sexual continuum (Rist, 1995; Terry, 1997). Suggesting that homosexual behavior is acceptable only if a scientific explanation of its origin can be found is also problematic, since it justifies arbitrarily limiting basic individual freedoms in the sexual realm.

Despite these concerns, it is important to consider the political climate in which gays and lesbians find themselves in the first part of the twenty-first century. As a culture, we do not yet have the luxury of dismissing scientific explanations that are simplified, because they are necessary to inform public opinion. Most of us simply cannot understand the intricacies of molecular genetic or behavior genetic research, or the complex interplay of genes, neuroanatomy, and exposure to other biological, environmental, and cultural processes that lead to variations in sexual orientation. We can understand that the scientific evidence thus far points to the likelihood that many, if not most, homosexuals are, in fact, "born that way," or at least "born more likely to be that way," and that same-sex attraction is a natural variation of human sexuality and not a pathological aberration. Even though the determinants of sexual orientation have not been fully identified, we can conclude from the research to date that sexual orientation is, in most circumstances, unchosen and unchangeable. We need to resist explanations that are based on dogma or uninformed opinion and use reasoned scientific findings to inform our social policies and laws. As our history bears out, theories and explanations based on fear and lacking scientific foundation are dangerous and have no place in our courtrooms.

4

Gays and Lesbians as Parents and Partners: The Psychological Evidence

Elizabeth Cantor

Gay and lesbian adults' ability to raise well-adjusted children and create healthy homes has been called into question, at first within the context of divorce and custody proceedings twenty to thirty years ago, and still more recently within the debate over same-sex marriage. Does the psychological research bear this out? Are children raised in families with a homosexual parent likely to be maladjusted and shunned by their peers? Are they more likely than children raised by heterosexual parents to be homosexual themselves? Do homosexual parents create warm and nurturing homes for their children, or are they characterized by a lack of boundaries and moral clarity? Are gay and lesbian couples as capable of psychological intimacy and making long-term commitments as heterosexual couples? Many observers might find these questions absurd, if not offensive, since they presuppose that a parent's private sexual behavior is somehow more related to a child's development than other factors such as love, respect, and positive expectations, and that gay and lesbian adults either have deficient relationship skills or are simply uninterested in committing to intimate relationships. Nonetheless, psychologists have conducted numerous studies to determine how lesbian and gay parents parent, how children of lesbian and gay parents develop, and whether gay and lesbian couples function similarly to heterosexual couples in important ways.

When engaging in the debate over the "appropriateness" of lesbian or gay relationships or parenthood, it is important to remember that there are millions of gay and lesbian couples (Peplau & Cochran 1990), millions of children in families with gay or lesbian parents (Falk, 1994), and these families are not going to disappear regardless of public (or court) opinion. Even if the public (or some of the public) is uncomfortable with this fact, it is nonetheless a fact much the way that interracial marriage is a fact. Whether the numbers of children being raised by gay and lesbian parents will eventually increase or decrease over time is a matter of conjecture. Most gay fathers and lesbian mothers are currently raising children that were conceived within prior heterosexual unions that have dissolved. It seems likely that as homosexuality is more accepted within our culture, fewer homosexual adults will join heterosexual unions, and therefore that fewer children will be born under these circumstances. However, lesbian mothers are now choosing to adopt or bear (through donor insemination) children on their own or with a lesbian partner. Thus, while the number of children born to homosexual parents through heterosexual unions will likely decrease, the number of children born to, or adopted by, lesbian mothers as single or coupled parents will likely increase. Gay fathers are less likely than heterosexual fathers and all mothers to be primary custodial parents, either through divorce or not, so the number of children raised primarily by gay fathers will likely always remain relatively small. However, the number of children adopted by gay fathers will likely increase as laws prohibiting such adoptions diminish. Regardless of the numbers, the question that child advocates should be asking is what is in the best interest of the children given their situation. Is it to take them away from their parents? Or is it to increase awareness of children's specific needs and concerns and to construct social policies that will support them in their development?

What do we know about the well-being of children raised by gay and lesbian parents? What do we know about how gay fathers and lesbian mothers parent? What do we know about the stability and quality of gay and lesbian couple relationships? There is considerable research on children raised by lesbian mothers and about lesbian parents, while there is far less research on children raised by gay fathers and about gay parents. In the following sections, the research on lesbian and gay parents and their children is reviewed. Research has addressed both child outcomes and parenting variables, and these will be discussed separately, first for lesbian families and then for families with a gay father. A few longitudinal studies in the literature on lesbian families deserve special mention, since they provide a unique set of data regarding children's adjustment and perspective over time. There is also a body of research that addresses the quality and stability of gay and lesbian couple relationships, and this will be presented last.

Lesbian and Gay Parents and Their Children

Many reviews of the literature on gay and lesbian parenthood already exist (e.g., Anderssen, Amlie, & Ytteroy, 2002; Falk, 1994; Fitzgerald, 1999; Gottman, 1990; Green & Bozett, 1991; Parks, 1998; Patterson, 1992; Stacey & Biblarz, 2001), and reviewers overwhelmingly conclude that while there are methodological limitations to much of the research, the evidence consistently indicates that children living with homosexual parents are as "well off" as children living with heterosexual parents. Research has consistently failed to find differences between these groups that would suggest that lesbian or gay parents have a detrimental effect on their children because of their sexual orientation. Although this is also the conclusion that I have ultimately reached, a closer look at the research highlights important methodological limitations, especially with research on gay fathers, as well as some interesting possible differences that should not be overlooked.

Methodological Limitations

SAMPLING

Many of the early studies on gay and lesbian families used small, nonrepresentative samples because it was very hard to "find" homosexual parents except through gay-friendly organizations and through word of mouth (referred to in the literature as "snowball sampling"). Therefore, results are hard to generalize to the general population, and results have to be considered as being indicative of only the samples involved. In many cases, samples were comprised of white, affluent, and highly educated parents. The preferred method is always to find a "random" sample, which means that all people in the group of interest have an equal chance of being in the study. This rarely happens in research, since people who volunteer for research are probably different from people who don't, but it is the standard that researchers try to meet. Sampling methods have become more robust as the population of gay and lesbian parents is less "hidden." For example, studies with families using donor insemination have used more representative samples of families using sperm banks (e.g., Chan, Raboy, & Patterson, 1998; Brewaeys, Ponjaert, Van Hall, & Golombok, 1997), while other researchers have been able to gather data from families within larger population studies (e.g., Golombok et al. [2003] used subjects from the Avon Longitudinal Study, which is a geographic population study including more than fourteen thousand British families; Wainright, Russell, and Patterson [2004] used subjects from a national sample of adolescents through the Add Health study). It is also the case that children from earlier studies were all products of divorce, in both the lesbian and heterosexually parented homes, and it is difficult to tease out the effects of divorce on these groups of children. The newer studies looking at children born into lesbian-parented families eliminates the confounding divorce experience while also being able to evaluate how children develop with two mothers compared with children who are raised by heterosexual parents.

SOURCES OF DATA

Much of the early data was collected by parent report without corroborating evidence from teachers or the children themselves. Since the motivation to present one's children and one's parenting skills in a positive light is obvious (referred to as *response bias*), especially when the stakes are so high, it is hard to fully accept the data as representing an objective evaluation of children's functioning. To illustrate an extreme example of this in one study, whether a child had experienced molestation by the father was assessed by asking the father (Miller, 1979). Last, some of the earlier studies, especially with gay fathers, used a descriptive approach rather than an empirical one. That is, the researchers reported on information gathered from the subjects and the trends that were evident, without subjecting the findings to rigorous statistical analysis. This is not unusual when beginning to investigate a new topic, since it helps identify questions to ask and theoretical ideas to consider in future research efforts. However, it is again important to realize that the "results" may not fully represent the trends of the larger population.

Children of Lesbian Mothers

The majority of research on children with homosexual parents has been with lesbian-mother families. This is because most of the children with homosexual parents are children with lesbian mothers. Over the course of the past 20 years, the research has shifted from comparisons primarily involving divorced lesbian and heterosexual mothers to comparisons involving planned lesbian and heterosexual families through donor insemination (often referred to as the "lesbian baby boom"). There are still relatively few studies examining within-group differences for this group of children, but those that do, raise important issues for further study. This course of study will likely provide much more useful results, as it acknowledges that children with lesbian parents are interesting to study in their own right. It will hopefully lead to awareness of the specific issues these families might be facing and ideas about how to help them develop and function optimally. In addition, research involving this population will contribute to the general field of family studies and child development by identifying mechanisms related to parental gender and sexuality as they affect parenting and child development.

Three main areas of concern dominate the literature on children of lesbian mothers: children's sexual and gender development, their overall social-emotional adjustment (including self-esteem, behavior problems, etc.), and their peer relationships. In custody disputes, it has been argued that children with homosexual parents would be more likely to become homosexual themselves or at least experience gender confusion, become maladjusted, and experience more stressful peer relationships (due to harassment and stigma) than would children raised in heterosexually parented homes.

SEXUAL AND GENDER DEVELOPMENT

A variety of specific issues arise in discussing children's sexual and gender development. *Gender* or *sex role* behavior refers to behavior that is typically male or female, as determined by one's culture. *Gender* or *sexual identity* refers to the subjective feeling of being either female or male. *Sexual orientation* refers to sexual partner preference. Obviously, determining sexual orientation of subjects is limited to older adolescent and adult offspring.

Gender Role and Gender Identity   Children of lesbian mothers have not demonstrated more gender identity or sex role confusion than children of heterosexual mothers regardless of whether the children were living with divorced parents or born into a lesbian family (Brewaeys et al., 1997; Golombok et al., 2003; Golombok, Spencer, & Rutter, 1983; Gottman, 1990; Green, Mandel, Hotvedt, Gray, & Smith, 1986; Hoeffer, 1981; Javaid, 1993; Kirkpatrick, Smith, & Roy, 1981; MacCallum & Golombok, 2004; Patterson, 1994). Most of the children studied tend to play with gender-specific toys, understand their own gender identity (am I a boy or a girl?), and demonstrate gender-typical preferences and behaviors. These constructs have been examined in a variety of studies, through a variety of measures, in several countries, and results consistently show that children with lesbian mothers do not differ in important ways from children living with heterosexual mothers.

For example, Golombok et al. (2003) administered a questionnaire to children from heterosexual and lesbian-led families to evaluate their preferences for a variety of "feminine" and "masculine" activities (The Activities Inventory). They found no significant difference between the two groups as a function of the mother's sexual orientation. Kirkpatrick et al. (1981) examined children's gender development using an inkblot technique and drawings, and they found that the two groups did not differ as a function of their mothers' sexual orientation. Hoeffer (1981) measured sex role behavior by asking children to divide pictured toys into groups of most, somewhat, or least preferred. The toys fell into one of three categories: feminine, masculine, and neutral. The children were also asked to explain their choices. Again, no differences were found between the two groups of children, but there were significant differences between the genders, as expected, with boys picking more "masculine" toys and girls picking more "feminine" toys regardless of the mother's sexual orientation. Of interest as well is that mothers were asked to identify preferred toys for their children, and it was found that heterosexual mothers were more likely to prefer sex-typed toys for their children than were lesbian mothers. Interestingly, despite the difference in mothers' attitudes, the children from the two groups did not differ from each other.

Green et al. (1986) interviewed children born to heterosexual and lesbian mothers and asked them which gender they would choose if they could be born again, and no differences were found between groups, with most children choosing the gender that they already were. Children were asked to draw a person (using the Draw A Person scoring system), and the groups did not differ in their scores and in the number of children who chose to draw the same or opposite gender figure. Green et al. also asked the children to identify toy preferences using the "It-Scale" (using a neutral figure, "It," to choose the activities), and both groups of boys and girls scored within the "masculine" and "feminine" ranges respectively. Last, they interviewed the children and their mothers about actual toy and activity preferences at school and home, and about thoughts of future jobs, and both similarities and differences emerged. While boys did not differ between groups (both consistently chose traditional masculine activities and job choices), the girls differed somewhat, with the children of lesbian mothers demonstrating a wider range of possibilities. About one-half of the lesbians' daughters identified possible careers such as doctor, lawyer, astronaut, or engineer, compared to about one-fifth of the heterosexuals' daughters. (Note that this study was conducted in the 1980s, and it would be expected that these numbers would be higher for all girls today.) In terms of activity choices, it was found that daughters of lesbian mothers were more likely to be involved in both feminine and gender-neutral activities, while daughters of heterosexual mothers were more likely to be restricted to feminine activities.

In a longitudinal study in England, MacCallum and Golombok (2004) evaluated "gender role orientation" when the children were 12 years old. The researchers compared children born to lesbian mothers with children from both single- and two-parent heterosexual households on a variety of adjustment variables. Results from the Children's Sex Role Inventory (CSRI), which is a questionnaire that was administered *to the children*, indicated that boys did not differ on the "masculinity scale" across groups, and girls did not differ on the "femininity" or "masculinity" scales across groups. However, boys from single-parent (i.e., father absent) homes scored significantly higher on the "femininity" scale than did boys from two-parent heterosexual homes regardless of mother's sexual orientation. The researchers explain that "during [the] interview, several of the mothers in father-absent families spoke about how they were trying to teach their children, both sons and daughters, to be considerate and appreciate the feelings of others" (p. 1416).

Although there are several more studies examining children's gender role behavior and gender identity (cited earlier), the results are consistent and suggest that there are more similarities than differences, and the differences found do not indicate detrimental effects. If anything, they suggest that daughters of lesbian mothers may be exposed to a wider range of gender-neutral activities and career options in a positive way, and sons in father-absent families may be more likely to develop increased emotional sensitivity while maintaining their masculine identity.

Sexual Orientation   Several researchers have examined whether children who live with a lesbian mother are more likely than children living with heterosexual parents to grow up with a homosexual orientation. Since we already know that sexual orientation is primarily genetically and biologically determined (see chapter 3 in this volume), this line of research is unlikely to tell us that homosexual parents pass on homosexuality like a contagious virus, or

Elizabeth Cantor

that children can "decide" to be gay in order to be like their parents. It is also the case that even asking these questions assumes that becoming or being a homosexual is a negative thing in and of itself. This points to the unfortunate pattern of heterosexist bias determining research questions.

These points aside, the research on this question indicates no elevated incidence of homosexuality in offspring living with a lesbian parent (Golombok et al., 1983; Gottman, 1990; Green, 1978; O'Connell, 1993). However, some evidence (from one more recent longitudinal study) suggests that daughters of lesbians may be more likely to *experiment* with lesbian relationships during adolescence and young adulthood (Tasker & Golombok, 1997a), even though the majority of these adolescents develop a heterosexual orientation. This finding suggests that some daughters of lesbian mothers are more open to the possibility of same-sex relationships even when they have a primarily heterosexual orientation. Further research is necessary to evaluate whether same-sex experimentation during adolescence or early adulthood influences adult functioning and, if so, how.

EMOTIONAL ADJUSTMENT

Research has compared children of lesbian mothers with children of heterosexual mothers on a variety of measures of well-being, and data all indicate that the groups are basically not distinguishable from each other. Studies have examined variables such as self-esteem in adolescence (Huggins, 1989); IQ (Flaks, Ficher, Masterpasqua, & Joseph, 1995; Green et al., 1986; Kirkpatrick et al., 1981); and behavior problems in school (Golombok et al., 1983) and at home (Patterson, 1994). While much of the earlier research focused on comparisons between divorced single mothers, more recent efforts have examined the adjustment of children born to (or adopted by) and raised in lesbian homes (e.g., Chan, Raboy, & Patterson, 1998; Dundas and Kaufman, 2000; Flaks et al., 1995; MacCallum & Golombok, 2004; Patterson, 1994; Wainright et al., 2004). The following are examples of more recent research studies in which certain interesting group differences were found.

Patterson (1994, 1996) studied a group of children born to, or adopted by, lesbian mothers in the San Francisco Bay Area by administering a variety of measures of psychosocial functioning. Although she did not employ a control group, she compared the subjects' scores to the norms established for each of the measures. Mothers completed the Child Behavior Checklist (CBCL), which is a widely used measure of children's social competence and behavior problems, and the children were interviewed using several scales of the Eder's Children's Self-View Questionnaire, which measures self-concept. Results from the CBCL indicated no differences between the subjects and the "normal population" and expected significant differences between the subjects and the "clinical population" as determined by questionnaire normative data. In the area of self-concept, results are less clear. Significant differences between the subjects' scores and those of the normative sample were not found on three of the five scales: Aggression, Social Closeness, and Social Potency. However, the subjects did score significantly higher on two of the five scales, Well-Being and Stress Reaction. Patterson (1996) notes that scores were still within the normal range (according to the scale's scoring procedures) despite the difference, but a look at the mean scores (shown in Patterson, 1994) suggests that the scores were not in the "normal" range but were greater than one standard deviation above the mean. In addition, Patterson's sample of children ranged in age from four to nine, but they were compared to a normative group of five-and-one-half-year-olds. Although these issues do not necessarily render the results meaningless, they do suggest that cautious interpretation is in order. The results indicate that "children of lesbian mothers said that they more ʋ felt angry, scared or upset but also said that they more often felt joyful, comfortable with themselves than did children of heterosexual ʋ ʋ (p. 16ʋ). It is possible that these results indicate that children of lesbian mothers are more likely, or more willing, "to report a variety of intense emotional experiences, whether positive or negative" (p. 170). Regardless of the reasons for the difference, this group of children was judged by others to demonstrate normal adjustment in a variety of areas.

Brewaeys and her colleagues in the Netherlands and Belgium have studied children born into lesbian homes via donor insemination (e.g., Brewaeys et al., 1997; Vanfraussen, Ponjaert-Kristoffersen, & Brewaeys, 2003). In one study (Brewaeys et al., 1997) the researchers compared children born to lesbian mothers via donor insemination, children born to heterosexual mothers via donor insemination, and children born to heterosexual couples in the conventional way on a number of parenting, couple, and child variables. They also used the Child Behavior Checklist (CBCL) to evaluate overall behavioral functioning of the children, and results indicated that the children born to lesbian mothers did not differ significantly from the two heterosexual groups; however, results did indicate that the *two heterosexual groups* differed from each other, with the children born via donor insemination demonstrating relatively more behavior problems than the children conceived naturally. It was found that many more children in the heterosexual donor insemination group scored in the clinical range than did the children in the other two groups. Results from this study and others (e.g., MacCallum & Golombok, 2004) suggest that the concern that "father absence" necessarily has a detrimental effect is not supported and that children raised from birth in lesbian-parented homes appear to develop similarly to their well-adjusted peers.

PEER RELATIONSHIPS

Friendships   In reviewing the research on children's peer relationships, two distinct questions emerge. First, do children of lesbian parents have satisfying peer relationships? And second, do these children experience more stressful social interactions due to teasing or feeling stigmatized compared to children in heterosexually parented homes? As with many child variables in this body of research, peer relationship quality is probably not best evaluated through parent report, since there may be a strong bias toward presenting children's social skills in a positive light. In fact, the studies that have employed this strategy have found that children in lesbian homes are rated as having peer relationships that are as strong as those of their peers (e.g., Green et al., 1986; Patterson, 1994). However, it appears that children from lesbian-parented homes also report themselves that their peer relationship quality is similar to that of their peers (Golombok et al., 2003; Green et al., 1986). Teachers have also reported on social problems and prosocial behavior, and results are consistent and suggest that children's peer relationships do not differ based on their mothers' sexual orientation (Chan, Raboy, & Patterson, 1998; Flaks et al., 1995; Golombok et al., 2003).

Two studies have specifically addressed peer relationships with adolescents (MacCallum & Golombok, 2004; and Wainright et al., 2004). MacCallum and Golombok compared children born to lesbian mothers with children from both single- and two-parent heterosexual households in the longitudinal study described earlier. Data were gathered from parents, the children (at age 12), and their teachers. Results indicate no significant differences between the groups on the children's peer relationships across measures. Wainright et al. compared groups of adolescents identified through a national sample of over 12,000 adolescents from across the country. Forty-four adolescents, ages 12 to

18, raised with lesbian parents were compared to a control group of 44 adolescents raised by heterosexual parents, and the groups were matched on a variety of demographic variables (e.g., parents' ages, income, racial background, etc.). Information was gathered from a variety of sources, including the adolescents, their parents, and their teachers. The two groups of adolescents did not differ with regard to a range of psychosocial variables (such as anxiety, depression, and self-esteem), which is consistent with previous reports. However, the group of children raised by lesbian parents reported more "school connectedness" than their counterparts, and this did not vary based on gender. School connectedness was assessed with interview questions about the degree to which the adolescents "felt close to other students, felt like a part of their school, felt safe in their school" (p. 1891). One gender difference also emerged in the adolescents' reports of how much they perceived that adults, teachers, and friends cared about them, with girls reporting higher levels of care than did boys, regardless of the mother's sexual orientation. In examining romantic relationships among the adolescents, there were no differences between the two groups in whether they had had a romantic relationship during the previous 18 months, or the frequency of sexual intimacy. Too few subjects reported same-sex interest or experience to be able to use the data for statistical analyses. The researchers also compared the children of lesbian mothers to the larger (i.e., unmatched) sample of adolescents from which they were chosen, and all comparisons were nonsignificant.

Stigmatization   Whether children of lesbian mothers experience more teasing or bullying, or feel stigmatized because of their alternative family structure, is the second question raised in the area of peer relationships. Research described earlier indicates that children with lesbian mothers have peer relationships and social skills that are as strong as those of children from heterosexually parented homes. Some of the measures used include items that specifically address "peer acceptance," and group differences have not been found. But it still seems quite likely that they, like all children who are "different" on any salient dimension, are at greater risk for teasing and feeling stigmatized. Research findings are very limited in this area, since peer relationships are often evaluated through questionnaires, but feeling stigmatized per se is not addressed directly.

One study has been conducted examining how coping strategies may guard against low self-esteem in the face of perceived stigma among children of lesbian mothers (Gershon, Tschann, & Jemerin, 1999), but results from that study do not include the level of teasing or stigma that these children report actually facing. Another study suggests that children of lesbian mothers do not necessarily experience significantly more teasing or harassment than their peers, but they may be more likely to *worry* that they will be teased (O'Connell, 1993); however, this study is based on a sample of only 11 subjects (young adult children of lesbian mothers). An older study conducted in Denmark involved interviews with 13 children of lesbian mothers, and the researchers report that the children experienced "direct negative reactions" from peers because of their mother's lesbianism. However, actual numbers were not reported (Haack-Moller & Mohl, 1984, as translated and cited in Anderssen et al., 2002). In an even older study, Green (1978) interviewed 21 children of lesbian mothers, and 3 of the children reported being teased one time by a classmate.

The only study that involves extensive information about teasing and bullying is Tasker and Golombok's (1997a) longitudinal study with children raised by postdivorce lesbian mothers. In the second phase of the study (Time 2), 25 adult subjects were interviewed about their experiences as adolescents as well as their current attitudes. Subjects, who were compared to a control group of offspring raised by heterosexual mothers, were asked about incidents, extent, and content of teasing by peers. There were no significant group differences, but there was a trend (meaning that the difference approached significance) toward children of lesbian mothers reporting more teasing regarding *their own* (versus their mothers') sexuality. Worth mentioning is that fully 76 percent of *all* subjects reported experiencing some bullying or teasing about something during their school years. It is also important to point out that these data are based on retrospective reports and so may not fully reflect the adolescents' actual experience.

The issue of stigmatization, maybe more so than other research variables mentioned, would seem to be particularly sensitive to time and place. One would assume that children with homosexual parents are more likely to be teased in certain communities than in others, and more 20 years ago than today. Children living and going to school in more educated or liberal communities (e.g., the Bay Area) might experience less stigmatization and direct teasing than children living and going to school in less sophisticated areas. It would seem to be the same for interracial families—the less discrepant the family's structure is from the norm of the community, the more accepted the family.

What is clear from the evidence, however, is that regardless of the degree of stigmatization and teasing, the children of lesbian mothers from a number of studies appear to be as well-adjusted as their peers.

In sum, the research on children of lesbian mothers is replete with methodological limitations, most notably nonrandom, small samples. However, more recent efforts have been successful in using more representative samples from larger population studies both in the United States and abroad. As many of the other reviewers of this literature have also concluded, the evidence overwhelmingly suggests that children raised by a lesbian mother do not appear to be suffering any obvious detrimental effects as a function of their mother's sexual orientation. Some research studies have identified possible differences, including less rigid gender roles for girls, more same-sex experimentation of some girls in adolescence, and more teasing in certain settings, but these differences have not been found across studies. Children of lesbian mothers do not appear to be significantly different from their peers in terms of sexual orientation, self-esteem, behavioral adjustment, or social skills.

Lesbian Mothers

Numerous studies exist examining lesbian mothers' parenting styles and family functioning, although more recent studies have examined parenting in the context of a planned lesbian family rather than in families with a divorced lesbian mother. Overall, results from earlier and later studies suggest that lesbian mothers demonstrate as much warmth and sensitivity as heterosexual mothers, and their children are as well cared for, but interesting differences have been found in how some lesbian couple families function compared to families with heterosexual parents.

Early research on lesbian mothers suffered from the same methodological problems stated earlier in relation to child outcomes. For example, in one study comparing divorced lesbian mothers to married heterosexual mothers, subjects were administered questionnaires and asked to respond to a slide presentation of several parent-child situations in order to evaluate basic parenting skills (Miller, Jacobsen, & Bigner, 1981). These two groups were not matched on important variables (income, marital status, occupation), and results indicated significant differences between the groups of mothers, with lesbian mothers appearing more "child-oriented" overall than the heterosexual mothers. A similar study, conducted by Mucklow and Phelan (1979), found no differences between lesbian and "traditional" mothers on a slide-show measure of parenting attitudes.

Since a growing body of evidence on lesbian mothers has been derived through more carefully controlled studies, results from more recent research will be the focus in this section. The research on children born to, or adopted by, lesbian mothers has explored questions regarding the role and influence of biology. For example, researchers have investigated whether children are more likely to have contact with biological extended family than nonbiological extended family (Patterson, Hurt, & Mason, 1998; Fulcher, Chan, Raboy, & Patterson, 2002), how names are chosen (Patterson, 1998), and how child care responsibilities are divided (Brewaeys et al., 1997; Chan, Brooks, Raboy, & Patterson, 1998; Patterson, 1998). Some research has also been done comparing lesbian parents of biological versus adopted children on a variety of parenting variables (Ciano-Boyce & Shelley-Sireci, 2002).

CONTACT WITH EXTENDED FAMILY

Patterson et al. (1998) studied 37 lesbian families in the San Francisco Bay Area (66 lesbian mothers with 37 children, ages four to nine), and the overall project is referred to as the Bay Area Families Study. The researchers found that the children of lesbian mothers in their study were in regular contact with grandparents, and children in two-parent homes were more likely to be in contact with biological versus nonbiological relatives. That is, children were more likely to see their biological mother's relatives than the relatives of their second, nonbiological, mother. In looking at contact with maternal grandmothers specifically, the majority of children (74 percent) did have contact with their nonbiological mother's mother (compared to 97 percent with their biological maternal grandmother). The researchers also found that more contact with grandparents was associated with fewer behavior problems, as measured by parent questionnaires. In addition, children who were reported to have more contact with adult nonrelatives (i.e., mothers' friends) reported "greater feelings of well-being" (p. 396), as measured through self-report questionnaires.

Fulcher et al. (2002) also examined the contacts of children living in lesbian families, but they used a sample of children conceived via donor insemination drawn from a single sperm bank in California. The larger study is referred to as the Contemporary Families Study. They also employed a control group from the same sperm bank for comparison study. Their sample included families headed by lesbian couples (49), lesbian single mothers (6), heterosexual couples (17), and heterosexual single mothers (8), for a total of 80 families. The researchers examined the contacts that children had with relatives and found no significant differences between the lesbian and heterosexual groups, or between the single- and two-parented homes. Consistent with results from the Patterson et al. (1998) study, the children were more likely to be in contact with biological (76 percent) versus nonbiological (47–50 percent) relatives, regardless of parents' sexual orientation.

In the Bay Area Family Study, Patterson (1998) also examined how names are chosen for the children in the lesbian families. Results indicated that the most common tendency was for the child to have the biological mother's surname, and the second most common solution was for the child to have a hyphenated surname, combining the surnames of both the biological and nonbiological mother.

Together these studies suggest that, contrary to popular belief, families with lesbian mothers are not more likely to be isolated from their families of origin than are families with heterosexual parents, and that biology plays an important role in determining how the family functions.

DIVISION OF LABOR

Using the same sample from the Bay Area Families Study, Patterson (1995) evaluated the division of labor among the couples in the study and its relationship to both parent and child outcomes. The sample consisted of 52 mothers and 26 children. There was no heterosexual comparison group, since the question was how the division of labor among these families related to various aspects of the families' own adjustment. Results indicated that lesbian mothers (biological versus nonbiological) did not differ in their report of the *ideal* division of labor between them, or in the *actual* division of labor, with regard to household tasks or decision making. However, they did differ in their report of *actual child care* responsibilities, with both groups of mothers reporting that the biological mother was, in fact, more responsible for child care than was the nonbiological mother. The study also found that nonbiological mothers, as a group, spent more time in paid employment than the biological mothers. Reports of parental satisfaction were also obtained, and results indicate that both groups report equal satisfaction with division of labor and their couple relationship. When these variables were examined in relation to children's adjustment, it was found that they were significantly associated with each other. Specifically, the data suggest that "the more satisfaction expressed by nonbiological mothers with their participation in child care, the greater the sense of well-being reported by their children" (p. 119). And "the most positive outcomes for children occurred in families that reported sharing child-care tasks relatively evenly between parents" (p. 119).

Chan, Brooks, et al. (1998) also evaluated the division of labor among families with lesbian versus heterosexual parents using data from the Contemporary Families Study. Thirty lesbian couples and 16 heterosexual couples and their families participated. As anticipated, lesbian couples were generally more equitable in the sharing of child care tasks than were heterosexual couples, although both groups reported fairly equal division of household tasks and decision making. In general, regardless of sexual orientation, mothers (compared with fathers) desired a more equal division of child care duties, but the lesbian mothers were more likely to actually practice this. When these variables were related to child adjustment (as measured by both teachers and parents), results were consistent with previous research on lesbian families (Patterson, 1995a) and suggest that children in lesbian-mother families had fewer behavior problems when the nonbiological mother participated more in child care. It was also the case that both groups reported equally high satisfaction with their couple relationship and the division of labor in their homes. All children, from both groups, scored within the normal range on adjustment measures.

Brewaeys and her colleagues (1997) have studied family relationships and children's development in groups of children born to families via donor insemination in Europe. In one longitudinal study, at Time 1, children born to lesbian mothers (30) were compared with children born to heterosexual parents through donor insemination (38) and with children conceived naturally to heterosexual parents (30). The children's average age was five years old. The researchers evaluated the parental relationship, the parent-child relationship, division of labor, discipline, the child's perception of his or her family, child adjustment, and gender role behavior, some of which has already been described earlier in this chapter. In terms of findings related to division of labor, results indicated that more lesbian biological mothers worked full time (58 percent) than heterosexual donor-inseminated biological mothers (24 percent) and the mothers of naturally conceived children (9 percent). The nonbiological lesbian mothers did not differ from the two groups of fathers in this respect (86 percent versus 94 percent and 86 percent respectively). In terms of child care, nonbiological lesbian mothers were significantly more involved with child care, and helped significantly more often with discipline, than were the fathers. Equitable distribution of child care occurred in 50 percent of the lesbian families and in none of the heterosexual families.

PARENT-CHILD INTERACTIONS AND RELATIONSHIPS

A number of studies have examined the quality of parent-child interactions and relationships, and results consistently indicate that lesbian mothers are as likely to develop a warm and secure bond with their children as are heterosexual mothers (Gartrell et al., 2000; Golombok, Tasker, & Murray, 1997; Harris & Turner, 1986; MacCallum & Golombok, 2004; O'Connell, 1993; Tasker & Golombok, 1997b; Wainright et al., 2004). There have also been some interesting findings regarding the relationship between nonbiological mothers and their children (e.g., Brewaeys et al., 1997; Vanfraussen et al., 2003).

In the longitudinal study mentioned earlier (Brewaeys et al., 1997; Vanfraussen, et al., 2003), the quality of the biological parent-child relationship, as well as the quality of the relationship between the "social" or nonbiological mother and her child, has been studied over time. Results at Time 1 indicated that biological lesbian mothers did not differ significantly from their heterosexual counterparts in the quality of mother-child interactions. However, the social mother was rated as demonstrating significantly better parent-child interactions than the fathers in either of the other two groups (Brewaeys et al., 1997). In looking at children's perceptions of their parents, there were no differences between groups. In a test involving attributing feeling cards to various family members (Family Relations Test), children consistently gave their biological mother the most positive responses. There were no group differences between how the children perceived the social mother versus the father.

At Time 2 (Vanfraussen et al., 2003), parent-child interactions were evaluated (including the social mother and the father) in the lesbian-mother families and a control group of heterosexually parented families. The children's average age was about 10 years. Families were evaluated on a range of parent-child interaction variables, as reported by both the children and the parents, and results indicated that the two groups of families did not differ on most of the variables included in the study. The researchers found an interesting gender difference, however, with parents generally reporting more positive interactions with their daughters than with their sons, and daughters, in general, reporting higher levels of acceptance with their parents than did the sons. Other differences included the ongoing division-of-labor differences, with more equal division of child care tasks in the lesbian versus the heterosexual households. And children in lesbian-parented homes did not indicate a preference for one parent over the other in discussing emotional topics, while children with heterosexual parents preferred having these kinds of discussions with their mother versus their father.

In the only study thus far comparing lesbian adoptive parents to lesbian and heterosexual biological parents (Ciano-Boyce & Shelley-Sireci, 2002), results are consistent with prior research on division of labor (i.e., that lesbian birth couples share child care tasks more evenly than do heterosexual couples). However, there were also some interesting differences among these groups with regard to parent-child interactions. The researchers found that birth mothers and heterosexual adoptive mothers "are more often sought by the child for going to bed, feeding and mealtime, when the child is afraid, tired, cranky, sick or hurt" (p. 6), while nonbirth mothers and adoptive fathers are more often sought out by the child for rough-and-tumble play. In the lesbian adoptive families as well, one parent was generally sought out for more nurturing activities, while the other was more frequently sought out for rough-and-tumble play, reading, or watching TV. What is different about the lesbian adoptive couples, however, is that they were more likely to report that "their child's preference is occasionally a source of conflict" (p. 7). It is also interesting that the lesbian adoptive mothers experienced more dissatisfaction with the child care division of labor, even though their division was egalitarian, than did the parents of the other two groups. As already mentioned, the role of biology in determining "who does what" is quite apparent in studies of lesbian and heterosexual parents who conceive via donor insemination; it appears that lesbian adoptive parents may have more "negotiating" to do in the realm of parenting than do lesbian couples that include a biological parent. It is important to note that the sample of lesbian adoptive parents in this study was quite small (18), compared to larger samples of the other two groups (49 lesbian biological parents and partners, 44 heterosexual adoptive parents). It is also important to note that child outcomes were not measured, and the results do not suggest that these differences have any identifiable detrimental effect on the children in these families.

As part of a longitudinal study in England, researchers compared children's play narratives to evaluate the parent-child relationship "from the child's point of view" (Perry et al., 2004). Narratives from children of lesbian-mother families were compared with those of children from the general population. The families in the lesbian sample consisted of both single mothers and couples, and the two control groups used included heterosexual two-parent and single-parent families. Results indicated that "children from lesbian-mother families and children from heterosexual families represented their mothers as equally positive and showed their mothers to have similar levels of discipline" (p. 474). The researchers concluded that the attachment security of the children was no different between the two groups of children.

The same sample was used to evaluate the parent-child relationship using interview data (Golombok et al., 2003). Lesbian-mother families were again compared to heterosexual-mother families, and groups of both single and coupled parents were included. Results indicated a few differences between the two groups of biological mothers and between the co-mothers and fathers, but the groups were not significantly different on most variables. Mothers were rated as equal in their expressed warmth, emotional involvement, supervision, frequency of disputes, and most areas of play involvement. Differences were found between the single- and two-parent families in that overall parenting quality and overall enjoyment of motherhood were higher among the mothers with partners compared to the single mothers. Single mothers reported more severe disputes (but not more frequent), and heterosexual parents reported more "smacking" than did lesbian mothers. In the area of play, lesbian mothers and single mothers engaged in more imaginative play, and lesbian couples engaged in more domestic play, than did mothers from the other three groups.

PARENTING SKILLS AND CHARACTERISTICS

There are no observational data examining lesbian mothers' parenting behaviors, but some studies have attempted to measure lesbian parents' parenting skills by asking them to make judgments about child care situations. Some of these studies have found that lesbian mothers tend to demonstrate more child-oriented responses than their heterosexual counterparts (Flaks et al., 1995; Miller et al., 1981), while others have found no differences between groups (Mucklow & Phelan, 1979). In the most recent study, Flaks et al. (1995)

compared 15 lesbian couples with 15 matched heterosexual couples who had children via donor insemination on a variety of variables, including parenting skills. Parenting skills were assessed with a measure (Parent Awareness Skills Survey) administered through an interview that evaluates how parents respond to a variety of child care scenarios. There was an overall significant difference between the two groups, with lesbian mothers demonstrating more parenting awareness skills than heterosexual parents; however, it was also the case that heterosexual fathers demonstrated significantly lower scores than the three groups of mothers. Results must be interpreted carefully, however, since parenting skills in this instance were evaluated by being able to verbalize issues and probable responses, and because the sample size is so small. The researchers acknowledge that observational data would be helpful.

PARENTING STRESS

In several studies, the degree of parenting stress experienced by lesbian mothers has been evaluated using the Parenting Stress Index (PSI) (e.g., Chan, Raboy, & Patterson, 1998; Dundas & Kaufman, 2000; Golombok et al., 2003) or other measures (Bos, van Balen, & van den Boom, 2004). Results have varied between studies, with some samples demonstrating no differences for reported stress among groups of lesbian, heterosexual, single, or coupled parents (e.g., Bos et al., 2004; Chan, Raboy, & Patterson, 1998; Golombok et al., 1997), and others reporting that parental stress was higher among single than coupled parents, regardless of sexual orientation (Golombok et al., 2003). Dundas and Kaufman (2000) administered the PSI to a group of 27 lesbian mothers (within the context of a larger study) and found that only 4 of the 27 scored high enough on the PSI to warrant follow-up.

MISCELLANEOUS

Other studies have demonstrated no or nonmeaningful differences between lesbian and heterosexual mothers on questionnaires measuring various aspects of parenting, such as dyadic adjustment, family and relationship problems, parent-child relationship, and family competence (McNeill, Rienzi, & Kposowa, 1998). These researchers do not provide information about what the scores mean in absolute or practical terms, but they emphasize that the scores are not statistically different between the two groups of mothers. Another example is the Siegenthaler and Bigner (2000) study examining lesbian and heterosexual mothers' responses to the Value of Children questionnaire, which is intended to help explain why parents decide to have children. Of the six subscales, the two groups differed on only one, Goals and Incentives, so that heterosexual mothers scored slightly higher (i.e., agreed slightly more that their reasons for having children included providing incentive to succeed, because having a child is one of the highest purposes, and because having children strengthens the partners' bond). The two groups were indistinguishable on scales indicating the following reasons: being a parent is personally satisfying, deriving adult status, affection, children perceived as source of pleasure, sense of accomplishment, being able to influence another human being, achieving a sense of family, and because children can help provide for parents when older. Again, the researchers do not explain how the two groups scored on any of the other subscales, but they emphasize that what matters is that the groups did not differ from each other.

Longitudinal Studies on Lesbian Families

The last set of data to consider in the discussion of lesbian parents and their children consists of the few longitudinal studies conducted, with some still in progress, to examine various experiences of lesbian-parented families. Some of the studies were cited earlier in relation to specific variables, but they will be briefly reviewed here with the focus on issues raised over time. Golombok and her colleagues in England have conducted two longitudinal studies, one examining the development of children's sexual identity and attitudes about their lesbian-led families (Golombok et al., 1983; Golombok & Tasker, 1996; Tasker & Golombok, 1995; Tasker & Golombok, 1997a, 1997b), and the other regarding children's socio-emotional development and parent-child relationships in homes of children raised without a father from infancy (Golombok et al., 1997; MacCallum & Golombok, 2004).

The focus of the first study was to examine the children's attitudes about their families over time and what factors influenced their attitudes. The first set of data was collected in the 1970s, when the average age of the children was about 9 years old; the follow-up study was conducted more than a decade later, when the average age was 23½. All children had been conceived within a heterosexual relationship and were products of divorce, and lesbian families were compared to a group of heterosexual single-mother families on certain variables, while within-group differences were also explored. Results from the first longitudinal study (at Time 2, when the subjects were young adults) indicated that for both groups, the young adults became "more positive about their family identity as they reached young adulthood, and this was especially so for those from lesbian families" (Tasker & Golombok, 1997b, p. 190). Within the lesbian group, negative feelings in adolescence were related to the mother's being too open about her lifestyle in front of friends, as well as negative responses from peers; positive feelings were associated with the mother's having long-term stable relationships and her being accepting of the adolescents' own relationship partners. However, in young adulthood, these variables were no longer related to feelings of family acceptance, and the subjects reported positive feelings overall. As already mentioned, children of lesbian mothers were not more likely to develop a homosexual orientation than children raised in heterosexually parented homes, but adolescent girls from lesbian homes were more likely to experiment with same-sex relationships than were girls from heterosexual homes.

The second British study (Golombok et al., 1997; MacCallum & Golombok, 2004) has focused on the experiences of children raised in fatherless families from infancy. Three groups have been employed for this study: lesbian-mother families (both single and coupled), single heterosexual mother families, and two-parent heterosexual families. The children were first evaluated at ages 3 to 9 (mean age was 6 years) and then again at about age 12. Importantly, these families were all highly educated and relatively affluent, so the confounding impact of low socioeconomic status was removed from the analysis. Although the groups did not differ on most variables measured, the differences that did emerge in this study, at both Time 1 and Time 2, were related to whether there was a father in the home and not to the sexual orientation of the mother. For example, single heterosexual and lesbian mothers were found to interact more with their children than mothers in heterosexual two-parent families, but there were more severe (but not more frequent) disputes reported in single and lesbian mother homes. As already mentioned, boys raised in fatherless families also demonstrated more feminine characteristics, but no fewer masculine characteristics, as measured by a questionnaire. The groups of children did not differ with respect to school adjustment, behavior, and peer relationships.

Three longitudinal studies have been undertaken to examine the development of children born to lesbian mothers via donor insemination, one in the

Netherlands (Brewaeys et al., 1997; Vanfraussen et al., 2003), one in Canada (Dundas & Kaufman, 2000), and one in the United States (Gartrell et al., 1996; Gartrell et al., 1999; Gartrell et al., 2000). The focus of the European study has been on the role of the social, or nonbiological, mother in lesbian families. Results have shown that children raised with two mothers develop a relationship with the social mother that is as strong as that of children with their fathers, and that the social mother plays a larger role in child care activities than do fathers.

The Canadian study has thus far only published data from the first phase (Dundas & Kaufman, 2000). Subjects are a cross section of lesbian families (16 families, 27 mothers, 20 children); most children (14) were conceived via donor insemination, but some (6) were conceived within a prior heterosexual relationship. Parents completed a variety of questionnaires to measure a range of personal and parental functioning. Parents and children were also interviewed to assess both the children's and the mother's perceptions about being in a lesbian-parented family, and knowledge and feelings about the fathers. Children's responses "suggest that they were content with their family makeup and did not feel stigmatized by having two mothers" (p. 77). The researchers plan to follow the children into adolescence.

The American study intends to follow a group of lesbian families over the course of 25 years through interviews with mothers. Data have been gathered from the mothers before or during pregnancy (Gartrell et al., 1996), when their children were toddlers (Gartrell et al., 1999), and when the children were five years old (Gartrell et al., 2000). At Time 1, the researchers found that the prospective children were "highly desired and thoughtfully conceived" (Gartrell et al., 1996, p. 279). At Time 2, children were equally well bonded to both mothers, and mothers were found to share parenting responsibilities (Gartrell et al., 1999). At Time 3, children continued to be bonded equally to both parents, and most of the families were determined to be functioning well. The majority of the children were reported to be developing good peer relationships, but a substantial minority (18 percent) had experienced homophobia from teachers or peers. The researchers do not further explain the nature of the "homophobia," so it is hard to know what this means (single incident versus chronic; name-calling versus physical attacks; etc.). Because mothers anticipated homophobic reactions, they reported working very hard to prepare their children for prejudice and how to deal with these situations. Seventy-five percent of the mothers also reported being actively involved in political or educational efforts in the community to help increase tolerance of diversity (Gartrell et al., 2000).

Summary of Research on Lesbian Parents and Their Children

The research on lesbian parents and their children has evolved from focusing on families of divorce to families that are planned after the mother has assumed her lesbian identity. Methodological limitations, primarily because of small and nonrepresentative samples, have made generalizations of results difficult. However, some more recent studies have used larger and more representative samples derived from specific sperm banks, and longitudinal studies have provided interesting insights regarding the development of lesbian-led families over time. Taken together, results overwhelmingly indicate that children of lesbian mothers are as well-adjusted as their peers, and they are not more likely to become homosexual adults. In addition, lesbian parents appear to be no less effective than heterosexual parents. Many of the differences found between lesbian and heterosexual parents are more related to gender than to sexual orientation, and many differences favor lesbian mothers. Children of lesbian mothers may experience more teasing regarding their family's difference, but it is not clear that they experience more teasing than children from any other stigmatized group. And research suggests that even if these children do get teased, they still develop healthy peer relationships and positive psychological adjustment.

Children of Gay Fathers

Empirical research on the children of gay fathers is virtually nonexistent. I could identify no studies that involved comparing children of gay fathers to children of heterosexual fathers on adjustment variables. However, some research examines the sexual orientation of adult sons of gay fathers (Bailey, Bobrow, Wolfe, & Mikach, 1995), and there are some older reports of interviews with gay fathers and their children on a variety of topics (e.g., Miller, 1979; Bozett, 1987). Most of the attention in research on gay fathers has been on their parenting experiences: for example, the reasons for wanting to be a parent (Bigner & Jacobsen, 1989a), or child-rearing attitudes (Bigner & Jacobsen, 1989b; Scallen, 1981, as cited in Bozett, 1987). There does not seem to have been any empirical psychological research conducted over the past 10 years, in contrast to the ongoing and dynamic process that has been evident in research involving lesbian parents and their children. Perhaps this simply mirrors the fact that women are more often parents than are men, and that women are usually the primary caregivers. Nonetheless it is still surprising that so little attention has been paid to this population given the ongoing struggles of gay men to adopt children and provide foster care.

Bailey et al. (1995) interviewed 55 biological fathers who reported on the sexual orientation of their 82 sons, and the researchers subsequently interviewed 43 of the 82 sons. Results indicate that about 9 percent of the sons were nonheterosexual (i.e., homosexual or bisexual). The researchers acknowledge that their sample likely is not representative and that fathers with gay sons may have been more interested in participating in the research project than fathers with heterosexual sons. In addition, there was no control group for the study. The researchers used previous samples as well as population base rate estimates to conclude that their results are consistent with other findings, and that whatever "environmental transmission" exists cannot be very strong given that the vast majority of sons develop a heterosexual orientation.

Miller (1979) conducted a study over the course of three years examining relationships between gay fathers and their children. Note that this study took place 25 to 30 years ago, and the experiences of gay fathers are likely to have changed over time. Miller wanted to address four issues frequently raised in custody disputes: whether gay fathers have children to cover up their homosexuality; whether they are likely to molest their children; whether their children grow up to become homosexual; and whether the children are exposed to homophobic harassment. Miller interviewed 40 fathers and 14 of their children in a number of American and Canadian cities. He concluded that none of these concerns appear to be true for these families. Miller also found that fathers anticipated negative reactions by their children in finding out about their father's homosexuality, but in most cases the children were positive and accepting. In addition, it appeared that girls were more accepting, overall, than boys. As already mentioned, this kind of descriptive study was useful in helping dispel some long-held beliefs regarding the experiences of gay fathers, and it paved the way for future research. From an empirical standpoint, the small sample size and likelihood of response bias are major concerns.

Bozett has done the most extensive research with gay fathers and their children over the years. Through extensive interviews, he has been able to identify relevant patterns, issues, and challenges that gay fathers and their children face. In one study, he interviewed 19 children of gay fathers and found that the "overriding concern of these children was their fear that others would think that they, too, were gay if their fathers' homosexuality became known" (Bozett, 1987, p. 40). He described "social control strategies" that these children use to manage their image presented to others, especially peers. These include *boundary control* (e.g., asking the father to limit public displays of affection with a partner), *nondisclosure* (i.e., not telling others about the father's sexual orientation), and *disclosure* (i.e., telling select others to prepare them to meet the father). Bozett also identified factors that influence the degree to which children employ social control strategies. These include *mutuality* (i.e., the extent to which children feel identified with their father), *obtrusiveness* (i.e., how obvious the father's homosexuality is, as perceived by the child), *age* (i.e., how old the child is, as well as when the child is told of the father's homosexuality), and *living arrangements* (i.e., whether the children live with their father).

Bozett also found that gay fathers were very sensitive to their children's needs and would limit overt homosexual behavior to make their children more comfortable (Bozett, 1987). They were confronted with having to balance the children's need for protection with the need to develop tolerance for difference. Interview data from two of Bozett's studies (as cited in Bozett, 1987) indicated that very few of the offspring of the gay fathers were gay themselves.

Gay Fathers

Bigner and Jacobsen (1989a, 1989b, 1992) have conducted some of the few empirical studies on the topic of gay fathers, but the results have not consistently yielded meaningful information. They compared a group of gay fathers to a group of heterosexual fathers (33 fathers in each group) on a measure of the reasons for wanting to become a parent (the Value of Children scale) (Bigner & Jacobsen, 1989a). Results indicated that the two groups did not differ overall, but they did score differently on two of the six subscales. The group of heterosexual fathers disagreed less with reasons on the Security-Continuity-Tradition subscale, while the gay fathers disagreed less with reasons on the Social Status scale. The researchers point out that both groups rated the reasons for having children negatively (i.e., both groups tended to disagree more than agree with reasons presented). While the researchers concluded that both groups therefore seem to value children negatively, it would seem more plausible that the questionnaire simply did not capture the reasons why these groups of men had children. Methodological problems of this study also include the fact that the heterosexuality of the control group was assumed, and the sample of gay fathers was restricted to those in a support group for gay fathers.

Their second study (1989b) again compared two groups of fathers (possibly the same sample) on another parenting questionnaire, the Iowa Parent Behavior Inventory, and the groups were found to differ on three of the five scales: limit setting, reasoning guidance, and responsiveness. Results indicated that gay fathers were more strict, more likely to explain rules and regulations to their children, and more responsive to their children's needs than were heterosexual fathers. Heterosexual fathers were more willing to be physically affectionate with their spouses, but they were less egalitarian. Out of the 36 items on the scale, the two groups significantly differed on about one-third of them, suggesting that there was a lot of overlap in parenting style and attitude between the two groups, especially in the areas of involvement and intimacy.

Bigner and Jacobsen (1992) also compared groups of homosexual and heterosexual fathers on two other measures of parenting. One involved responding to child situations presented in slide form (intended to assess "parenting style"), and the other was a parenting questionnaire intended to measure "traditional" versus "developmental" attitudes toward parenting (Attitude Toward Fathering scale). This distinction appears to describe more child-oriented (developmental) versus authoritative (traditional) attitudes. Because these instruments had not yet been subjected to standardization procedures, and because the sample was nonrandom, the authors did not present any of the quantitative data. They summarized that the groups responded similarly on both measures, and that both groups of fathers tended to demonstrate a more developmental (rather than traditional) attitude toward fathering.

In sum, research on gay fathers and their children is very limited in both quantity and quality, and general conclusions cannot be drawn directly from these studies. Gay fathers and their children report positive relationships with one another, and the research has not identified important differences in gay versus heterosexual fathers' parenting abilities. More importantly, the research has helped identify issues that gay fathers and their children face, and there are certainly clinical implications, especially from Bozett's work, for how to help gay fathers and their children cope with being in a nontraditional family.

Gay and Lesbian Couples

If gay and lesbian couples marry, are they likely to stay together for as long as heterosexual couples? Are their relationships as stable? This question cannot be answered directly through empirical research, since gay and lesbian couples have not been able to marry, and so any comparisons between gay/lesbian and heterosexual couples have to be made between groups of unmarried couples or between gay/lesbian unmarried couples and heterosexual married couples. However, even the former comparison is not equivalent, since heterosexual couples inhabit a very different social context from gay and lesbian couples. Heterosexual couples exist in a society where they are accepted and supported, and they live with the knowledge that they, as a couple, can opt for marriage. Gay and lesbian couples live in a society that largely condemns their relationships, and they, historically, have not been able to opt for marriage. Despite the inevitable apples-to-oranges comparisons, some research has been conducted to try to address the question of stability (or "durability"), and the factors that might predict whether a homosexual relationship is likely to dissolve.

There is no question that many gay and lesbian adults are involved in committed couple relationships. Estimates of the numbers of homosexual adults in couple relationships, based on older (1970s) survey research, range from 40 to 60 percent for gay men and 45 to 80 percent for lesbian women (see Peplau & Cochran, 1990). However, the actual numbers may have risen over the last three decades as gay and lesbian adults enter fewer heterosexual marriages.

There are not a lot of data concerning actual dissolution rates of homosexual couples. However, a few studies have attempted to address the issue. In a classic study of American couples, Blumstein and Schwartz (1983) collected questionnaire and interview data on hundreds of couples across the United States regarding the areas of money, work, and sex. The study included married couples, heterosexual cohabiting couples, and gay and lesbian couples. The researchers requested follow-up questionnaires from about half of the subjects 18 months after the interview, and among other things, they reported on the number of couples from each category who broke up. Not surprisingly, the lowest rate of dissolution was among the married couples (14 percent total). However, the rates of dissolution for gay and lesbian couples were very similar to that of married couples for those who had been together more than 10 years (married, 4 percent; gay, 4 percent; lesbian, 6 percent). (The researchers note that there were so few heterosexual cohabiting couples who had been together for more than 10 years that the numbers were not reported.) The rates of dissolution for the three nonmarried groups were similar to each other for couples who had been together for 0 to 2 years, at the beginning of the study (heterosexual, 17 percent; gay, 16 percent; lesbian, 22 percent), and for 2 to 10 years (heterosexual, 12 percent, gay, 16 percent; lesbian, 20 percent). Since there are no statistical analyses to determine whether the differences in the rates are statistically significant, it is unclear whether the slightly higher rate among the lesbian group is meaningful.

In a longitudinal study, Kurdek (2004) found that gay and lesbian couples had similar rates of dissolution over the course of 12 years (19 percent and 23.8 percent respectively), but the rates of dissolution for heterosexual married couples *without* children (18.7 percent) and married couples *with* children (3.1 percent) were statistically different. The gay/lesbian and heterosexual groups could not be compared directly because of differences in the two samples and the timeline of data collection. However, it is clear that the rate of dissolution for homosexual couples in this study was very similar to that of the married couples without children. More importantly, Kurdek (2004) found that the "processes that led to dissolution" were similar for both homosexual and heterosexual couples. In other words, the dimensions of the relationships that were important for stability were the same for both homosexual and heterosexual couples.

Research has also consistently demonstrated that gay and lesbian couples are at least as *satisfied* with their relationships as are their heterosexual counterparts regardless of whether they are parents or are childless (e.g., Bos et al., 2004; Chan, Brooks, et al., 1998; Kurdek & Schmitt, 1986b; Mackey, Diemer, & O'Brien, 2004; Metz, Rosser, & Strapko, 1994; Patterson, 1995a; Peplau & Cochran, 1990), the *quality* of their relationships is at least as strong as those of heterosexual couples (Flaks et al., 1995; Julien, Chartrand, & Begin, 1999; Kurdek & Schmitt, 1986b), and their relationships appear to go through similar *stages* (Kurdek & Schmitt, 1986a).

Further, research indicates that the factors that can contribute to relationship quality, satisfaction, and stability are similar for heterosexual and homosexual couples (Kurdek, 1991, 1992, 1994b, 1994c, 2003; Peplau & Cochran, 1990). These factors include social support (Elizur & Mintzer, 2003; Julien, Chartrand, Simard, Bouthillier, & Begin, 2003; Kurdek, 1991), barriers to leaving the relationship (Peplau & Cochran, 1990), cognitive beliefs (Kurdek, 1992), income (Elizur & Mintzer, 2003), the presence of major conflict (Blumstein &

Schwartz, 1983), and conflict resolution skills (Julien et al., 2003; Kurdek, 1991, 1994b). Homosexual and heterosexual couples have been found to have similar areas of conflict in their relationships (Kurdek, 1994a), and similar general conflict resolution styles (Metz et al., 1994). As expected, higher levels of relationship conflict have been found to be related to higher rates of relationship dissatisfaction (Kurdek, 1994a) and dissolution (Blumstein & Schwartz, 1983; Kurdek, 1994b).

Methodological concerns regarding much of the research on gay and lesbian couples include the same sampling issues raised with regard to gay and lesbian parents. Much of the research is based on white, educated subjects who complete questionnaires. Therefore results are likely limited in their generalizability to other gay and lesbian couples. Some more recent observational studies have been conducted (e.g., Gottman, Levenson, Gross, et al., 2003; Julien et al., 2003), and results are consistent with previous findings that relationship satisfaction and durability are related to similar relationship factors in heterosexual and homosexual couples.

One observational study (Gottman, Levenson, Swanson, et al., 2003) evaluated committed homosexual and married heterosexual couples in their conflict interactions, and results indicated that the homosexual couples tended to be more positive in conflict discussions than were heterosexual couples. The researchers speculate that the reasons for the difference might be related to higher relationship equality in homosexual couples, as well as the fact that there are fewer barriers to leaving the relationship, so that homosexual couples might therefore be more careful in their discussions of conflict. Although Metz et al. (1994) found, through questionnaires, that homosexual and heterosexual couples were similar in many ways in terms of self-reported conflict resolution styles, the differences they found were more related to gender than to sexual orientation.

Some research has been conducted with homosexual and heterosexual couples who had been together for many years to better understand what factors contributed to the stability and satisfaction of their relationships (Mackey et al., 2000, 2004). Using a sample of 108 diverse couples (two-thirds heterosexual, one-third homosexual) who had been together for an average of 30 years, the researchers conducted in-depth interviews. They found that there were no differences between the groups in level of relationship satisfaction, and that most couples reported being satisfied in their relationships. In addition, factors that were most highly associated with relationship satisfaction in recent years, intimacy and conflict, were the same for all groups. The researchers did find that lesbian couples "were more likely to report that their relationships were psychologically intimate in recent years" than were gay or heterosexual couples (Mackey et al., 2000, p. 219).

Although the legalization of same-sex marriage in Canada, Belgium, the Netherlands, and Massachusetts (and of civil unions in Vermont) is very recent, some research has examined couples who have taken advantage of this new opportunity (Alderson, 2004; Solomon, Rothblum, & Balsam, 2004). Alderson conducted interviews with married or soon-to-be-married couples from different countries to better understand the "phenomenological" experience for these couples. Subjects commented that the benefits and disadvantages to marriage were the same for them as for heterosexuals. They felt that marriage "solidified" their commitment to their partners, and they recognized the fact that their marriage might end in divorce.

Solomon and her colleagues (2004) compared lesbian and gay couples who had civil unions in Vermont with two other groups: lesbian and gay couples who did not have civil unions, and married heterosexual couples who were related to the couples in civil unions. There were very few differences between the two groups of lesbians. Lesbians in civil unions reported being more "out" than lesbians who were not in civil unions, and they reported having less contact with their mothers than did lesbians not in civil unions. There were many more differences as a function of sexual orientation among the women. For example, lesbian couples were more educated, more equal in their division of labor, and more likely to report engaging in leisure activities with their partner than were heterosexual women. Heterosexual couples had been together longer, were more likely to have children, and reported more family support. In comparing the groups of men, there were also more differences as a function of sexual orientation than due to partner status. Gay men perceived significantly more social support from friends than did heterosexual men, but heterosexual men were more likely to report positive contact with their partner's father. Gay men in civil unions were the most likely to report that they share mutual friends with their partner. Gay men not in civil unions were more likely to report having considered ending their current relationship than were men in the other two groups.

In summary, much of the research on gay and lesbian couples has identified that they function much the same way that heterosexual couples do, and the same factors that predict heterosexuals' relationship quality and stability also predict the quality and stability of homosexual couples. Where differences have been found, they are often related to lesbian couples' greater intimacy, sense of cohesion, and positive conflict resolution skills. Another important difference that is sometimes identified is in the area of social and family support, with homosexual couples in some studies reporting receiving less support than heterosexual couples. Rates of dissolution appear similar between homosexual couples and heterosexual couples without children. Heterosexual couples with children appear to have the lowest rate of dissolution. It is important to remember that much of this research has been conducted with samples of primarily white and educated individuals, and so generalizing the data to the larger population is not possible.

The "Opposition"

The fact that so much of the research described in this chapter indicates that children raised by homosexual parents do not suffer significant and systematic detrimental effects and that homosexual couples are as healthy as heterosexual couples raises the question of whether there is *any* compelling research that challenges these conclusions. The answer is no. However, some researchers whose agendas are explicitly hostile to the cause of gay rights have written articles severely criticizing the existing research base, misrepresented the evidence, and gathered data of questionable value. The most notable example is Paul Cameron and his colleagues of the Family Research Institute in Colorado. Dr. Cameron was dropped from the membership of the American Psychological Association for ethical violations over twenty years ago, the Nebraska Psychological Association has "disassociated" itself from him, and the American Sociological Association has "condemned" him for "his consistent misrepresentation of sociological research" (ASA Motion, 1986). Despite being discredited by these professional associations, he has continued to conduct and publish research and opinion that have influenced court decisions and social policy (Stacey & Biblarz, 2001). An extensive review and analysis of Cameron and Cameron's recent large-scale survey and interview study (1996) has been conducted by an eminent scholar (Herek, 1998) and will not be detailed here. The main methodological problems with the study (which concluded that children with homosexual parents were more likely to have sexual relations with their parents and other caregivers than were children raised by heterosexual parents) included a very low response rate, an absurdly low subsample size of adversely affected subjects raised by homosexual parents (5 out of 17 from a total sample of over 5,000), interviewer bias, and inadequate questionnaire validity.

What Have We Learned?

In an attempt to lend more power to the data of the earlier studies on children with gay and lesbian parents, Allen and Burrell (1996) conducted a meta-analysis of several of the studies conducted through the mid-1990s that compared children of homosexual and heterosexual parents. Since many of the studies heretofore had small sample sizes, they were criticized as not necessarily having enough power to detect differences even if differences did exist in the general population. A meta-analysis is used to help determine whether the *combination* of results can reasonably be generalized. Allen and Burrell included 18 studies in their analyses, including a few on children of gay fathers, and they evaluated the data based on three global areas: sexual orientation and development, adjustment ("satisfaction with life"), and intelligence and moral development. The researchers note that their analyses did have "sufficient power to detect large or medium effects" (p. 30), and their results indicated no differences between the groups on any of the variables measured.

Although there are many limitations to much of the research on gay and lesbian families, the studies are consistent in failing to show detrimental effects of parental sexual orientation on children's adjustment. Even though it is impossible to "prove the null hypothesis" (i.e., prove the no-difference hypothesis), it seems unlikely that detrimental effects would remain hidden if children were, in fact, systematically harmed by living with a homosexual parent. It is true that most samples consist of well-educated white families, and the generalizability of many findings is limited by this fact. Nonetheless, if the argument is that gay and lesbian parents *by definition* are a bad influence on children, then even results from restricted samples are relevant. In fact, if we identify even one normally developing child with a gay or lesbian parent, the argument is rendered false.

The American Psychological Association has issued resolutions on gay and lesbian parents and their children, and on same-sex couples, after professional review of the literature, and they clearly support "the protection of parent-child relationships" regardless of parents' sexual orientation, as well as marriage between same-sex adults.

We know through decades of research on the family and parenting that what matters most for children and families is risk factors such as mental illness, poverty, and isolation, and family processes such as discipline approaches and attachment styles. Why, then, have researchers conducted so many studies to demonstrate that children raised in homes with same-sex parents are no different from children raised by heterosexual parents? It seems to be a very defensive research approach whose purpose is to counteract an "opposition" that claims that homosexual parents are a bad influence on children and should not be allowed to parent. Since the courts have not consistently carefully considered the research base for such claims, researchers who are "gay friendly" have undertaken the task of producing empirical evidence to support gay parents. It is unfortunate that this is the reason for embarking on this research path, but without it, gay and lesbian parents would probably not be making the strides they are in being allowed to exercise their right to parent their own children and build their own families.

Others have noted the "defensiveness" in this research area (e.g., Green & Bozett, 1991; Stacey & Biblarz, 2001) and have suggested that examining differences could yield useful information for all families. As Green and Bozett (1991) note, "Until we begin to value healthy difference we miss the opportunities for growth and knowledge that having different family structures gives us" (p. 214). And, we are reminded, differences do not necessarily translate into deficits (Baumrind, 1995; Stacey & Biblarz, 2001). The research reviewed here has not identified detrimental effects of being in a homosexual relationship or of having a homosexual parent; however, it has identified possible differences in the area of gender and sexual development of children (i.e., a wider range of acceptable roles and behavior for girls and boys, possibly more female adolescent same-sex experimentation), and with regard to gender-specific parenting behaviors (i.e., fathers versus mothers). It has also been argued that the "traditional" family (i.e., breadwinning father, stay-at-home mother) should not be the standard by which other families are measured, given the high divorce rate among heterosexuals[1] and the number of "nontraditional" families already in existence (Stacey, 1996), and given the fact that this "traditional" 1950s family structure is a relatively new construct (and, therefore, not traditional at all) within our culture's history (Coontz, 1992, 1997).

5

Same-Sex Parents and Their Children's Development

James C. Black

As our society explores and defines the rights and roles of gays and lesbians, it is their real or perceived limitations as parents that generate the most public controversy and concern. Civil society has a strong and valid interest in parental competency. Whatever good or ill that emanates from healthy or maladaptive family functioning, whatever good or ill that cultural change brings, it is children who will first and most fully reap the benefits or suffer the consequences. Although all children are born with idiosyncratic constitutional assets and liabilities, it is in the crucible of parental performance that their ultimate character will be forged.

While parental competency is clearly not the sole determinant of children's development and the ultimate arbiter of their adult mental health, one can certainly argue that it is a crucial factor in their development and a strong predictor of their adult mental health. Consequently, we must guard their emotional well-being, but we must not be driven by anxiety and prejudice. Both the law, and the opinions of judges in individual cases deciding custody for biological and adoptive parents alike, have been largely informed by fear, suspicion, and unconscious as well as conscious bias. Where innate prejudice—in the form of unexamined, self-evident assumptions disguised as common sense—has not been sufficient to deny or restrict custody by gay and lesbian parents, it has been manufactured by wild and apocalyptic speculation, similarly without

The author gratefully acknowledges the editorial assistance of Dr. Timothy Black, who helped to clarify and beautify this chapter's language.

reference to actual data or research. As a last resort, limitations on gays and lesbians assuming normal parental roles have been predicated on the deleterious effects on their children of society's own prejudicial attitudes, an ironic justification that in the past was similarly used to limit the parental participation of interracial couples and that even now is the principal stated basis for the prohibition on military service by gays and lesbians.

But if speculation and presumption are to be replaced by scientifically informed rationales for rendering custody decisions, then it is clear that the first step, as in any scientific inquiry, is to identify the relevant questions: "Are children's developmental needs addressed differently by heterosexual and homosexual parents, and if so, how?" and "Do any such differences negatively affect the adult mental health of the children of gay and lesbian parents, and if so, how?" Having posed these questions, we must look to the evidence to answer them. As we will see, if society then continues to make public policy on the basis of bias, and if the judicial system continues to determine custody on the basis of hostility to gays and lesbians, it cannot do so under cover of "the best interests of the child."

While considerable research has been done on lesbian parenting, much less has been conducted on gay parenting.[1] This difference arises from the limited pool of research subjects in the latter case, which in turn is partly a consequence both of the general difficulty that homosexual parents have in obtaining custody, and the extent to which courts have been willing to let an even more powerful preference for mothers over fathers override discrimination based on sexual orientation. Gay fathers, being both homosexual and male, are therefore at a double disadvantage when attempting either to obtain custody of their biological children or to adopt nonbiological children. Another possible factor in the relative paucity of families with male homosexual parents is the unknown extent to which lesbians who wish to raise children procure the services of a male associate to impregnate them. For obvious biological reasons, this avenue is much more complicated for male homosexuals to pursue.

But whatever the origin of the discrepancy, it is a present fact of life, and we are therefore forced to some extent to generalize from research on families headed by lesbian parents to the broader class of homosexual parents. We must also admit that this generalization is not rigorously justified, both because the gender identities of parents are at least as, and likely much more, powerful influences on their parenting practices as are their sexual orientations, and also because it is becoming clear that male and female homosexuality are distinct states that likely arise from completely different genetic and developmental origins (Bearman & Brückner, 2002; Hershberger, 1997). Nonetheless, inasmuch as both public policy and the personal predilections of family court judges have framed the debate as one of heterosexual versus homosexual, and furthermore out of a necessity at least partly engendered by the very prejudice that science seeks to enlighten, we are forced to overlook this lack of rigor for the time being, and for the purposes of this discussion.

Children's psychological development is an evolving process in which we can identify distinct periods whose successful or unsuccessful completion provides the environment in which subsequent developmental tasks are pursued, in accordance with the epigenetic principle (Erikson, 1950). The effect of parental qualities and characteristics—including a parent's sexual orientation and lifestyle—is therefore specific to each developmental stage. It is inadequate to speak broadly of good or bad parenting without addressing how parental qualities facilitate or inhibit a child's ability to master the tasks peculiar to these crucial epochs that mark the journey from infancy to adulthood. For the purposes of our analysis, this journey will be broken into three phases, with the understanding that the boundaries between these phases are somewhat porous and demark categories of developmental tasks; particular tasks may well transcend the borders between phases or lie latent within an intervening phase, only to reappear as developmental issues in a later period.

These three developmental epochs will be defined as (1) the preschool phase, which incorporates infancy, toddlerhood, and early childhood, from birth to 6 years of age; (2) the late childhood or latency phase, from 6 to 12 years of age; and (3) adolescence, from 12 to 19 years of age (Gemelli, 1996).

The Preschool Years

The principal relevant developmental tasks of the preschool years are *attachment* and *separation-individuation*. It is undisputed that attachment or bonding to a parent is of vital importance to the infant and toddler, since under the umbrella of attachment, essential personality ingredients such as trust in the world, a sense of confidence, the ability to separate reality and fantasy, and control over one's impulses are formed and organized. The specific parental qualities that promote optimal attachment are the ability to provide nurturance and empathy to infants and small children. Nurturance fosters the sense of security and well-being that leads to trust in the world and in oneself. Empathy is the capacity to instinctively and intuitively put oneself in another's place, and to share another's feelings. To do so is to temporarily suppress one's own self-interest for the sake of another. Self-esteem and the ability to value others apart from the purpose they serve are prerequisites for the development of nurturance and empathy (Black & Cantor, 1989); nurturance and empathy require a sufficiently large measure of self-worth to remain confident that one's own needs will be met in good time, making sacrifice for the sake of a child both possible and worthwhile.

Numerous studies of lesbian and heterosexual mothers reveal more similarities than differences in their maternal attitudes and approaches to child care and child rearing (Kweskin & Cook, 1982; Lyons, 1983; Miller, Jacobsen, & Bigner, 1981; Mucklow & Phelan, 1979; Pagelow, 1980; Rand, Graham, & Rawlings, 1982; Thompson, McCandless, & Strickland, 1971; Golombok et al., 2003; Brewaeys, Ponjaert, Van Hall, & Golombok, 1997; Vanfraussen, Ponjaert-Kristoffersen, & Brewaeys, 2003). On maternal variables such as warmth, sensitivity, emotional involvement, and the ability to develop and promote a secure parent-child bond, there were no significant differences between the two groups. In fact, in one study, a stronger child-centered orientation was seen in lesbian mothers than in heterosexual mothers (Miller, Jacobsen, & Bigner, 1981).

Attachment has not been studied in gay fathers. Apart from the aforementioned difficulties involved in doing any parental studies with gay fathers, attachment studies have always focused on mothers. It has been assumed that mothers were the exclusive principal attachment figures for infants and small children, a consequence of the predominance of women as the caretakers of the very young in our society. The extent to which children "naturally" bond with women as opposed to men is as yet unclear. The naturalist thesis, that infants are "monotropically matricentric"—exclusively attached to mothers rather than fathers—was explored by Kotelchuck, who studied 12- to 21-month-old children. He found that in such children, maternal preference was dominant, but not by any means exclusive, a conclusion that is supported by the findings of Schaffer and Emerson (Bowlby, 1969; Kotelchuck, 1972; Lamb, 1976; Spiro, 1958).

In Western societies, fathers are increasingly devoting themselves to the care of their children. This cultural trend makes it both possible and important to conduct further research into paternal attachment. Any such studies should also investigate gay parenting. One must take care in interpreting research into attachment in gay fathers, however. Inasmuch as the naturalist thesis may be true in some degree, the attachment of infants to gay fathers cannot fairly be directly compared to infantile attachment to either straight or lesbian mothers.

The term *separation-individuation* refers to two distinct developmental tasks that, however, proceed simultaneously and reinforce each other. Separation is the child's evolution of physical and emotional independence from others, principally the mother (Mahler, 1968). It implies that the child can tolerate both a physical separation from the principal attachment figure, as well as situations in which the attachment figure diverts her attention and emotional investment away from the child. Individuation refers to the child's development of a sense of having a unique existence (Pine & Furer, 1963). Individuation requires the child to acknowledge, endorse, and take responsibility for its own fears, thoughts, and decisions. But the child does not face this task alone. The project of separation and individuation is a collaborative one. A child's ability and willingness to separate from a parent are usually contingent on the parent's ability and desire to do the same.

It is therefore axiomatic that the psychological fitness of the parent in separating from the child determines a child's success with the twin developmental tasks of separation and individuation. Optimally, parents will not project inordinate or unreasonable fears onto their child and will recognize that all emotional growth is accompanied by some tolerable level of anxiety. They will avoid overprotection and will not foster dependence, recognizing that overprotectiveness and dependency promote the avoidance of normal conflict and facilitate psychological regression. In addition, they will take pleasure in their child thinking for herself, even when the child's thinking differs from their own. They will relish their youngster's growing autonomy and willingness to make independent decisions.

The process of individuation entails unconsciously adopting another's personality characteristics through identification, and using these characteristics as the basis from which the child evolves his or her own unique personality. The personal qualities of others—principally those of the attachment figure—provide the template, but once adopted, they become part of the child's own integrated personality and evolve and diverge from the model according to the child's own unique life experiences. A parent who is successful in helping a child through this developmental phase not only fosters independence in the child but takes pleasure in the child's pride in his or her own uniqueness. A parent committed to this transition must be free of conscious or unconscious attempts to mold and shape the youth according to some preordained image. I will defer further discussion of personality uniqueness to the section on adolescence, because it is during that time frame that children fully become themselves, both psychologically and sexually, but it should be clear that healthy child development requires a parent who is fully committed to his or her child's physical, emotional, and characterological autonomy.

A number of researchers have conducted comparative studies of separation and individuation with heterosexual, gay, and lesbian parents. In a 1985 study, Steckel compared three basic factors in these different populations: independence, ego functions, and object relations. *Independence* in the child comprises both external and internal autonomy. It entails the ability to physically separate from a parental figure as well as the capacity to identify and cope with one's own emotions and make one's own decisions, at least to a limited degree. *Ego functions* are the cognitive processes—ego defenses, perception, learning, memory, et cetera—that mediate between the internal and external world. The term *object relations* refers to the psychological representation of the self and others in the external world, and the interactions between them. Healthy object relations and ego functions promote separation and individuation by clearly demarking the boundaries between one's own feelings and desires and the desires and feelings of others, and by accurately translating and analyzing interactions between one's self and others.

Steckel found no significant differences in these personality factors between gay and straight parents. In particular, she concluded that the children of gay parents did not manifest psychopathology related to separation and individuation at a statistically higher rate than did the children of straight parents, although she found qualitative differences between the manner in which the two groups of parents interacted with their children. Similarly, Patterson et al., in comparing gay and heterosexual fathers, found no important disparities between the two groups in promoting intimacy with, and autonomy in, their children (Patterson, Fulcher, & Wainwright, 1987).

Other researchers comparing straight and lesbian mothers have obtained somewhat surprising results. Siegelman (1972) found that lesbian women scored higher on tenderness and lower on depression, submission, and anxiety than their straight counterparts. In a study that used the Adjective Checklist, Green et al. likewise determined that lesbian mothers outperformed heterosexual mothers in a number of psychological parameters relevant to healthy separation and individuation. They scored higher than straight mothers on self-confidence, dominance, and exhibition, whereas straight mothers exhibited a higher degree of abasement and deference (Green, Mandel, Hotvedt, Gray, & Smith, 1986). To the extent that this research accurately depicts the two populations, as a whole, lesbian mothers are less likely to defer to others and are more likely to see themselves as dominant and independent than heterosexual mothers. Presumably they are therefore more likely to promote their children's independence by modeling independent thinking and behavior themselves.

A more nuanced picture emerges from a study conducted by Patterson in 1994 of children born to, or adopted by, lesbian and heterosexual mothers. The children were examined using instruments that measured their psychological functioning. In addition, the mothers completed the Child Behavior Checklist. While the children in the lesbian-led homes indicated that they experienced anger, fear, and upset more often than the children of heterosexual mothers, they also experienced joy and contentment to a greater degree. Furthermore, they were more comfortable with themselves than were the children in homes led by heterosexual mothers. As Dr. Cantor noted in the previous chapter, it is possible that the children of lesbian mothers were more willing to report more intense emotional experiences, both positive and negative.

All mental health professionals agree that the ability to be in touch with one's emotions is a personality asset of great value to parents and children alike. Because self-awareness enhances one's capacity for appropriately experiencing and acting on emotions, it is a key marker of successful separation and individuation. A person who is unable to adequately identify and analyze his or her own internal state is always to a greater or lesser degree an automaton whose feelings and behaviors are controlled by others, not themselves. Those who can accurately distinguish their own emotions, thoughts, needs, and desires from those of others are thereby capable of a genuinely separate and independent existence. The extant data lead us to tentatively conclude that lesbian mothers are at least the equals of heterosexual mothers in promoting the kind of self-awareness that independence requires.

The various comparative studies of parenting in the preschool years consistently yield the same general findings: gay and lesbian parents are as able as straight parents to love and commit to their children, and to provide them with a sense of security in the world in which they are growing up. They are as adept as heterosexual parents in facilitating the development and maturation of the psychological skills that will help them become healthy and independent adults. These include separating from their parents to go to school and make friends; being aware of and appropriately experiencing their own emotions; thinking for themselves; and enjoying, within sensible bounds, the freedom to make their own decisions.

Late Childhood, or the Latency Age Years

As children grow out of their early childhood, and away from total dependence on their parents, they enter a phase of development that Erik Erikson characterized by the surrender of the child's attachment "to the womb of their family," and an introduction to "the tool world" and "the weapons used by big people" (Erikson, 1950). By this, Erikson meant that children are required to separate from home, accept the constraints and stimulation of going to school, and develop ties to their peer society. Formal schooling requires the ability to concentrate and to absorb information, tasks that require self-control and the acceptance of adult authority. And while the preschool child draws esteem and approval almost exclusively from his or her parents, the latency age child broadens the universe of influential others to include, first, teachers and other adult authority figures, and then peers. Ultimately, the child who successfully navigates this developmental phase acquires self-esteem and is motivated in large part by pride in his or her own accomplishments. The essential tasks that confront latency age children—whose successful mastery forms the components of their sense of self-worth—are academic achievement and acceptance by other children.

No research has as yet been conducted that compares the school performance of children from families led by homosexual and heterosexual parents. We do know, however, a great deal about the impact of parental sexual orientation on the ability of children to successfully enter their peer groups, and to acquire and sustain friendships. These studies, which have been conducted almost exclusively with lesbian mothers, show that across a wide range of measures of peer and self-acceptance, the children of lesbian mothers do not differ from the children of intact families with heterosexual mothers. Research investigating the relative strength and nature of peer relationships in children from homes with heterosexual and lesbian parents found no disparities between the two categories of children (Golombok et al., 2003; Green et al., 1986). Likewise, teacher reports on prosocial and antisocial behavior demonstrated no differences between the two sets of children (Chan, Raboy, & Patterson, 1998; Flaks, Ficher, Masterpasqua, & Jospeh, 1995; Golombok et al., 2003). Other studies showed that regardless of whether a child's parent was gay or straight, the child chose gender-same friends and peer groups rather than gender-opposite friends and peers, indicating that both groups of children exhibited behavior consistent with the development of a heterosexual orientation and a gender identity consistent with their physiology (Golombok, Spencer, & Rutter, 1983; Green, 1978).

Investigations of peer-group popularity and social adjustment found that 80 percent of the daughters of lesbian mothers, compared with 75 percent of the daughters in the heterosexual group, described themselves in relation to their peers as "much more, somewhat more, or as" popular (Green et al., 1986). The same study had 80 percent of the boys in both groups reporting similarly high degrees of popularity. Hotvedt and Mandel (1982) found that the daughters of lesbian mothers in fact reported higher levels of popularity within their peer groups than did their counterparts from heterosexual homes.

Acceptance by peers, while not wholly determined by self-esteem, is certainly contingent on adequate self-acceptance and self-regard. Children who are unpopular with themselves are almost uniformly unpopular with others as well. Numerous studies demonstrated no differences between the children of lesbian and heterosexual mothers in their levels of self-esteem and in the nature of their self-concept (Hotvedt & Mandel, 1982; Patterson, 1992, 1995b).

Another matter that has been considered of such great importance by the courts that it has often formed the basis for denying custody to lesbian mothers has been the extent to which children may be teased and stigmatized by their peers on account of their parent's sexual orientation (Kraft, 1983). It is not altogether surprising that such children have, in fact, been harassed by their peers on these grounds, although the actual incidence of harassment has varied from study to study. Green (1978), for example, stated that only 4 out of 21 children from lesbian mother families had been teased, but that these were isolated incidents rather than long, organized campaigns of mockery. An even lower incidence of teasing was uncovered by Susoeff (1985), who found that only 5 percent of children raised by openly gay parents had been subjected to harassment by their peers. Riddle and Arguelles (1981), in their investigation of the families of gay men and women, noted that 63 percent of the children in those families received some "negative input" on account of their parents' sexual orientation, while 79 percent of the children from heterosexual families received "negative input" for other reasons.

A longitudinal study in which data were first collected in the 1970s from children with an average age of 9, and again collected when they were 23, found no significant differences in peer group teasing when compared to a control group parented by heterosexual mothers. All the children were asked about the extent and nature of teasing by peers. It is interesting to note that the children of lesbian mothers were teased more often about their own sexuality than about that of their mothers. In any case, 76 percent of all subjects reported some teasing or bullying (Haack-Moller & Mohl, 1984). In general, these studies find that all children are teased a lot, but the children of gay parents are likely teased somewhat more. Further, teasing by peers is likely to center on the children's or their parents' sexual orientation. The result of this research is consistent with the common observation that teasing in childhood is rampant and tends to focus on conspicuous, albeit superficial, characteristics.

A small study found the children of lesbian mothers worrying more than the children of straight mothers about teasing, whether or not they were, in fact, teased (O'Connell, 1993). Bozett described "social control strategies" that the children of gay parents use to protect themselves from harassment, such as trying to limit public displays between themselves and their gay fathers, not disclosing their gay fathers' sexual orientation, and only telling select others in preparation for an anticipated meeting with their fathers (Bozett, 1987).

Ultimately, however, the important issue is not whether the children of gay parents are disproportionately victimized through teasing, harassment, and bullying; it is the outcome of this victimization. We know that peer provocation is a common phenomenon among children of this age. Dealing with this type of adversity calls on the personality strengths of the victimized child. Whether the teasing is friendly or hostile, it is the strength of the child's self-concept and personality that determines whether or not teasing affects his or her self-esteem and acceptance by the peer group as a whole. It was one court's view that the struggle with societal disapproval might preferentially enable these children to develop independent moral convictions upon reaching adulthood (Kraft, 1983). Even though the children of gay and lesbian families may have a more difficult road, it does not seem to adversely impact their self-confidence. Self-images in boys and girls are a product not just of peer acceptance but also of parental modeling of family values and parental investment.

Besides the formation of satisfactory peer relationships, another important developmental task for the latency age child is the creation and maintenance of strong and healthy relationships with adult figures besides the primary caregiver. Of particular importance are relationships within the nuclear and extended families, which constitute a vital source of modeling, learning, and value development in children. Furthermore, because identity formation in the school-age years relies strongly on modeling the behavior of parents and other significant adults, both the quality of the child's ties with these adults, and the nature of the values that such adults reinforce through their behavior, are salient constituents of healthy identity formation in this developmental epoch.

Although it was likely the case that, in the past, children residing in homes headed by a gay parent were relatively deprived of contact with members of their extended families—most importantly grandparents—owing to the family's rejection of the gay parent's sexual orientation, this does not seem to be the case today. While the quality of relationships with grandparents is far less important to the child's development than the quality of parent-child relationships, relationships with grandparents are nonetheless influential in some degree. Such relationships give children an alternate avenue whereby they can seek nurturance and security, and constitute another source of values with which the child can identify. Patterson studied this matter and learned that 97 percent of the children of biological lesbian parents, and 74 percent of nonbiological lesbian parents, had contact with their maternal grandparents (Patterson, Hurt, & Mason, 1998).

In families disrupted by divorce, the relative willingness of the custodial parent to provide the noncustodial parent with appropriate access to the child is both a measure of the custodial parent's own psychological maturity and an important factor in the child's healthy development (see Black & Cantor, 1989). Golombok and her colleagues demonstrated that divorced lesbian mothers made their children more available for contact with their fathers than did divorced heterosexual mothers (Golombok et al., 1983). Contrary to the image of lesbians in the minds of many, a different investigation noted that in fact, relative to their heterosexual counterparts, lesbian mothers were more likely to value their children's opportunities for relationships with men in general, and in particular with their fathers (Kirkpatrick, Smith, & Roy, 1981).

What is most striking about role relationships within gay families is how similar they are to those found in heterosexual families. One study of families headed by lesbians found, for instance, that the biological mother did more caretaking than did the nonbiological parent (the so-called social mother), who in turn spent more of her time in paid employment (Patterson, 1995a). Although child care tasks seem to be more equitably shared in lesbian families than in heterosexual families, both types of families divide household tasks and decision making reasonably equally (Chan et al., 1998). A number of findings emerged from a comparative exploration of the familial roles adopted by lesbian adoptive parents, biological lesbian parents, and heterosexual biological parents. As shown in the earlier study by Patterson, the lesbian birth couples shared child care tasks more equitably than did the heterosexual parents. In families that had biological mothers, these were the parents most sought out by the child for nurturance, whether the mother was lesbian or straight. The nonbirth mothers in the adoptive families seem to occupy the same role as that of fathers in the heterosexual biological families, being more likely to be sought out for rough-and-tumble play. Intriguingly, a traditional "division of labor" evolved within the lesbian adoptive families, wherein one of the two parents was expected by the children to be available for nurturing, and the other for rough-and-tumble play (Ciano-Boyce & Shelley-Sireci, 2002). In these families, either the parents or the children—it is not clear which—create the same role relationships in gay families as exist in traditional families. The only distinction between the functioning of the families headed by lesbian and heterosexual parents is that whereas the biological lesbian mothers provided the same quality and character of parent-child interactions as did the heterosexual biological mothers, the social mothers in the biological lesbian families were better than heterosexual fathers at social interactions. This probably reflects nothing more than the relatively better social adeptness of women than men in general, rather than something specific to sexual identity.

Among the many components of family functioning that contribute to a child's sense of well-being and his or her healthy development, few are as important as parents' ability to control their impulses (Black & Cantor, 1989). Parental impulse control is especially important to children in the later latency phase years who, as part of their development of satisfactory peer relationships, must learn, through parental modeling as well as by other means, to assert themselves without becoming aggressive. Poor parental impulse control leading either to physical or sexual abuse can have a devastating impact on an abused youngster's self-image, leading to depression, behavioral difficulties, and possibly to becoming a physical or sexual abuser in later years.[2]

Few are concerned about the potential danger of physical aggression on the part of gay parents. The research data bear out this general lack of concern, inasmuch as gay and heterosexual parents exhibit no significant differences in their application of discipline and child control. While one study indicated that gay fathers were more likely to be strict than heterosexual fathers, gay fathers were also more likely to explain rules, and to respond to their children's needs (Bigner & Jacobsen, 1989b). The same researchers demonstrated in a later report that modern gay and straight fathers alike adopted developmentally appropriate, child-oriented disciplinary practices as opposed to more traditional, authoritative approaches (Bigner & Jacobsen, 1992). And although one study found children from lesbian and heterosexual families reporting similar levels of discipline (Perry et al., 2004), in another, heterosexual parents reported smacking their children more often than did lesbian mothers (Golombok et al., 2003). An investigation that measured no differences between moral development of the children of lesbian and straight mothers corroborates the fundamental equivalence of disciplinary practices employed by both groups (Rees, 1979).

By contrast, many have voiced concern that children raised in gay families are at a heightened risk of being sexually molested by their parents, or by their parents' friends. Some opponents of gay marriage and gay families have treated this unexamined but widely held belief as a self-evident fact and used it not only to generate alarm about the supposed threat of gay marriage and parenting but indeed to cast a shadow of suspicion on gays in general. But like so many beliefs that are grounded in contagious fear rather than in empirical evidence, it is a myth. Although societal concerns seem to focus more on gay fathers than on lesbian mothers, we will here address both areas of concern.

Authoritative studies of sex crimes involving children demonstrate that 90 percent of such crimes involve female children and male adults (DiLapi, 1989). DiLapi further stated that incidents of sexual abuse involving adult women and children of either sex were statistically insignificant. The same results were reported by Hall, who noted the absence in judicial records of sexual incidents between women and children (Hall, 1978), and Richardson, who could not identify any cases of female pedophilia, homosexual or heterosexual (Richardson, 1981).

The case for gay fathers being inclined to molest their children is almost as weak. In 1979, Miller studied, among other things, whether gay fathers were likely to molest children. He concluded that the concern was unfounded. To take the matter one step further, court statistics have demonstrated that sexual molestation occurs more frequently in the heterosexual male population than in the homosexual male population, leading one commentator to refer to the crime in the United States as "essentially a heterosexual male act" (Riley, 1975). The noted researchers Groth and Birnbaum studied 175 randomly selected males convicted of sexual assault. None had a primary homosexual orientation. In the authors' words, "It appears, therefore, that the adult heterosexual male constitutes a greater risk to underage school children than does the adult homosexual male" (Groth & Birnbaum, 1978).

As to whether the friends or partners of homosexual parents are more likely to molest a parent's child than the friends or partners of heterosexual parents, we can immediately eliminate consideration of abuse by the (female) partner of lesbian parents, since female pedophiles do not exist or are so rare as to be virtually nonexistent. In fact, on the same grounds, we can focus our attention entirely on the male friends or partners of either gay or lesbian parents. In the absence of any hard data exploring this topic, we can make the following theoretical arguments: First of all, inasmuch as gay and lesbian parents as a group are as psychologically healthy as heterosexual parents, they will be equally keen to the possible presence of a predator in their midst who may be invading their lives for the primary purpose of victimizing their child. Furthermore, every indicator points to the fact that gay parents love and cherish their children as much as straight parents. For gays and lesbians to obtain custody of a child—whether by adoption or through divorce—is an arduous process that demands a high level of commitment to parenting. Such a parent will certainly be at least as vigilant as the average and will take action if there is a reasonable indication that his or her child is in danger. Finally, statistics have clearly shown that heterosexual, rather than homosexual, males are more likely to be sexual predators of children, so the friends of gay fathers are likely to pose a heightened risk of predation only insofar as they are straight. Inasmuch as it is likely that heterosexual males are more likely to have heterosexual friends than are homosexual males, it follows that it is straight, rather than gay, parents whose friends are most likely to sexually abuse their children. This discussion ought to put to rest the fear that gay parents, or their partners or friends, are more likely to sexually abuse their children than straight parents and their partners and friends, but after many years of psychiatric practice, I am well aware that fear and suspicion do not die easily, especially when they are rooted in deeply ingrained prejudice.

The presumption that heterosexual parenting defines the template against which homosexual parenting must be compared—generally to the disadvantage of the latter—overlooks the possibility that the children of gay parents may benefit in some ways by virtue of their parents' sexual orientation. Patterson, for instance, suggested that such children could possibly approach their own sexuality with greater acceptance, develop more empathy for others, and have a greater tolerance for alternative points of view (Patterson, 1992).[3] Many children of lesbian mothers have noted that they were proud of their mothers for challenging society's rules and for standing up for what they believed. Obviously these children profited from modeling by mothers who subscribed to the belief that being true to oneself had a higher priority than succumbing to cultural traditions when it required living in dishonesty and deception. They learned the following lesson very well:

> This above all: to thine own self be true,
> And it must follow, as the night the day,
> Thou canst not then be false to any man.
> (Shakespeare, *Hamlet*, act 1, scene 3)

In summary, the available research data show little difference between homosexual and heterosexual parents in their ability to guide their children through the latency age period. Both groups are equally adept at helping their children navigate the path from childhood into adolescence and healthy adulthood. The only significant differences between the experiences of children raised in the two types of families are special challenges in forming and maintaining peer relations that stem mainly from prejudice itself. However, there is no evidence that the children of homosexual parents are at greater risk of any psychological damage as a consequence of these challenges, and there is indeed some evidence that some are strengthened by them. We can therefore conclude that there is no psychiatric basis for discriminating against gay parents on the basis of their ability to successfully shepherd their children through the latency age years.

Adolescence

There is no phase of childhood that parents anticipate with greater anxiety or look back on with as much frustration as that of adolescence. It is during this period that their children apparently move farther away from them, wholeheartedly embracing the culture of their friends and peers. Adolescents

often adopt unusual modes of speech and dress and develop strange fasci-
nations with peculiar music that represent as much of a polar extreme from
their parents' choices as they can possibly find. All of this is in the service of
consciously severing the tie of dependence on their parents, even though in
reality these unseen bonds continue to exist as strongly as ever. Teenagers are
simultaneously engaged in attempts both to explore, and also to crystallize,
their identities, defining not merely who and what they are but also who and
what they are to become. Included in this crystallization process is the resolution of their sexual identities. If they have not done so already, young men
and women will declare themselves as heterosexual or homosexual—perhaps
prematurely—as part of their coming of age.

The teenager's peer group and its judgments become even more important
in adolescence than in earlier childhood. It is therefore vital to look at the extent to which teenagers who have a gay parent feel stigmatized on this account
by their age-mates. In a study investigating 12-year-old preadolescents born
to either lesbian or heterosexual mothers, no difference in the quality of peer
relations between the two groups was observed (MacCallum & Golombok,
2004). Other researchers who looked at older adolescents from the same two
groups found no difference between them on a range of psychosocial variables
related to peer acceptance, including anxiety, depression, and self-esteem. It
is in fact noteworthy that the teenagers from lesbian families reported greater
"school connectedness" than their counterparts from heterosexual families,
regardless of their gender. Specifically, they more likely "felt close to other
students, felt like a part of the school, felt safe in school" (Wainwright, Russell,
& Patterson, 2004). Comparing the self-esteem of older adolescents who were
raised by lesbian mothers to those raised by heterosexual mothers, Huggins
(1989) also found no differences between the groups of teens. Thus, although
the adolescent children of gay parents continued in adolescence to endure
greater levels of teasing than their cohort from heterosexual families (Tasker
& Golombok, 1997b), just as in late childhood, this teasing had no significant
effect on either their general level of peer acceptance or their psychological
well-being as measured by their levels of self-esteem, anxiety, and depression.

The age at which children learn of their parents' sexual identities appears
to strongly influence their healthy development. Those who learned about
their parents' gay, lesbian, or bisexual orientation in early to mid-adolescence
had more difficulty coping with that knowledge than those who learned in

earlier childhood or in late adolescence (Paul, 1986). Huggins corroborated this observation, concluding that children whose parents came out before adolescence had relatively higher self-esteem than those who learned of their parents' sexual orientation during adolescence (Huggins, 1989). It is widely agreed that early adolescence is an especially difficult time for children to learn that a parent is gay or lesbian (Bozett, 1980; Pennington, 1987; Schulenberg, 1985). Pennington posited that until the time children acquire established sexual identities of their own and separate from their mothers, as they grow older, they become increasingly aware of their lesbian mothers' sexual orientation and fear ostracism on that account (Pennington, 1987). It is notable, however, that this same "time-sensitivity" also applies to the age at which children learn of their parents' divorce. It may simply be that early and middle adolescence age children are poorly equipped to cope with *any* surprises regarding their parents' romantic lives, inasmuch as during this time they are most deeply immersed in constructing their own sexual and romantic identities and ideals.

For those interested in the ultimate impact of gay parenting, one critical issue in particular generates great controversy: does the sexual orientation of gay parents influence their developing children's sexual identities and orientations? To be absolutely clear about the issue before us, let me reiterate the distinction between gender identity and sexual orientation. Gender identity is the conscious awareness of being male or female. Many transsexuals report believing at an early age that they were born into the wrong body. Gender role denotes those interests and behaviors that are stereotypically regarded as male or female. Gender identity develops very early, so that by two and one-half to three years of age, boys and girls will typically identify themselves as males or females, respectively. Sexual orientation, on the other hand, is the preference for a heterosexual or homosexual relationship. Whereas gender role (which is an understanding of who one is) unfolds in early childhood, sexual orientation (which defines whom one desires) commonly evolves in mid- to late adolescence.

When Green interviewed the children of heterosexual and lesbian mothers in 1986, asking what gender they would choose if they could be born all over again, for the most part they chose their anatomical gender, regardless of the sexual orientation of their mothers (Green et al., 1986). Likewise, in a comparison of lesbian and heterosexual families, Golombok and colleagues found no evidence that children from either group were statistically more likely to assign themselves a biologically anomalous gender (Golombok et al., 1983). Another study involving the adult daughters of mated lesbian, mated heterosexual, and single heterosexual mothers also uncovered no differences in gender identity between the experimental populations (Schwartz, 1985).

A variety of research investigations have explored the extent to which the attitudes and activities of homosexual and heterosexual parents differentially influence their children's gender-role behavior. One study found that while heterosexual mothers were more likely than lesbian mothers to prefer gender-stereotypical toys for their children, no differences between the gender role self-assignments of the two groups of children emerged as a consequence (Hoeffer, 1981). Another compared children's idealized gender-role behaviors with their mothers' description of their own gender-role behaviors in families having either heterosexual or lesbian mothers. The children's description of ideal gender roles was correlated to that of their mothers, rather than to their mothers' sexual orientation (Kweskin & Cook, 1982).

While children born to lesbian mothers did not differ from those living in either single-parent or two-parent heterosexual households on measures of "masculinity" and "femininity," boys from "father absent" heterosexual homes scored higher than boys from two-parent heterosexual homes on the femininity scale. This latter result might be explained by the attempts of single-parent mothers to teach their sons, in particular, to be considerate and appreciative of the feelings of others (MacCallum & Golombok, 2000). In one study, boys raised by heterosexual couples appeared to be slightly more aggressive than those raised by lesbian parents (Steckel, 1985). Another showed that although boys born to both heterosexual and lesbian mothers selected traditionally masculine activities and careers, the girls who had lesbian mothers chose a wider range of possibilities than their counterparts from heterosexual homes. These girls were more likely to be involved in both feminine and gender-neutral activities than their counterparts, who most often restricted themselves to traditionally feminine activities (Green et al., 1986). No coherent or significant pattern seems to emerge from the research, beyond the uncontroversial observation that children at least mildly base their gender-role expectations on those of their same-sex parent. Across the board, research assessing gender-role behavior in children from gay, lesbian, and heterosexual families has not uncovered any obvious differences between these groups (Golombok et al., 1983; Hoeffer, 1981; Kirkpatrick et al., 1981; Kweskin & Cook,

1982; Moses & Hawkins, 1982; Nungesser, 1980; Ostrow, 1977; Rees, 1979; Turner, Scadden, & Harris, 1990).

In any case, it is not gender identity but sexual orientation, and its presumed transmissibility, that is the source of greatest anxiety on the part of those who fear the influence of gay and lesbian parents on developing children. This presumption that sexual orientation is somehow contagious, the so-called "universal latency fear" (Riley, 1975), is contradicted by our current, well-established understanding that sexual orientation is primarily genetically and biologically determined, at least in the case of male homosexuality (Bailey & Pillard, 1991, 1995; Blanchard, 1997; Hamer et al., 1993; Hershberger, 1997; LeVay, 1991).

Some research, however, shows that girls raised by lesbian mothers are more likely to experiment with lesbian relationships during adolescence and young adulthood than the daughters of heterosexual mothers. Experimentation, however, does not equal orientation. The majority of the girls in this study ultimately adopted a heterosexual orientation (Golombok & Tasker, 1996; Tasker & Golombok, 1997b). In all research conducted to date that compares the sexual orientation of children raised by lesbian parents, transsexual parents, and gay fathers, and those raised by heterosexual mothers, no significant differences emerged between the various populations, and the vast majority of the children from all groups adopted heterosexual orientations (Bailey, Bobrow, Wolfe, & Mikach, 1995; Bozett, 1980, 1982, 1987, 1989; Golombok et al., 1983; Gottman, 1989; Green, 1978, 1982; Miller, 1979; O'Connell, 1993; Paul, 1986; Rees, 1979; Schwartz, 1985).

For instance, in one study comparing adolescents from lesbian families with those from heterosexual families headed by single-parent mothers, only one teenager developed a homosexual orientation, and that adolescent was from the heterosexual mother group (Huggins, 1989). In another study of 21 gay parents, only 1 of the 21 adolescents in the group was homosexual, a number consistent with the incidence of homosexuality in the general population (Turner et al., 1990). Given these research data, it is safe to say that children raised in a gay or lesbian household are no more likely to become homosexual than those raised in a heterosexual family. Naturally, this is what we would expect, given that sexual orientation is primarily constitutionally determined. Homosexuality is divided roughly evenly across heterosexual and homosexual families of origin. We would not expect otherwise.

James C. Black

Conclusion

Based on the research cited in this chapter, on my 37 years of experience as a child and adolescent psychiatrist, and on my involvement with the legal system in innumerable cases as a child custody evaluator, I can state with conviction that children raised by one or more homosexual parents have the same likelihood of healthy development as those raised by one or more heterosexual parents. Those who argue against this assertion are motivated either by ignorance or by a prejudice that constitutes the greatest actual threat to those whose interests they claim to represent and serve.

6

Homosexuality and Adoption

Campbell D. Barrett

Before 1973, homosexuals were regularly denied the right to adopt.[1] Today that right is available to homosexuals in virtually every state. The debate over the issue hinges on the question of whether sexual orientation is a relevant consideration in determining an individual's ability to parent. Over the past three decades, the issue has played out in legislatures and courts across the country in the context of both "stranger adoptions" (adoptions where an individual or a couple adopts an unrelated child) and "second-parent adoptions" (adoptions where an individual adopts the adopted or biological child of a partner). The evolution of the issue has not been a linear progression but perhaps can be more aptly described as a series of distinct trends.

The issue has advanced in two distinct ways: (1) by the refusal of individual states to enact legislation establishing a blanket prohibition against homosexual adoption, thus permitting homosexuals to enter into stranger adoptions on a case-by-case basis; and (2) by a widespread pragmatic recognition that second-parent adoption serves the best interests of children already being raised in same-sex households. Nevertheless, the uniform acceptance of homosexual adoption has been hindered by the lingering presumption, as reflected in certain statutes and judicial decisions, that homosexuals are unfit to parent simply because of their sexual orientation.

The debate has been bracketed by two significant events in the state of Florida. First, in 1977, the commercial actress and Florida citrus spokesperson Anita Bryant commenced a vitriolic campaign against gay rights. Ms. Bryant's campaign, entitled "Save Our Children," sought to protect children from the influence of homosexuals. Bryant argued that "since homosexuals cannot reproduce, they must recruit and freshen their ranks."[2] In response to this argument, the Florida legislature enacted a statute expressly denying homosexuals the right to adopt. The Florida statute provides that "no person eligible to adopt under this statute may adopt if that person is a homosexual."[3] The statute was the first legal authority to overtly abridge the rights of homosexuals with respect to adoption.

Twenty-eight years later the same Florida statute stood at the epicenter of American legal debate. Specifically, on July 21, 2004, the United States Court of Appeals for the Eleventh Circuit (the federal appeals court with jurisdiction over federal cases originating in the states of Alabama, Florida, and Georgia) rendered a decision in the case of *Lofton v. Secretary of Department of Children and Family Services*,[4] upholding the constitutionality of the statute. The case basically stands for the proposition that individual states have the right to prohibit homosexual adoption. On January 10, 2005, the United States Supreme Court declined to review the decision. The denial of review was somewhat of a surprise, given the Supreme Court's decision in 2003 in the case of *Lawrence v. Texas* (discussed more thoroughly in chapters 1 and 2).[5]

Although the *Lofton* case represents a significant setback to the gay rights movement, it is, in a sense, an aberration in the evolution of the legal battle for homosexual adoption rights. This chapter will address how this legal battle has played out over the past thirty years in the various courts and legislatures across the country.

Early Cases (1980–1990)

The 1980s represented a confusing time with respect to the legal right to gay adoption. In many instances, the early cases addressing the issue did so in the context of stranger adoptions—meaning the type of adoption where an individual seeks to adopt an unrelated child. The reasoning of these early cases differed greatly from state to state. In many respects, these cases mirrored the judicial decisions that were being rendered during the same time frame addressing the rights of gay parents in contested custody cases, which likewise varied greatly from state to state.

In 1981 the Virginia Supreme Court touched on the issue of gay rights in the context of adoption in the case of *Doe v. Doe*.[6] In *Doe*, a woman petitioned to adopt her stepchild based on the claim that the child's biological mother was a lesbian. A lower court permitted the adoption and terminated the biological mother's parental rights, based on a finding that her lesbian relationship would be detrimental to the child.[7] The Virginia Supreme Court reversed this decision, reasoning that there was no scientific evidence entered to support the trial court's conclusions.[8] The court concluded that no matter how offended it was by the lesbian relationship, it could not find, as a matter of law, that homosexuals are unfit to parent.[9]

The *Doe* case was consistent with a series of court decisions that were issued during the same time period concerning the rights of gay parents in custody cases—all of which were based on the recognition that homosexuality by itself is not a controlling factor in determining an individual's ability to parent. In the case of *Nadler v. Superior Court*,[10] for example, a California court determined that it was impermissible to find that a mother was an unfit parent based solely on the fact that she was a lesbian. In the case of *People v. Brown*,[11] a Michigan appellate court determined that there was no proof that a woman's lesbian relationship rendered her home an unfit place to raise foster children. In *MP v. SP*,[12] a New Jersey appellate court reversed a lower court's decision where custody was awarded to a father based solely on the fact that the mother was a lesbian. Similarly, in *Bezio v. Patenaude*,[13] a Massachusetts court determined that there was no correlation between a mother's status as a lesbian and her fitness as parent. Likewise, in *DH v. JH*,[14] an Indiana appellate court found that homosexuality standing alone does not render a homosexual parent unfit. In *In re Marriage of Cabalquinto*,[15] a Washington court determined that "homosexuality in and of itself is not a bar to custody rights or to visitation" and that the appropriate inquiry is the needs of the child rather than the sexual preference of the parent. Finally, in *SNE v. RLB*,[16] the Alaska Supreme Court recognized that there was no suggestion that a mother's homosexuality would adversely impact her child.

Nevertheless, there were many cases issued during the same period that found that homosexuality was directly relevant to an individual's ability to parent.[17] Curiously, in 1985, the Virginia Supreme Court, the same court that had decided *Doe v. Doe* in 1980, rendered a decision in the case of *Roe v. Roe*,[18] which held in the context of a custody case that a father's homosexuality, standing alone, would have a negative impact on his child.

The reasoning of these cases was adopted by several courts addressing the issue of gay adoption. For example, in the case of *In re Appeal in Pima County Juvenile Action B-10489* (1986),[19] an Arizona appeals court determined that a lower court properly rejected an adoption petition filed by a bisexual man.

The court, expressly citing *Bowers v. Hardwick* (discussed in chapters 1 and 2),[20] noted that homosexual conduct was illegal in the state of Arizona and that as a result the petitioner's "ambivalence" concerning his sexual preference was an appropriate concern when determining whether the adoption was in the child's best interest.[21] Similarly, in the case of *In re Adoption of JMG* (1987),[22] the Montana Supreme Court upheld a stepfather's adoption, reasoning that the evidence of the biological father's homosexuality was a relevant consideration to his emotional health and mental well-being.

The position that homosexuals as a class may be unfit to adopt was also embraced on the legislative level. Specifically, in 1987, the state of New Hampshire established a statute prohibiting homosexuals from adopting.[23] This was the first time since Florida had enacted its statute in 1977 that a state legislative body had taken an affirmative stance against the right to homosexual adoption. The stated basis for the statute was that homosexuals do not provide a healthy environment for children.

The New Hampshire statute was significant because it established a blanket rule that homosexuals could not adopt. This is in contrast to the court decisions in *In re Appeal in Pima County Juvenile Action B-10489* and *In re Adoption of JMG*, which both held that an individual's homosexuality was a *factor* to be considered when determining whether he or she was fit to adopt. Arguably, homosexuals could still adopt under the reasoning of those two cases if they had sufficient positive attributes to outweigh the negative aspect of their sexual orientation. This was not the case in New Hampshire, which joined Florida in banning outright all homosexuals from adopting.

Moreover, in the case of *In re Opinion of Justices* (1987),[24] the New Hampshire Supreme Court found that the statute in question did *not* violate any constitutionally protected rights. This was the first time that an American court had addressed the gay adoption issue in the context of constitutional terms. The court first determined, in express reliance on the *Bowers v. Hardwick* decision, that there is no fundamental right to engage in homosexual acts.[25] The court further noted that there was no constitutionally protected right to adopt because it was a creature of statute.[26] The court then determined that the blanket exclusion of homosexuals from adoption accomplishes the legislature's stated goal of "promoting [a] healthy environment for children" and eliminating the "social and psychological complexities" that living in a "homosexual environment" could have on children.[27] The court acknowledged that its conclusions were based not on any empirical data evidencing that children are negatively impacted by exposure to homosexuals, but rather on the *possibility* that such harm *might* occur.[28]

The decision of the New Hampshire Supreme Court was not unanimous. One member of the court, Justice William Batchelder, issued a strong dissenting opinion. The dissent takes issue with the reasoning of the majority decision, noting that it improperly presumes that every homosexual is unfit to parent. The dissent also notes that there is no evidence whatsoever that exposure to homosexuals affects a child's development.[29] Justice Batchelder concluded that denying homosexuals the right to adopt violated both their state and federal due process rights because although "parenting an adopted child . . . is not a fundamental right, as parenting one's own biological child is . . . parenting is so engrained in our culture that to deny the opportunity to adopt . . . is a deprivation only in a lesser degree."[30] Nevertheless, the majority of the New Hampshire Supreme Court determined that it was constitutional for the state to deprive homosexuals of the right to adopt.

1990–2005: A Pragmatic Approach to the Issue

The 1990s presented a change from the 1980s in the approach that was taken with respect to the issue of homosexual adoption. More and more states began to accept the concept that homosexuals were fit to parent. More often than not, the recognition came in the form of judicial decisions establishing the right to second-parent adoption (the form of adoption where an individual seeks to adopt the adopted or biological child of his or her partner). These decisions generally took the pragmatic approach that permitting homosexuals to adopt the adopted or biological children of their partners served the best interest of the children because it created legal rights and stability. In addition, it is important to note that no state established any laws in the 1990s, either through the enactment of statutes or through the rendering of judicial decisions, establishing a blanket prohibition against gay adoption. In fact, by the end of the decade, Florida would stand alone as the only state with such a rule of law.

Ohio Recognizes the Right to Gay Adoption

In 1990 the Supreme Court of Ohio became the first court of last resort to determine that a gay individual has the right to adopt a child. The case of

In re Adoption of Charles involved a gay man's attempt to adopt a child with significant special needs.[31] The state administrator of social services recommended against the adoption because the petitioner, as a homosexual, did not meet "the characteristic profile of preferred adoptive placement."[32] An intermediary appellate court dismissed the petition based solely on the petitioner's sexual orientation. The state Supreme Court, however, reversed this decision, reasoning that nothing in the Ohio adoption statutes prohibited homosexuals from adoption. The court then determined that the best interest of the child was paramount, and that the adoption served this purpose.[33]

A similar result was reached in a number of decisions issued by lower courts in the state of New York. For example, in the case of *In re Commitment of JN* (1993),[34] a court allowed a lesbian foster mother to adopt a child over the child's biological grandmother because of the bond that had developed between the foster parent and the child. Likewise, in the case of *In re Adoption of Jessica* (1994),[35] a court allowed a lesbian to adopt a child based on the fact that the adoption served the child's best interests. Similarly, in the case of *In re Adoption of Anonymous* (1994),[36] a court held that applications for adoption may not be denied on the basis of an applicant's sexual orientation. The decisions in each of these cases were based on the core recognition that homosexuals can be fit parents, and serve as a sharp contrast to the legal authority from the 1980s that stood for the opposite proposition.

Second-Parent Adoption

In the 1990s, a spate of judicial decisions was issued addressing the issue of homosexual second-parent adoption. In these cases, an individual would petition to adopt the adopted or biological child or children of a same-sex partner. Problems arose, however, because the statutory scheme that most states had with respect to adoption required that a biological parent's parental rights be terminated before any adoption by a nonrelated third party. The statutes generally had "stepparent" exceptions that permitted the spouse of a biological parent to adopt a child with the termination, but these exceptions did not appear to apply, on their face, to same-sex couples. Many courts resolved this issue by extending the "stepparent" exception to include same-sex couples.

In 1993, for example, the Vermont Supreme Court became the first court of final resort to establish the definitive right to second-parent gay adoption when the court rendered a decision in the case of *In re BLVB*.[37] The case involved a challenge by a lesbian woman of a lower court's denial of her petition to adopt the biological child of her partner. The Vermont Supreme Court reversed the decision of the lower court, reasoning that the "family unit" in the case comprised the petitioner, the biological mother, and the children, and that nothing in the Vermont adoption statutes precluded the adoption.[38] Specifically, the court determined that the petitioner was the functional equivalent of a stepparent and that as a result she should be permitted to adopt in that capacity. The court stated that statutes must be interpreted to allow for changes in social mores.[39] The court concluded that "by allowing same-sex adoptions to come within the step-parent exception . . . we are furthering the purposes of the statute as was originally intended by allowing the children of such unions the benefits and security of a legal relationship with their *de facto* second parents."[40] The best interests of the children were the court's paramount concern.[41]

Later in 1993, the Massachusetts Supreme Court likewise expressly recognized the right to second-parent adoption in the case of *Adoption of Tammy*.[42] In that case a woman sought to adopt the biological child of her partner. The child had been conceived through artificial insemination, and the two women made a commitment to raise the child together. The court approved the adoption, reasoning that "there is nothing in the statute that prohibits adoption based on gender or sexual orientation."[43]

The Vermont and Massachusetts cases provided support for numerous other court decisions. For example, the concept of second-parent adoption was expressly recognized by two courts in the state of New Jersey. First, in the case of *Matter of Adoption of Child by JMG* (1993),[44] a court determined that the petitioner should be treated as a stepparent as a matter of common sense. Similarly, in the case of *Adoption of Two Children by HNR* (1995),[45] a New Jersey appellate court determined that "the stepparent exception to the natural parent's termination of rights should not be read literally and restrictively where to do so would defeat the best interests of the children and would produce a wholly absurd and untenable result."

A series of New York cases also endorsed the concept of second-parent adoption. In the case of *In re Evan* (1992),[46] a court approved the adoption of a child without terminating the rights of the biological parent. The New York court found that termination of the parent's rights "would be an absurd outcome which would nullify the advantage sought by the proposed adoption:

the creation of a legal family unit identical to the actual family setup." In the case of *In re Adoption of Caitlin*,[47] a court determined that New York law did not prohibit second-parent adoptions and that adoption by the lesbian petitioner would serve the child's best interests. The court noted that the committed relationship of the two mothers was a persuasive factor.[48] Similarly, in the case of *In the Matter of Jacob* (1995),[49] the court determined that although the New York legislature could not have envisioned the concept of homosexual second-parent adoption when it established the state's adoption statutes, a child should not be deprived of the benefits of having as a legal parent an individual who has acted as the child's de facto parent.

The second-parent adoption concept was similarly approved in the state of Illinois in the cases of *In re Petition of KM and DM* (1995)[50] and *In re CMA* (1998).[51] In both cases, the state appellate court determined that sexual orientation is not a valid consideration for purposes of Illinois's adoption statute, and that as a result it was appropriate to permit second-parent adoption. The *In re CMA* case demonstrates the heated nature of the debate over gay adoption. In that case, a particular trial court judge was barred from hearing the merits of the adoptions in question based on cause (presumably because of her own antihomosexual adoption position). The adoption petitions were then approved by a different judge. Nevertheless, the recused judge scheduled her own hearing and invalidated the adoptions. The appellate court determined, in strong terms, that the recused court lacked the requisite jurisdiction to take this action. For a judge to go to such lengths simply underscores the fervor that often exists in the debate over homosexual adoption.

A critical decision was rendered by the District of Columbia Court of Appeals in the case of *In re MMD*.[52] In that case, the court addressed the issue of whether a gay man could adopt a child that his partner had previously adopted. This factual scenario is distinct from the earlier cases, which all involved an individual seeking to adopt the biological child of a partner. The D.C. court determined that the adoption was appropriate based, in large part, on the fact that the two men were involved in a committed relationship and that they had historically jointly cared for the child.[53] The court found that the adoption would strengthen the family unit—a paramount goal in all adoption cases. As a result, the court extended the stepparent exception to parental termination and permitted both men to be the child's parents.[54]

Courts continued to sanction second-parent adoption after the commencement of the new millennium. The issue was addressed in two separate contexts in the state of Indiana. First, in the case of *Adoption of MMGC* (2003),[55] the Indiana Court of Appeals held that a woman could adopt the adopted child of her lesbian partner. The court reasoned that nothing in the Indiana adoption law precluded such a result and that allowing the second parent to adopt would serve the best interests of the child.[56] A year later, the same court expanded second-parent adoption to include cases where an individual wishes to adopt the biological child of his or her partner. In that case, *Adoption of KSP*,[57] the court determined that although such an adoption appeared to be prohibited by the plain language of the Indiana adoption statute (which would require the termination of the biological mother's rights upon the granting of her partner's adoption petition), the Indiana legislature could not have intended such an "absurd" result.[58] The court determined that the best interests of the children and the fostering of family relationships are the principal concerns of the adoption statute, and that these goals would be defeated by divesting the biological mother of her parental rights.[59] The court concluded that "when social mores change statutes must be interpreted to allow for these changes."[60]

In the case of *In re Adoption of MJS* (2000),[61] a Tennessee appellate court upheld an adoption stating that although a prospective adoptive parent's "lifestyle" is a considered factor, it "does not control the outcome . . . particularly absent evidence of its effects on the child." Similarly, in the case of *In re Hart* (2001),[62] a Delaware family court held that to deny an adoption petition by a lesbian when she had already actively participated in raising the children in question would be "illogical" and would "produce an absurd and unacceptable social result."[63] Moreover, in the case of *In re Adoption of RBF*,[64] the Pennsylvania Supreme Court found that it would be "absurd" to deny homosexuals the right to second-parent adoption.

The second-parent adoption cases take a pragmatic approach to the issue of homosexual adoption. They recognize that many children are already living in homes with committed, loving same-sex parents, and that it would be contrary to the best interests of these children to deny them the legal and practical benefits that flow from an adoption. At their core, however, these cases also all accept the fact that homosexuality is not a determinative factor in the question of whether an individual is fit to be a parent.

Campbell *D. Barrett*

Cases in Opposition to Second-Parent Adoption

The concept that homosexual parents should be permitted to participate in second-parent adoptions has not been adopted on a uniform basis. Courts from five states have expressly rejected the right to second-parent gay adoption. For example, in the case of *In re Angel Lace M* (1994),[65] the Supreme Court of Wisconsin determined that the state's adoption statutes prohibited a woman from adopting the biological child of her partner, despite finding that the adoption would serve the child's best interests. Similarly, in the case of *In re Adoption of TKJ* (1996),[66] a Colorado appellate court determined that a lesbian couple did not have the right, under the plain language of the relevant adoption statutes, to adopt each other's children. Importantly, both courts determined that there were no constitutional implications to their decision. Similar results were reached by courts in Nebraska,[67] Ohio,[68] and Connecticut (see discussion hereafter).[69] It is critical to note that the courts in each of these decisions expressly declined to consider the best interests of the children, resorting instead to a strict textual interpretation of the relevant adoption statutes.

This textual approach, as opposed to the more pragmatic approach employed by a majority of states, lends support, whether intentionally or not, to the notion that sexual orientation, in and of itself, may be a relevant factor in determining an individual's ability to parent. This concept has continued to find its way into some judicial decisions regarding contested custody cases. For example, in the case of *Larson v. Larson* (1995),[70] the Court of Appeals of Alabama determined that a mother's lesbian relationship constituted "deviant sexual activity." Similarly, in the case of *Ex Parte JMF* (1998),[71] the Alabama Supreme Court determined that a mother's status as a lesbian was an important consideration in determining her ability to parent because in the eyes of most citizens her orientation was neither legal nor moral. It is important to note, however, that these cases were rendered before the United States Supreme Court overruled *Bowers v. Hardwick*[72] in the case of *Lawrence v. Texas*.[73]

Legislative Actions

In 1999 the Connecticut Supreme Court determined in the case of *In re Baby Z* that there was no right to same-sex second-parent adoption under the state's statutory scheme addressing adoption.[74] In support of its holding, the court conducted the same type of strict textual analysis that was conducted by the courts in *In re Angel Lace M, In re Adoption of TKJ, Adoption of Luke,* and *Adoption of Doe.* The court also found that the adoption would serve the child's best interest. The Connecticut legislature immediately responded to this decision, however, and enacted legislation expressly permitting second-parent adoption.[75] This represents the first time that a legislative body has enacted a statute expressly addressing the issue.

Significantly, in 1999, the New Hampshire legislature repealed the statute outlawing gay adoption. Thus, at the turn of the century, Florida stood alone as the only state with an express prohibition against gay adoption. There are other examples, however, of state statutes that negatively impacted the right of homosexuals to adopt. For example, Mississippi[76] and Utah[77] have statutes that ban gay *couples* from adopting, but not gay individuals. Ironically, Connecticut law states that the sexual orientation of a prospective adoptive parent may be considered when making a placement.[78]

The Battle in Florida

Since its enactment in 1977, the constitutionality of the Florida statute prohibiting gay adoption has been addressed on a number of occasions. There are examples of lower-court decisions where the statute has been found to be unconstitutional. For example, in the case of *Seebol v. Farie,*[79] a trial court determined that the statute was unconstitutional. The court recognized that "society has become increasingly knowledgeable of homosexual behavior and more tolerant of this sexual orientation." Similarly, in the case of *In re Pearlman* (1989),[80] a Florida trial court permitted a lesbian woman to adopt the biological child of her deceased partner—clearly in contravention of the plain language of the operative statute. These cases demonstrate the willingness of the court system to recognize the core concept that homosexuals can be fit and appropriate parents.

The statute was ultimately found to be constitutional, however, by the Florida Supreme Court in the case of *Cox v. Florida Department of Health and Rehabilitative Services* (1995).[81] In the *Cox* case, a gay man seeking to adopt a special-needs child filed a lawsuit challenging the validity of the state statute. The trial court determined that the statute was unconstitutional on the basis that it violated homosexuals' right to equal protection, it was impermissibly vague (for purposes of due process), and it violated homosexuals' right to privacy.[82] The state of Florida appealed this decision. Ultimately the Florida Supreme Court disagreed with the analysis conducted by the trial court and determined that the statute did not violate any due process or privacy rights. The court determined, however, that there was not enough evidence for it to review the equal protection claim. As a result the Supreme Court ordered that a new trial be scheduled before the trial court for the limited purpose of providing additional evidence.[83] Mr. Cox, apparently exhausted with the process, chose not to pursue the new trial.[84]

As stated in the introduction to this chapter, in 2004 the United States Appeals Court for the Eleventh Circuit found the Florida adoption statute to be constitutional in the case of *Lofton v. Secretary of Department of Children and Family Services*.[85] This was the first time that a federal court had addressed the issue of homosexual adoption. It is important to note that while the *Lofton* case was pending, the United States Supreme Court issued a decision in the case of *Lawrence v. Texas*—a case in which the nation's highest court appeared to recognize that certain fundamental liberty interests applied to homosexuals as a class.[86]

The *Lofton* case involved a lawsuit filed by six homosexuals challenging the constitutionality of the Florida adoption statute. The petitioners argued that Florida's prohibition against gay adoption (1) impedes their fundamental right to family integrity as guaranteed by the Due Process Clause of the United States Constitution; (2) violates their fundamental right to sexual privacy; and (3) violates their right to equal protection.

The Eleventh Circuit Court rejected each of these arguments and expressly held that homosexuals do not have a constitutionally protected right to adopt. In support of its holding, the court reasoned that there is no fundamental right to adoption, and that homosexuals as a class do not have a right to heightened scrutiny of statutes abridging their rights. In support of this contention, the court expressly held that the *Lawrence* case does *not* establish a new fundamental right to sexual privacy. The *Lofton* court then found that the Florida adoption statute is rationally related to the state's stated goal of furthering the best interests of children by placing them in homes with both a father and a mother. Moreover, the court determined, in reliance on the New Hampshire Supreme Court decision in *In re Opinion of the Justices* that, notwithstanding a lack of empirical proof, being raised in a homosexual environment *could* be detrimental to a child.[87] The court stated that openly homosexual households represent a relatively recent phenomenon, and sufficient time has not passed for conclusive scientific studies on the impact that homosexual parents may have on children. The court concluded that the debate over gay adoption involves questions of policy and not constitutional law, and that the appropriate forum for the debate is with the legislature. The reasoning and holding of the *Lofton* case stands in sharp contrast to the marked progression that has defined the advancement of homosexual adoption over the past four decades.

Conclusion

There is no question that the issue of homosexual adoption has evolved a great deal in the past forty years. In the 1960s and 1970s, the concept was virtually unrecognized. The issue reached a nadir in 1977, when Anita Bryant successfully lobbied the Florida legislature to enter a blanket prohibition against gay adoption. Indeed, over the past three decades, commencing with Bryant's campaign and continuing through 2004 with the Eleventh Circuit's decision in the *Lofton* case, the state of Florida has stood as the standard bearer for the argument against homosexual adoption. Yet while Florida's views may have remained static, the views of the rest of the country, with limited exception, have evolved a great deal.

Significantly, no other state presently has any legislation that per se precludes gay adoption. New Hampshire enacted such a statute in 1987 but repealed it in 1999. In addition, an increasing number of states have issued court decisions that expressly allow homosexuals to participate in stranger adoptions as well as second-parent adoptions. The state of Connecticut enacted a statute expressly recognizing the right to second-parent adoption. These types of rights were virtually uncontemplated in the 1960s and 1970s.

This is not to say that homosexual adoption has become a uniformly accepted right. The vitriol expressed by Anita Bryant still finds its way into certain statutes and judicial decisions. But the trend is clear; homosexuals today have adoption options that were nonexistent in prior decades. There is no question that the driving force behind this evolution is the recognition that homosexuality does not per se define a prospective parent as unfit.

7

The Present Status of the Law of Marriage in the United States and Abroad

Campbell D. Barrett

As discussed in chapter 1, in 1967, the United States Supreme Court rendered the landmark decision of *Loving v. Virginia*.[1] In *Loving*, the Court struck down a Virginia state statute prohibiting interracial marriage, noting that "the freedom to marry has long been recognized as one of the vital personal rights essential to the orderly pursuit of happiness by free men." Thirty-eight years have passed since the watershed *Loving* decision was rendered, yet the "vital personal right" to marriage still has not been extended, on a uniform national level, to homosexual couples.

Over the past four decades, the battle for the legal recognition of same-sex marriages has been waged on every possible front of the American legal system. Indeed, the battle can be seen as a primer for the interplay between the various branches of the American government.

First, the issue is being addressed in America's courts. There is a burgeoning body of common law (judge-made law) interpreting the parameters of marriage (as established by legislatively enacted marriage statutes) and addressing whether it is constitutionally permissible for the government to limit the definition of marriage to a union between a man and a woman. To a certain extent, the same-sex marriage agenda is being pushed by the judicial branch.

Second, the issue is being addressed on the legislative level with state and federal lawmakers enacting statutes expressly defining marriage as a union between a man and a woman. These statutes have largely been enacted in response to the judge-made law. The statutes are susceptible, however, to constitutional scrutiny by the courts. In other words, the laws enacted by the legislative branch, which seek to limit the definition of marriage, can be invalidated by the courts on the basis that the exclusion of same-sex couples results in an impermissible encroachment on certain constitutional rights.

Third, the same-sex marriage battle is being waged on a constitutional level, with many states amending their individual constitutions (documents establishing the fundamental laws of a particular nation or state) to prohibit same-sex marriage. This is an extreme measure and protects against court intervention. Put plainly, when a state constitution itself expressly limits the right to marry to heterosexual couples, it would be virtually impossible for a state court to determine that it is unconstitutional to deny same-sex couples the right to marry.

This chapter will address how the debate over gay marriage has evolved in the context of all three of these battlefronts, and will show how the issue has played out differently from state to state. In addition, the chapter will compare the same-sex marriage debate in America with the various ways that the issue is being addressed on an international level.

1971–1993: The Traditional View That Marriage Is a Union between a Man and Woman

Before the 1990s there is a paucity of legal authority in the United States addressing the issue of same-sex marriage. The judicial decisions that were written during this time, however, uniformly dismiss the notion that people of the same gender have the right marry one another. The rationale behind these decisions is consistent: each argues that historically marriage has been limited to heterosexual relationships, and there is no constitutional justification to extend this right to same-sex couples.

The first challenge to the notion that homosexuals cannot legally marry was made in 1971, in the state of Minnesota in the case of *Baker v. Nelson*.[2] In that case, the Minnesota Supreme Court determined that under Minnesota law, homosexuals did not have the legal right to marry because the Minnesota statutory scheme, established by the state's elected legislative body, clearly defined marriage as being between a man and a woman. In addition, and perhaps more significantly, the *Baker* court determined that same-sex couples did not have any constitutionally protected right to marry. In support of its holding, the court found that homosexuality is incompatible with marriage, an institution whose central purpose—procreation and the raising of children—"is as old as the book of Genesis."[3]

Moreover, the Minnesota Court expressly distinguished the U.S. Supreme Court decision of *Loving v. Virginia* from the issue of gay marriage, noting that the Virginia statute outlawing interracial marriage was struck down on the grounds of its "patent racial discrimination" and that "in commonsense and in a constitutional sense, there is a clear distinction between a marital restriction based merely upon race and one based on the fundamental difference in sex."[4]

Although the *Baker* case was the first time that a court had *expressly* addressed the issue of whether it was legal for same-sex couples to marry, a similar issue had been addressed a year earlier, in the state of New York, in the curious case of *Anonymous v. Anonymous* (1970).[5] In that case, a man sought a divorce because his "wife," whom he had always believed to be a woman, turned out to be a man. The New York court refused to grant the divorce, reasoning that a marriage had never occurred because "marriage is and always has been between a man and a woman."[6] Although the case did not involve a same-sex marriage per se, it provides an interesting early judicial gloss on the issue—the concept of individuals of the same gender marrying was so antithetical to the traditional concept of marriage that it was dismissed without much serious consideration.

The reasoning used by the courts in the *Baker* and *Anonymous* cases set the tone for all the judge-made law in the 1970s and 1980s addressing the issue of same-sex marriage. Simply put, courts refused to recognize that homosexual couples had any statutorily delineated or constitutionally protected right to marry, reasoning, in each case, that same-sex relationships fell outside the historical definition of marriage, and that there was no constitutionally protected right guaranteeing gay marriage. The decisions were uniform in this regard, and all efforts to establish the legal right of gay marriage were summarily rejected. As discussed in chapter 3, this rationale was consistent with the widespread belief in the early 1970s that homosexuals were functionally different from other American citizens.

In the case of *Jones v. Hallahan* (1973),[7] for example, a Kentucky court held that two women were properly denied a marriage license by their local town clerk. The court noted that although the Kentucky marriage statute did not expressly define marriage as solely being between a man and a woman, the general dictionary definition of marriage was limited to a union between a man and a woman. The court reasoned further that "marriage was a custom long before the state commenced issuing licenses for that purpose," and that "in all cases . . . marriage has always been considered as the union of a man and a woman."[8] The court concluded, without any reference to the *Loving* decision, that there is no constitutional right of marriage between persons of the same sex because "in substance, the relationship proposed . . . is not a marriage."[9]

Similarly, in the case of *Singer v. Hara* (1974),[10] a Washington court held that the statutory prohibition against same-sex marriage did not violate the state constitution's equal rights amendment, nor did it violate any federally protected constitutional rights. The court rejected the argument that the *Loving* case was applicable to the issue of same-sex marriage:

> Given the definition of marriage [as being between a man and a woman] the distinction between [this case] and . . . *Loving* . . . is apparent. In *Loving* . . . the parties were barred from entering into the marriage relationship because of an impermissible racial classification. There is no analogous sexual classification involved in the instant case because appellants are not being denied entry into the marriage because of their sex; rather they are being denied entry into the marriage relationship because of the recognized definition of that relationship as one which may be entered into only by two persons who are members of the opposite sex. . . . [W]hat they propose is not a marriage.[11]

The court further noted that the state of Washington was justified in prohibiting gay marriage because the primary purpose of marriage is procreation and the rearing of children—situations that the court found incompatible, if not impossible, with same-sex marriage.[12]

The issue of same-sex marriage was first addressed by a federal court in the case of *Adams v. Howerton* (1982).[13] In that case, a federal appeals court determined that a marriage between an American man and his illegal alien gay partner was invalid for purposes of federal immigration law. The court reasoned that because the United States Congress, when establishing the applicable immigration statute, did not expressly state that an individual's spouse could be a member of the same sex, it could not have intended to expand on the historical definition of marriage—a union between a man and a woman—to include a union between two individuals of the same gender.[14] The court further reasoned that Congress could not have intended to sanction gay marriage because the same federal immigration statute that conferred benefits to spouses of American citizens barred persons "afflicted with sexual deviations" (which included homosexuality) from entry into the United States.[15] The court then concluded that there was no constitutional right to gay marriage, citing the fact that gay couples cannot procreate and stating that homosexual marriage "violates traditional and often prevailing societal mores."[16]

Finally, in *De Santo v. Barnsley* (1984),[17] a Pennsylvania court determined that two men did not have the right to enter into a common-law marriage (a form of marriage permissible under Pennsylvania law where individuals are considered married, without a formal ceremony and without the need of an officiant, after simply professing an intention to establish a marital relationship). The court reasoned that since statutory marriage in Pennsylvania (a ceremonial wedding performed by a religious or civil authority) was limited to heterosexual couples, by necessity common-law marriages must be as well.[18] Furthermore, the court found that there was no pressing need or compelling reason to expand the definition of common-law marriage to include a contract between two persons of the same sex.[19]

Significantly, in 1986, the United States Supreme Court rendered the controversial decision of *Bowers v. Hardwick*.[20] Although this case did not address the issue of same-sex marriage, it represented a monumental blow to the advancement of gay rights. As discussed in chapter 1, the *Bowers* Court upheld a Georgia statute outlawing certain acts of homosexual sodomy, reasoning that homosexuals did not have the fundamental right to commit the acts.[21] The *Bowers* case essentially sanctioned the judicial reasoning set forth in the *Baker v. Nelson, Anonymous v. Anonymous, Jones v. Hallahan, Singer v. Hara, Adams v. Howerton,* and *De Santo v. Barnsley* cases. Significantly, it did so in a direct way and with inflammatory language that demonstrated a refusal to recognize even the most fundamental concept of homosexual rights. The case stands as the nadir for the recognition of same-sex marriage.

In the early to mid-1990s, two judicial decisions were issued in strong reliance on the legal precedent from the 1970s and 1980s. In *Dean v. District of Columbia* (1995),[22] a Washington, D.C., court, relying on *Bowers v. Hardwick,* held that the denial of a marriage license to a gay couple was supported by the local marriage statutes and did not violate certain human rights laws. The court concluded that "same sex marriage is not a fundamental right" worthy of constitutional protection because the homosexual relationship is not "deeply rooted in this nation's history and tradition."[23] In *Matter of Estate of Cooper* (1990),[24] a New York court, relying on *Baker v. Nelson*, determined that a homosexual man could not be his deceased lover's "surviving spouse" for purposes of inheritance because only a lawfully recognized husband or wife could assume this legal designation and that "persons of the same sex have no constitutional rights to enter into a marriage with each other."[25] It is clear from these two decisions that the body of law addressing the issue of same-sex marriage had become stagnant and that America's courts had essentially become solidified in the view that marriage was limited to the union between a man and woman and that any constitutional arguments to the contrary, regardless of how they were framed, were unavailing.

1993–2005: The Evolution of the Issue

1993: Hawaii Breaks from Precedent

In 1993 the nation's fiftieth state became the first to recognize, albeit briefly, the right of same-sex couples to marry. In the case of *Baehr v. Anderson*,[26] the Supreme Court of Hawaii became the first court in the United States to recognize a constitutional right to same-sex marriage. The *Baehr* case set forth a chain reaction of legal maneuvering from all three branches of government. In a sense, the case broke the logjam that had developed with respect to the law regarding same-sex marriage. Although the recognition of the right to same-sex marriage was fleeting in Hawaii, the *Baehr* case pushed the debate on the issue to the forefront of American discourse and provided the necessary foundation and impetus for future judicial decisions and legislative acts addressing the issue.

In 1991 three gay couples sued Hawaii's Director of Department of Health (DDH), claiming that they were improperly denied marriage licenses. The lawsuit alleged that the Hawaii state marriage statute (which the DDH relied on when denying the licenses) should be invalidated because it violated certain rights guaranteed by the Hawaii State Constitution. The lawsuit was initially dismissed by a lower court for failure to state a valid claim. The plaintiffs appealed this decision, and the issue was ultimately addressed by the Supreme Court of Hawaii (the state's highest court, which has as one of its principal functions the final word in interpreting Hawaii's state constitution).

The Supreme Court of Hawaii addressed two separate constitutional questions in its decision: (1) whether the Hawaii marriage statute violated the same-sex couples' right to privacy; and (2) whether the statute violated the couples' right to equal protection. It is important to note that these issues were addressed in the context of Hawaii's individual state constitution, rather than in the context of the United States Constitution or the individual constitutions of the other states. This is significant for three reasons: (1) the decision of the court would not be subject to review by the United States Supreme Court; (2) the decision would not be binding on any other state; and (3) the analysis conducted would differ from an analysis under the United States Constitution because the rights afforded by the Hawaii Constitution were broader.

With respect to the first issue, the *Baehr* court determined that the right to privacy does *not* include a fundamental right to same-sex marriage. In coming to this conclusion, the court analyzed a number of decisions from the United States Supreme Court addressing the right to privacy, including *Roe v. Wade* and *Griswold v. Connecticut* (discussed in chapter 1). The court determined, after reviewing these cases, that the fundamental constitutional right to marry, within the context of the right to privacy, presupposed a marriage between a man and a woman.[27] The court determined that same-sex marriage did not constitute a "new fundamental right"[28] because it is not so deeply entrenched in the "traditions" and "collective consciousness" of society that the failure to recognize it would violate "fundamental principles of liberty and justice."[29] To a certain extent, the court's decision was reminiscent of the earlier decisions denying the right to gay marriage, that is, the right does not exist because of the traditional definition of marriage as being a union between a man and a woman.

The second constitutional issue addressed by the *Baehr* court, however, served as a significant departure from past precedent. Specifically, the court held that the denial of marriage to same-sex couples is presumptively a violation of their equal protection rights.[30] Of particular note is the fact that the Hawaii court expressly rejected the reasoning used by the earlier courts that had addressed same-sex marriage. For example, the court distinguished *Baehr* from both *Baker v. Nelson* and *De Santo v. Barnsley*, reasoning that *Baker* was limited to a federal constitutional inquiry and *De Santo* involved the concept of common-law marriage (a relationship not recognized in Hawaii).[31] The court then determined the reasoning used by the courts in *Jones v. Hallahan* and *Singer v. Hara*—that the definition of marriage must be limited to a union between a man and a woman because it has always been so—to be "circular and unpersuasive" and "tortured and conclusory sophistry."[32]

The *Baehr* court determined that a new trial was necessary so that a lower court could apply "strict scrutiny" to the statute and determine whether the state could prove that it had a "compelling state interest" to limit marriage to heterosexual couples. After the retrial, a Hawaiian lower court determined that the marriage statute was unconstitutional.[33]

The Hawaii legislature, however, rendered the *Baehr* case a nullity. In 1998 the Hawaii Constitution was amended to state that "the legislature shall have the power to reserve marriage to opposite-sex couples."[34] In response to this amendment, the Hawaii legislature enacted a statute stating that a "valid marriage contract . . . shall be only between a man and a woman."[35] The decision rendered in *Baehr* was therefore superseded because the constitutional deprivation found by the Hawaii courts was resolved by a new constitutionally protected definition of marriage. Nevertheless, the *Baehr* decision had a profound impact on the gay marriage movement at both the federal and state levels.

The Legislative Response: DOMA

In 1996, largely in response to the *Baehr* decision, the United States Congress enacted the Defense of Marriage Act (DOMA). The purpose of the bill is two-fold: (1) it defines marriage as being a union between a man and a woman for purposes of federal statutes,[36] and (2) it provides that individual states are not required to honor same-sex marriages from other states under the U.S. Constitution's Full Faith and Credit Clause.[37] In addition, following the enactment of the federal DOMA statute, at least forty-one individual states enacted their own DOMA statutes. Much like the federal statute, these state statutes seek to limit the definition of marriage to a union between a man and a woman. For the most part, the statutes are similar in nature—some define marriage as solely being between a man and a woman, whereas others expressly preclude marriage between individuals of the same gender. It is important to note, however, that all these statutes are susceptible to review by courts as to whether the limitations they impose violate constitutionally protected rights. In other words, much in the way that the Hawaii Supreme Court scrutinized the Hawaii marriage statute in *Baehr*, state courts will be able to determine the state constitutionality of the DOMA statutes.

Post-DOMA Judicial Interpretation

VERMONT

In 1999 the Vermont Supreme Court issued a decision in the case of *Baker v. Vermont*.[38] *Baker* involved a challenge by three same-sex couples who had been denied marriage licenses. The couples had lived together in committed relationships varying from four to twenty-five years. Two of the couples had raised children.[39] The case was initially dismissed by a Vermont lower court based on a finding that the Vermont marriage statute (which applied only to heterosexual couples) furthered the state's interest in promoting "the link between procreation and child rearing."[40] The same-sex couples appealed this decision to the Vermont Supreme Court.

The issue before the Vermont Supreme Court was whether the state could exclude homosexual couples from the "benefits and protection" that are offered by the state to married heterosexual couples. The court's inquiry was limited to whether there was a constitutional deprivation under the state's "Common Benefits Clause," which it characterized as being broader than the corresponding Federal Equal Protection Clause.[41] In coming to its conclusion, the court rejected the traditional arguments against gay marriage.

First, the court characterized the argument that marriage must be limited to heterosexual couples in order to "further the link between procreation and child rearing" as an "extreme logical disjunction."[42] The court reasoned that this "procreation argument" did not present a valid public interest because (1) many heterosexual married couples do not have children; (2) a significant number of children are being raised by same-sex couples; and (3) the Vermont legislature expressly recognized that same-sex couples conceive and raise children when it enacted statutes permitting same-sex couples to adopt, conceive, and rear children.[43] The court concluded that denying gay couples the benefits of marriage would actually serve to illegitimize the children of same-sex couples—the exact opposite of the state's rationale for limiting marriage to heterosexual couples.[44]

Furthermore, the *Baker* court rejected the argument that the historical intolerance of homosexual relationships provides a basis for denying same-sex couples the right to marry. The court reasoned that over the past thirty years, the Vermont legislature had enacted a number of statutes, including statutes repealing criminal sodomy statutes, prohibiting discrimination against homosexuals, and providing same-sex couples the right to adopt, that all demonstrate the growing acceptance of homosexual relationships.[45]

The *Baker* court, relying on the *Loving* decision, expressly recognized that "access to a civil marriage license and the multitude of legal benefits, protections, and obligations that flow from it significantly enhance the quality of life in our society."[46] Nevertheless, the court declined to find that same-sex couples had an absolute constitutional right to marry. Instead the court held that homosexual couples had the right to receive the same *benefits* that marriage provides to heterosexual couples.[47] The court then held that the Vermont legislature was the appropriate body to determine how these benefits would be provided, whether by marriage, domestic partnership, registered partnership, or some other means.[48]

In response to the *Baker* decision, the Vermont legislature enacted a statute establishing "civil unions"—a legally recognized relationship that provides gay couples with many of the same state-created benefits as married couples.[49] The statute was significant, even though it did not expressly recognize same-sex marriage, because it was the first time that a state legislative body in the United States had established a legal union for same-sex couples.

ALASKA

In 1998 two gay men in Alaska filed a lawsuit challenging the denial of their application for a marriage license. Before the trial commenced, a lower court in the case determined that the right to marry an individual of one's choosing is fundamental, regardless of whether the decision results in a traditional or nontraditional marriage union, and the state would therefore have to demonstrate a compelling reason for the existing marriage statute (which limited marriage to heterosexual couples) or it would be rendered unconstitutional.[50]

Much as in Hawaii with the *Baehr* decision, the Alaska court's decision in *Brause v. Bureau of Vital Statistics* was abrogated by an amendment to the Alaska Constitution, which provides that a valid marriage "may exist only between one man and one woman."[51] After the enactment of this amendment, the *Brause* matter was dismissed, and there were no further judicial proceedings with respect to the case.

OTHER DECISIONS OF NOTE

In addition to the *Brause* and *Baker* cases, numerous other judicial decisions were rendered in the aftermath of DOMA addressing the same-sex marriage issue. Many of these decisions rejected the notion that homosexual couples have the right to marry. In 2003, in the case of *Lewis v. Harris*,[52] for example, a New Jersey trial court dismissed a lawsuit filed by seven same-sex couples challenging the constitutionality of the state's marriage laws. Likewise, in the case of *Morrison v. Sadler* (also rendered in 2003), an Indiana trial court dismissed a lawsuit filed by three gay couples seeking marriage licenses.[53] In the case of *Rosengarten v. Downes*,[54] the Connecticut Appellate Court determined that a couple who had obtained a civil union in Vermont could not then obtain a divorce in Connecticut because "a civil union is not a family relations matter."[55] Both the *Lewis* and *Morrison* cases are presently on appeal. The *Rosengarten* case was rendered moot before being heard by the Connecticut Supreme Court because Mr. Rosengarten died.

2003–2005: The Impact of Lawrence v. Texas and Goodridge v. Department of Health

In 2003 two seminal judicial opinions were rendered with respect to the advancement of the same-sex marriage cause. In June of that year, the United States Supreme Court issued a decision in the case of *Lawrence v. Texas*.[56] As discussed more thoroughly in chapter 1, the Court in *Lawrence* declared a Texas statute criminalizing certain homosexual acts to be unconstitutional. Fundamentally, the Court recognized that the obligation of the court system is "to define the liberty of all, not to mandate our own moral code."[57] The case was particularly significant because it expressly reversed the 1986 decision of *Bowers v. Hardwick*. In this regard, the Court noted that "the petitioners are entitled to respect for their private lives. The State cannot demean their existence or control their destiny by making their private sexual conduct a crime."[58]

Five months later, in November 2003, the Massachusetts Supreme Court issued a decision in the case of *Goodridge v. Department of Public Health*.[59] The court held that barring gay couples from the protections, benefits, and obligations of civil marriage violates the Massachusetts Constitution. The decision is profoundly important because for the first time since the Hawaii Supreme

Court decision in *Baehr v. Lewin*, a court of final resort had determined that same-sex couples had a fundamental right to marry (in contrast, the Vermont Supreme Court determined in *Baker v. Vermont* that gay couples had the right to the legal *benefits* of marriage, but not necessarily to the right of marriage itself).

The *Goodridge* case involved a challenge by seven same-sex couples from throughout Massachusetts. In each case, the couple was denied a marriage license by the local town clerk.[60] The relationships of the couples ranged in duration from four to thirty years, and several of the couples were in the process of raising minor children.[61] The case was dismissed by a lower court on the basis that Massachusetts law does not guarantee the right to same-sex marriage. The trial court further found that a prohibition against same-sex marriage serves the "legitimate interest" of "safeguarding procreation."[62] The case was appealed to the Massachusetts Supreme Court.

The Massachusetts Supreme Court held that "marriage is a vital social institution" that provides "an abundance of legal, financial, and social benefits" to the married couple and their children.[63] Moreover, the court recognized that the Massachusetts Constitution guarantees the "dignity and equality" of all citizens and prohibits the establishment of "second class citizens."[64] Importantly, the court held that there was no adequate reason to deny same-sex couples the right to marry.[65] As a result, the court held that same-sex couples had a fundamental right to marry under the state's constitution.

The *Goodridge* court recognized that the existing Massachusetts marriage statute could not be read to include gay couples, because the conventional definition of marriage contemplates only a union between a man and a woman.[66] The court determined, however, that the statute was unconstitutional because it violated the gay couples' equal protection rights and their rights to due process. In support of its holding, the *Goodridge* court relied heavily on the U.S. Supreme Court's decisions in *Griswold v. Connecticut* (recognizing that marriage is "an association that promotes a way of life, not causes") and *Loving v. Virginia* (recognizing that with the issue of gay marriage, as with the historical statutes barring interracial marriage, "history must yield to a more fully developed understanding of the invidious quality of discrimination").[67] The court concluded, much like the courts in *Baehr v. Lewin* and *Baker v. Vermont*, that a ban on gay marriage unnecessarily denies gay couples and their children significant benefits without a rational basis.[68]

Moreover, the *Goodridge* court rejected each of the arguments raised in support of the position that marriage should be limited to heterosexual couples. First, the court rejected the assertion that the primary purpose of marriage is procreation, reasoning instead that "it is the exclusive and permanent commitment of the marriage partners to one another, not the begetting of children, that is the *sine qua non* of marriage."[69] The court noted that fertility is not a requirement of marriage, nor is it grounds for divorce. Second, the court found no basis to the claim that the "optimal" setting for children was a family with two parents of the opposite sex, reasoning instead that the best interests of a child cannot be determined simply by his or her parent's marital status or sexual orientation. The court expressly found in this regard that there are countless same-sex couples who have children for the same reason as heterosexual couples, "to love them, care for them and nurture them," and that to preclude gay couples from marrying will subject these couples, and more importantly their children, to significant unnecessary hardship. Third, the court rejected the claim that limiting marriage to heterosexual couples would conserve scarce state and private financial resources, and that gay couples do not need the financial benefits that attend marriage because on the whole they are less dependent on one another. The court found this claim to be conclusory in nature and without any rational basis in fact.[70] Finally, the court rejected the state's claim that broadening the definition of marriage to include same-sex couples would trivialize marriage as it has historically been defined. The court found instead that although the decision might drastically change the definition of marriage, it in no way disturbs the fundamental value that marriage offers to society—"if anything extending civil marriage to same-sex couples reinforces the importance of marriage to individuals and communities."[71]

The decision in *Goodridge* was far from unanimous. Three of the seven justices who heard the case disagreed with the holding of the court and issued dissenting opinions. The tenor of the dissenting opinions is reminiscent of the earlier court rulings addressing the same-sex marriage issue. Like the court decisions from the 1970s, 1980s, and early 1990s, the dissenting justices relied on the historically accepted definition of marriage as a union between a man and a woman and concluded that the Massachusetts legislature "could rationally conclude that it furthers the legitimate State purpose of ensuring, promoting, and supporting an optimal social structure for the bearing and raising of children."[72] Nevertheless, the majority of the *Goodridge* court held the Massachusetts marriage law to be unconstitutional and ordered the state legislature to amend the relevant statute to provide for gay marriage.

The *Goodridge* case was not the only significant gay marriage decision to be issued in the wake of the *Lawrence v. Texas* decision. In the case of *Standhardt v. County of Maricopa*,[73] the Arizona Court of Appeals determined that the state's DOMA statute was constitutional under both the Arizona State Constitution and the U.S. Constitution. Significantly, the Arizona court expressly found that the *Lawrence* decision did not require a different result. The court did not find that *Lawrence* required that Arizona formally recognize same-sex marriage.[74] The court then determined that the history of the Arizona marriage statute, coupled with the Arizona DOMA statute, demonstrates that the right to gay marriage is not a fundamental liberty interest protected by due process.[75] The court concluded that the state had a legitimate interest in limiting the definition of marriage to a union between a man and a woman in order to encourage procreation and child rearing.[76] The *Standhardt* decision is on appeal.

In addition, in February 2004, the county clerk in San Francisco began issuing marriage licenses to same-sex couples at the direction of the city's mayor, notwithstanding the fact that California had established a DOMA statute in 2000. In August 2004 the California Supreme Court ruled that the clerk did not have the requisite authority, under the California marriage statute, to issue the licenses. As a result, all 4,037 of the marriage licenses issued to gay couples in San Francisco were rendered void. The California court did not address the issue of whether the California DOMA statute (which expressly limits marriage to heterosexual unions) violates the California Constitution.[77]

The Constitutional Backlash of 2004

In November 2004, in the wake of the *Lawrence* and *Goodridge* decisions, eleven states (Arkansas, Georgia, Kentucky, Michigan, Mississippi, Montana, North Dakota, Ohio, Oklahoma, Oregon, and Utah) joined Hawaii and Alaska, as well as Louisiana, Missouri, Nebraska, and Nevada, as states that have expressly enacted constitutional amendments limiting the definition of marriage to a union between a man and a woman (or, in the case of Hawaii, establishing a constitutional amendment permitting the legislature to define marriage as such). In addition, in April 2005, the state of Kansas likewise established a constitutional amendment barring gay marriage.

These state constitutional amendments functionally make it illegal for couples of the same sex to marry. Although the underlying basis of each is the same, the individual amendments often differ in the specific language used and in the reach of the prohibition. A few of the amendments are simply limited to establishing marriage as being a union between a man and a woman. In Oregon and Montana, for example, the amendments simply state that "only a marriage between one man and one woman shall be valid or legally recognized as a marriage."[78] Similarly, Nevada's amendment states, in its entirety, that "only marriage between a man and a woman shall be valid or recognized in Nevada,"[79] and Missouri's amendment states that "to be valid and recognized in this state a marriage shall exist only between a man and a woman."[80]

Several of the states' amendments take an additional step and include language that appears to be expressly designed to thwart any attempt to have a same-sex marriage or civil union from another state (i.e., Massachusetts or Vermont) recognized in their individual state. Ohio's amendment, for example, says that "this state and its political subdivisions shall not create or recognize a legal status for relationships of unmarried individuals that intends to approximate the design, qualities, significance or effect of marriage."[81] Nebraska's amendment states that "the uniting of two persons of the same sex in a civil union, domestic partnership, or other similar same-sex relationship shall not be valid or recognized in Nebraska."[82] Likewise, the amendments from North Dakota and Utah both state that "no other domestic union, however denominated, may be recognized as a marriage or given the same or substantially equivalent legal effect,"[83] and Kentucky's amendment states that a "legal status identical or substantially similar to that of marriage for unmarried individuals shall not be valid or recognized."[84]

Still other amendments recite, with great specificity, the long reach that they are intended to have. In Georgia, for example, the amendment says that the state will not honor "any public act, record, or judicial proceeding of any other state or jurisdiction respecting a relationship between persons of the same sex that is treated as a marriage under the laws of such other state or jurisdiction" and that Georgia courts will not have the requisite jurisdiction to divorce gay couples "or rule on any of the parties' respective rights arising as a result of or in connection with such relationship."[85] The Michigan amendment expressly states that its purpose is "to secure and preserve the benefits of marriage for our society and for future generations of children."[86] Oklahoma's amendment even goes so far as to provide that any individual who knowingly issues a marriage license to a same-sex couple will be guilty of a misdemeanor.[87] In contrast, the amendment from Arkansas says that the state's legislature "may recognize a common law marriage from another state between a man and a woman."[88]

Although the language used in the respective amendments differs, the amendments all share one common thread—they were designed and implemented to take the issue of same-sex marriage out of the control of lawmakers and the courts.

2005 and Beyond

In 2003, 2004, and 2005, a plethora of lower-court decisions supported both sides of the gay marriage debate. Although these cases are not binding and are subject to review, and potential reversal, by courts of higher resort, they represent the newest front on which the legal battle over same-sex marriage is being waged.

For example, in late summer of 2004, two decisions were issued in the state of Washington—*Anderson v. King County*[89] and *Castle v. Washington*[90]—both finding the state's DOMA statute to be unconstitutional. Both relied heavily on the reasoning employed by the U.S. Supreme Court in *Loving v. Virginia* and *Lawrence v. Texas*, the Vermont Supreme Court in *Baker v. Vermont*, and the Massachusetts Supreme Court in *Goodridge v. Department of Public Health*. In addition, each of the Washington state decisions took great pains to distinguish and minimize the importance of the earlier Washington state court case of *Singer v. Hara*, which prohibited marriage between same-sex couples. Similarly, in February 2005, a New York trial judge, relying extensively on *Loving*, *Goodridge*, and *Baker*, determined that five same-sex couples had the constitutional right to be married.[91]

To a certain extent, these recent lower-court decisions encapsulate the evolution of the legal debate over gay marriage. Unlike the cases rendered in the early 1990s, *Dean v. District of Columbia* and *Matter of Estate of Cooper*, which were limited to the rationale employed by the earlier cases addressing the gay marriage issue, the cases rendered in 2005 show a more developed view of the constitutional dimensions of the issue. The *Baehr*, *Baker*, and *Goodridge* decisions, which form the foundation of the more recent decisions, have clearly pushed the debate to the next level, so that there is a growing recognition that the "vital personal right" to marriage, as recognized by the U.S. Supreme Court in *Loving v. Virginia*, extends to same-sex couples.

In April 2005 the Connecticut legislature enacted a civil union statute. The statute provides same-sex couples with all of the legal benefits that are afforded to heterosexual married couples. The statute includes a provision expressly limiting marriage to a union between a man and woman. The Connecticut statute is significant for two reasons: (1) it makes Connecticut the second state to enact civil union legislation (joining Vermont); and (2) it represents the first time that a state legislature has enacted a same-sex civil union or marriage statute without any judicial prompting.[92]

The Debate on the International Stage

The battle over the issue of same-sex marriage is not only being waged in the United States. The issue is being addressed by courts and elected bodies around the world. To a large extent, the international debate is more evolved than the debate in the United States.

Canada

There is no question that Canada is taking a lead position in the debate over same-sex marriage. The positions taken in Canada are particularly important because Canada (like the United States) operates under a common-law legal system and provides its citizens with certain inalienable constitutional rights. The same-sex marriage issue has been addressed in the highest courts of several Canadian provinces. The Canadian courts addressed many of the same arguments that have been raised in the American court cases rejecting the concept of same-sex marriage.

For example, in the case of *Halpern v. Attorney General of Canada* (2003),[93] the Court of Appeals for Ontario determined that denying same-sex couples the right to marry violates the Canadian Charter of Rights and Freedoms (the equivalent of the U.S. Constitution). The court expressly rejected the argument that marriage should be limited to heterosexual couples because that has always been the traditional definition of the union. Specifically, the *Halpern* court stated that "an argument that marriage is heterosexual because it 'just is' amounts to circular reasoning. It sidesteps the entire analysis."[94] The court then redefined marriage as "the voluntary union for life of two persons to the exclusion of all others."[95]

Likewise, in the case of *Hendricks v. Quebec* (2002), the Quebec Court of Appeals determined that same-sex marriage was constitutionally required. The *Hendricks* court expressly rejected the argument that homosexual couples should be denied the right to marriage because they lack the ability to procreate. Specifically, the court held that marriage is no longer necessarily defined by the children born of the union, and that as a practical matter many heterosexual married couples do not procreate, while many homosexual couples, with the assistance of new technology, do have children.

Similarly, in the case of *Egale v. Canada* (2003),[96] the Court of Appeals for British Columbia held that a common-law bar to same-sex marriage contravenes the Charter of Rights. In coming to its conclusion, the *Egale* court noted that the establishment of Registered Domestic Partnerships (the equivalent of civil unions) was inadequate. In support of this holding, the court recognized:

> The redefinition of marriage to include same-sex couples . . . is the only road to true equality for same-sex couples. Any other form of recognition of same-sex relationships, including the parallel institution of [civil unions], falls short of true equality. This Court should not be asked to grant a remedy which makes same-sex couples "almost equal," or to leave it to governments to choose amongst less-than-equal solutions.[97]

Thus the court reformulated the common-law definition of marriage to be a union between "two persons" as opposed to a union between "one man and one woman."[98]

Finally, in July 2004, the Supreme Court of the Yukon Territory rendered a similar decision in the case of *Dunbar v. Yukon.*[99] The holding in that case was based entirely on the decisions rendered in the Ontario, Quebec, and British Columbia cases. In December 2004 the Canadian Supreme Court determined that same-sex marriage is constitutional.[100] In February 2005, a bill was proposed in the Canadian Parliament, seeking to establish a nationwide right to same-sex marriage.[101] The bill was passed on July 19, 2005.

Europe and Elsewhere

Presently, same-sex marriage is legal in Belgium, the Netherlands, and Spain. Moreover, numerous other countries in Europe provide same-sex couples with many of the rights offered to heterosexual married couples, for example, Croatia (property rights for same-sex couples who have lived together for more than three years); the Czech Republic (certain property and inheritance rights); Denmark, Finland, Iceland, Norway, and Sweden (all offer extensive rights for "registered partners" including most rights associated with marriage such as insurance, retirement, taxes, and adoption); France (a "Civil Solidarity Pact" is allowed after three years of committed relationship, which provides many rights offered to heterosexual married couples, such as tax and immigration advantages, welfare benefits, and inheritance); Germany ("Life Partnerships" provide inheritance rights, taxes, and other financial benefits); Hungary (numerous economic benefits); and Switzerland (many local states have enacted laws similar to those entered in France and Germany).[102]

In addition, numerous other countries around the world are addressing the same-sex marriage issue. For example, in Argentina, the city of Buenos Aires has enacted local ordinances providing same-sex couples with many of the rights offered to heterosexual married couples. Likewise, in Brazil, same-sex couples have been provided inheritance and property rights.[103] In 2004, New Zealand passed legislation establishing civil unions that provide same-sex couples the same rights as married couples in areas like child custody, tax, and welfare benefits.

Conclusion

Forty years ago the idea that American law, or for that matter the law anywhere, would allow homosexual marriage was close to unthinkable. To many it remains unthinkable. But today the United States has such marriage rights in Massachusetts and civil unions in Vermont and Connecticut. Canada, Belgium, the Netherlands, and Spain have instituted these rights, and lesser but important rights and benefits have been granted to same-sex couples in many other parts of Europe and elsewhere. The tide of public opinion favoring these rights for same-sex couples is already rising quickly both here and abroad.

8

The Practical Benefits of Marriage

Donald J. Cantor

Why don't homosexuals just live together? Why do they need the right to marry?

Until allowed to do so in Massachusetts in 2004, gays and lesbians had never had the right to marry in the United States, and only recently has their desire to obtain this right obtained sufficient attention to reach the public ear. Because the denial of their right is so old and the public perception of the desire to change it so new, because it has so long been taken as a given that homosexuals should not be allowed to marry, the great majority of Americans have yet to think deeply about the issue and most assuredly have never investigated what this inability has meant and still means to gay and lesbian couples.

There are, of course, those who believe that inhibiting the happiness of homosexuals is morally acceptable and therefore consider the unhappiness caused to be irrelevant because unavoidable and deserved. But we suspect, and profoundly hope, that the great majority of Americans would care if they knew the price the inability to marry has exacted from gay and lesbian couples.

The answer to the questions that opened this chapter is because the state of marriage carries with it in our society a multiplicity of rights, obligations, and benefits that heterosexuals take for granted and single-sex couples would like to share.

Consider spousal visits to a hospital—not an issue to heterosexual couples. If your spouse is seriously ill, your right to visit him or her in the hospital is presumed. But if you are gay and the man you would have married, had the law allowed it, is seriously ill, you may well not be allowed to visit him, because the rules only allow spouses and immediate family to visit. The lead editorial in the *Boston Globe* on July 8, 2003, wrote of "David Wilson, who was treated as a stranger by emergency medical personnel when his partner of 13 years suffered a fatal heart attack," and also of "Hillary Goodridge . . . whose health care proxy document was little help when her partner of 15 years gave birth and she tried to see her newborn daughter in a neonatal intensive care unit." We knew of two gay men who were business partners, very successfully, as well as lovers for more than a dozen years. One of them had AIDS, and for as long as possible, the other nursed him at home, bathing him, cleaning feces his partner could no longer control, until hospitalization was unavoidable. Once in the hospital, where he died, his partner no longer could see him—hospital rules.

I don't know how to evaluate the pain of being denied access to an ill same-sex partner, of not being able in that partner's last days to ease somewhat his or her pain, to assure that person that he or she at least dies loved. Because I can marry, I'll never have that happen. But who can fail to project sufficiently into that horrible potential situation not to appreciate at least somewhat how dreadful an experience it would be?

Let us assume that a spouse dies without a will, either because drawing one was forgotten or because the one drawn was somehow defective. The law of intestacy controls. Connecticut, for example, provides that if one dies intestate, the surviving spouse receives minimally one-half of the estate.[1] If a gay or lesbian partner dies intestate, since he or she cannot legally have a surviving spouse, the natural recipient, or at least one of the natural recipients, of the estate of the decedent inherits nothing. The purpose of the law of intestacy is to leave the decedent's estate to those persons to whom the decedent would probably have left it had he or she died with an effective, timely will. This body of law is totally frustrated where the intestate decedent is gay or lesbian and leaves behind a same-sex partner that the decedent would have married had the law so allowed.

Married persons qualify for country club membership discounts and special privileges. A person from another country can obtain residency in the United States upon marrying an American citizen. Traveling spouses can file joint customs declarations. A married person can sue for loss of consortium or for wrongful death of a spouse. Married persons may enjoy a legal privilege not to have to testify against each other. A married person can make decisions for an incompetent spouse. None of these rights and privileges inure to same-sex couples.

Curiously, perhaps the greatest legal benefit that married couples have is the ability to get divorced. Three of the authors of this book have had extensive experience with divorce, one as a child custody evaluator, two as attorneys. We are acutely mindful of the suffering and cost that divorce often entails. We can practically hear divorced readers scream, "How can you say getting divorced is a benefit?" and we are empathetic with that reaction. But imagine what post-married life would be if there were no divorce.

Consider a hypothetical marriage. Harry and Joan are married fifteen years. They own a home jointly with an equity of about $100,000. Joan graduated from college with a degree in marketing, worked for three years after marriage, then gave up working to be a housewife. Harry went into manufacturing, became successful, and at the end of fifteen years owned his plant individually and had 60 percent of the stock in the corporation that owned the manufacturing business. He declares $200,000 per year as income from the corporation, including $52,000 the corporation pays him as rent for the plant and the land it sits on. Harry and Joan have two children, ages eleven and seven, a joint brokerage account with $50,000, and a joint checking account that empties monthly; Harry has a pension, and there are no other assets of special value. The marriage breaks down because Harry falls in love with his secretary.

When a divorce action occurs, Joan will be able to do the following:

1. Hire an attorney even though she lacks access to funds because the court will be able to compel Harry to pay her reasonable counsel fees.

2. Hire an actuary to determine the present value of Harry's pension.

3. Hire a real estate appraiser to determine the present fair market value of the plant and the land it is on, and the residence, and whether the rent Harry receives is a fair rental.

4. Hire an accountant to investigate whether $200,000 is indeed Harry's true income or whether he actually makes other income that he labels as a corporate expense.

5. Hire a business appraiser to determine the fair market value of Harry's stock in the corporate business, as well as other corporate assets, if any, and to seek these fees from Harry pursuant to the same power the court has to order counsel fees.

Because Joan has the protection of the many aspects of divorce law, this hypothetical case would probably result in orders awarding legal custody of the children to one party solely or to both parties jointly, determining which party should have primary residential custody and what rights of visitation the other party should have, dividing the assets of the parties between them equally based on their fair market value, or in some states unequally for equitable reasons, providing child support assistance for the primary parent, and in most states ordering alimony for varying periods from Harry to Joan. Joan is also the beneficiary of federal law that allows interests in real estate to be transferred pursuant to court orders in a divorce judgment without triggering a capital gain tax; to orders that similarly allow the transfer of all or a part of retirement plans and pensions through Qualified Domestic Relations Orders; and to law that guarantees three years of health insurance for the spouse who, during the marriage, was insured under a policy covering the other spouse.

All of this, and other subsidiary orders, occurs because Harry and Joan, having been married, are automatically subject to a large body of philosophy and law that applies when their marriage is dissolved and that seeks to clothe that dissolution in fairness.

But what happens when relationships between unmarried couples break up? This body of law is not available. To be sure, certain other legal remedies exist. For instance, if there are children, legal actions are available to determine issues of custody, visitation, and child support. But these do not provide orders for asset divisions or alimony payments. If this same general situation applied to an unmarried Harry and Joan or to Harry and Jim or to Emily and Joan, the partner who had given up his or her work career and stayed home would have no opportunity to share in the assets built up via the working partner's business success and no chance for postbreakup spousal support to compensate for lost earnings, career damage, or even to assist until that partner had reentered the workforce.

Those with a superficial knowledge of law might here interpose an objection and point out that "palimony" exists without marriage. But it is irrelevant because the fact that one partner can sue his or her partner for money owed after the breakup of a domestic relationship depends on being able to prove that an explicit agreement governed the relationship that entitles the plaintiff to money (explicit agreements rarely are made), or that there was an implied agreement, or that the principles of constructive trust or unjust enrichment apply. These are not alternative remedies where divorce does not apply. Lawsuits based on implied agreements, constructive trust, or unjust enrichment will usually not fit the facts and, even where they appear to, will be expensive to litigate, imposing a burden of proof on the plaintiff that is difficult to bear successfully; and even if the plaintiff prevails, such litigation will usually not produce all the orders that are commonplace in a divorce action. In reality there is no alternative to divorce.

Divorce, like most law, is a means of dispute resolution, a substitute for self-help, an arena without violence where lawyers, not gladiators, contest, where the weapons are knowledge and words instead of lethal weapons and intimidation. About one-half of American marriages result in divorce. Imagine our social landscape if divorce was not there to soak up the enmity divorces present, if all financial resolutions left by broken marriages ended up being settled in favor of the stronger or the wealthier or the faster or the trickier partner. It is not hyperbolic to suggest that the absence of divorce would dramatically increase the incidence of heterosexual assaults, probably homicides, certainly anger and frustration. Divorce is a social necessity. Of course, many heterosexual couples choose to cohabit without the protection of divorce, but this is their choice. They are entitled to make that choice. Same-sex couples are also entitled to make that choice. Now they have no choice.

On January 31, 1997, Barry R. Bedrick, associate general counsel of the United States General Accounting Office, sent to representative Henry J. Hyde, chairman of the House Judiciary Committee, a lengthy report in response to Mr. Hyde's request that the GAO "identify federal laws in which benefits, rights and privileges are contingent on marital statutes."[2]

The report classifies these federal laws into thirteen categories:

1. Social Security and related programs, housing, and food stamps
2. Veterans' benefits
3. Taxation
4. Federal civilian and military service benefits
5. Employment benefits and related laws
6. Immigration, naturalization, and aliens
7. Indians
8. Trade, commerce, and intellectual property
9. Financial disclosure and conflict of interest
10. Crimes and family violence
11. Loans, guarantees, and payments in agriculture
12. Federal natural resources and related laws
13. Miscellaneous laws

While Attorney Bedrick is careful to make explicit that this report does not claim to "capture every individual law in the United States Code in which marital status figures," he nonetheless states that "we believe that the probability is high that it has identified these programs in the Code in which marital status is a factor." While he also makes a point to state that one should not conclude from the mere fact that a law is identified as one in which marital status is a factor that the law is advantageous to those who are married, it is obvious from even a cursory look that these laws do overwhelmingly confer benefits on married persons.

It is, however, true that married couples can pay more in income taxes than two cohabiting single persons of whatever gender. If two cohabiting unmarried persons each had taxable income of $68,800 in 2003, and each filed singly, each would owe a tax of $14,010.00 and thus together would pay $28,020.00, whereas if they were married, they would jointly pay $28,708.50 on their joint income of $137,600—a total of $688.50 more as a result of being married. This occurs because the marrieds pay at a 28 percent rate on the upper part of their joint income whereas the top rate for each of the unmarrieds would be 25 percent.

If each taxpayer had taxable income of $311,950, the married couple would pay $12,542.50 more in taxes than the unmarried couple. Gay and lesbian advocates of the right to marry may well be the first people in history striving to increase their taxes.

The first category listed earlier has a broad impact on Americans. The *Social Security* Program (Old Age, Survivors, and Disability Insurance) is constructed for the protection of husbands and wives, widows, and widowers. This law created a basic right of an individual participant to retirement benefits and created as well derivative rights in the present and former spouse of such participant. This area of law, because of its broad impact, deserves more than generalized treatment.

Section 402(a) of the Social Security Act outlines the requirements for individuals to qualify for Old Age Insurance benefits.[3] Section 402(b) provides for benefits for wives, and every divorced wife of an individual entitled to Old Age Disability Insurance benefits so long as the wife is sixty-two years old and meets other standards such as "in the case of a divorced wife, is not married." The benefit that is available to a qualifying wife, or former wife, is one-half of the amount paid to the husband or the ex-husband. While the major benefits for ex-wives go to those where marriages lasted at least ten years, there are also benefits possible for ex-wives who were not married ten years. The same rights granted to wives and ex-wives are later in the statute granted to husbands and divorced husbands "of an individual who is entitled to an old-age insurance benefit."

Medicare is a part of the Social Security Act, and it also provides benefits that arise from the marriage of a husband and wife. Under this act, a person may qualify for benefits who, inter alia, "was married (and had been married for the previous 1 year period) to an individual who had at least 30 quarters of coverage under such title"; or "had been married to an individual for a period of at least 1 year (at the time of such individual's death) if at such time the individual had at least 30 quarters of coverage under such title"; or "is divorced from an individual and had been married to the individual for a period of at least 10 years (at the time of divorce) if at such time the individual had at least 30 quarters of coverage under such title."[4] Similar benefits are contained later in the act for persons "receiving cash benefits under a qualified state or local government retirement system." Again, the beneficiaries derive, as divorced persons or widows or widowers, these benefits from marriage.

The second category of federal statutes listed in the Bedrick report to Representative Hyde was *veterans' benefits*. In this area, the spouses of veterans are entitled to several different forms of assistance by the government. Consider:

1. Spouses of certain veterans can receive government-provided medical care.

2. Spouses of veterans may qualify to be beneficiaries of National Service Life Insurance.

3. Spouses of eligible veterans are themselves eligible for burial in national cemeteries.

4. Spouses who survive a veteran who died of a service-connected disability are entitled to educational assistance for up to forty-five months and to job counseling, training, and placement services.

5. Spouses and widows or widowers of certain veterans receive preferential treatment in federal employment.

6. Spouses of veterans may be compensated if the veteran has disappeared.

7. Veterans with at least a 30 percent disability receive additional disability if they have a spouse.

8. If a veteran dies from a service-connected cause, a surviving spouse gets monthly dependency and indemnity compensation payments and monthly pension payments if the veteran's death was not service connected. In sum, husbands or wives of veterans have many rights and privileges by virtue of the marital relationship.

The gay soldier, no matter how courageously he may have died, no matter how loving a relationship he had with his surviving partner, no matter how much he and his partner may have wished to marry, can leave his or her partner nothing in veterans' benefits.

The third category is *taxation*. We have already spoken of the anomalous situation regarding income taxes that can favor nonmarried couples. But the laws regarding gift and estate taxes are quite favorable to married persons; for instance, property transferred to a spouse in a will is deductible for the purpose of fixing the value of the decedent's estate. In other contexts, the law allows interspousal transfers of property without taxing any gain—a privilege unavailable to single taxpayers.

The fourth category is *federal civilian and military service benefits*. The Bedrick report identified 1,049 provisions in the United States Code in which marital status was a factor; over 270 of them were found in this category. They pertain to United States civilian employees (Title 5), military personnel (Title 10), Foreign Service officers (Title 22), Central Intelligence Agency employees (Title 50), Lighthouse Service employees (Title 33), and Coast Guard members (Title 14). Examples of the laws in this category include

1. a law that establishes health benefits and service benefits for spouses of federal employees and officers;
2. a law designating spouses in the order of preference in the payment of final paychecks and life insurance benefits of employees or officers who die without having named their beneficiaries;
3. a law concerning the rights of present or former spouses to retirement annuities after the death of an employee;
4. a law granting increased compensation to an employee disabled by work-related injuries if that employee is married;
5. a law entitling Federal Civil Service employees to unpaid leave if they have a spouse with a serious health condition; and
6. laws applicable to military personnel that provide employment assistance and transitional services for spouses of members separating from the military service, as well as certain commissary privileges and free secondary education for specific classes of spouses.

The fifth category is *employment benefits and related law*. There are many federal laws that relate to private employment. Most of these appear in Title 29 of the United States Code (Labor). However, others appear in more specialized form in Title 30 (Mineral Lands and Mining), Title 33 (Navigation and Navigable Waters), and Title 45 (Railroads). Examples of these special spousal benefits are the following:

1. The spouse of a coal miner who dies of black lung disease qualifies for benefits.

2. The spouse of a public safety officer killed in the course of duty may qualify for a death benefit up to $100,000.

Curiously, the Employee Retirement Income Security Act has provisions that protect spouses from the subject employees. The act prohibits an employee from changing a beneficiary in a retirement plan or from waiving the joint and survivor form of retirement benefit unless his or her spouse consents in writing. The intent of ERISA to protect spouses is clear from 29 USCS no. 1055 (a):

Required contents for applicable plans. Each pension plan to which this section applies.

1. In the case of a vested participant who does not die before the annuity starting date, the accrued benefit to such participant shall be provided in the form of a qualified joint and survivor annuity, and

2. In the case of a vested participant who dies before the annuity starting date and who has a surviving spouse, a qualified pre-retirement survivor annuity shall be provided to the surviving spouse of such participant.

The Job Training Partnership Act makes "family" a relevant concept and defines it thus:

Two or more persons related by blood, marriage or decree of court, who are living in a single residence, and are included in one or more of the following categories:

(A) A husband, wife and dependent children.

(B) A parent or guardian and dependent children.

(C) A husband and wife.

The Family and Medical Leave Act provides for twelve work weeks of leave during any twelve-month period in the event that the employee, inter alia, has to care for a spouse who has a "serious health condition."

The sixth category is *immigration, naturalization, and aliens*. The laws in this category are much less likely to affect the numbers of people affected by the prior categories, but the effects of these laws can be crucial, even to the point of life or death. Title 8 of the United States Code (Aliens and Nationality) provides, in part, that spouses of aliens who are granted asylum in the United States qualify for the same status if they accompany or join their spouses. How many people craving asylum would forgo it if they could not bring and keep their spouses in the land offering it? How many spouses left behind would be endangered if their spouses obtained asylum? Just to pose these questions is to understand the enormous benefit provided to those who seek asylum and are married. Just to pose these questions is to understand the tragedy imposed on those who seek asylum without the legal right to marry those they would bring with them if they could. Secondarily, but importantly, aliens who qualify to work in the United States may bring their spouses without the spouse being subject to usual immigration limitations.

The seventh category deals with *Indians*. The treaties and laws that make up Title 25 of the United States Code contain certain provisions that grant rights to tribal property of white men who marry Indian women or of Indian men who marry white women. The law also grants the right to a surviving spouse who is not an Indian or a member of the deceased spouse's tribe to elect a life estate in property that he or she was living in at the time of the other spouse's death.

The eighth category consists of laws regarding *trade, commerce, and intellectual property* involving Titles 116 (Bankruptcy), 12 (Banks and Banking), 15 (Commerce and Trade), 17 (Copyrights), and 19 (Customs Duties) of the United States Code. The Bankruptcy Code allows spouses to file jointly for bankruptcy, which necessitates only one filing fee. More importantly, a former spouse of the person filing is given a major benefit in that a discharge in bankruptcy will not normally relieve the debtor of the obligation to pay alimony or child support arising out of a prior divorce decree or separation agreement.

Spouses also have a noteworthy privilege under the National Housing Act. This act prohibits banks from declaring a mortgage loan fully due if an owner transfers the property to a spouse even where the bank has the right to do so in the event of a sale by the mortgagor to another person without the bank's prior approval.

The Consumer Credit Protection Act, in its regulation of wage garnishments, gives special protection to spouses. Normally the act restricts garnishment withholding of an individual's wages to at most 25 percent of the disposable income, but if the garnishment is to enforce an order for the support of a spouse, the maximum rises to 60 percent—unless the wage earner is supporting a new spouse, in which case the maximum is 50 percent.

Title 19 (Customs Duties) has a provision whereby certain countries that do not allow their citizens to immigrate to the United States to join spouses (and other "close relatives") can be penalized by restrictions on their trade with the United States.

The ninth category, *financial disclosure and conflict of interest*, provides no spousal benefits relevant to this work.

Laws in the tenth category, *crimes and family violence*, extend legal protections to spouses both for their protection and for the protection of the officials they are married to. It is a federal crime to attempt to influence an official of the United States by threatening the spouse of that official. This philosophy extends to threats against the spouses of persons protected by the Secret Service. Another provision gives to the spouses of American citizens who have been victims of terrorism outside the United States the right to sue for treble damages.

The eleventh category is *loans, guarantees, and payments in agriculture*. In this area of law, marital status can be a factor in both determining a person's eligibility for many federal loan programs and determining the amount of federal assistance the applicant can receive. With respect to borrowing for housing, eligibility for such assistance extends to the surviving spouses of veterans who have died from a service-connected disability, have been missing in action, captured, or forcibly detained by a foreign government.

Laws in the twelfth category, *federal natural resources and related laws*, affect relatively few persons, but the governmental solicitude for spouses is evident. For instance, when the government purchases land for purposes such as parks or monuments, it not only allows the sellers to use it during their lifetimes but extends this right to the sellers' spouses. The Bedrick report found more than forty provisions in Title 16 (Conservation) alone in which marital status was a factor.

The last category—*miscellaneous laws*—is, according to the report, a mix of provisions from fourteen titles of the United States Code. They include fourteen statutes that prohibit discrimination on the basis of marital status. The reach of this prohibition, of course, does not include protection for same-sex couples. This category includes laws that charter patriotic societies that assist, inter alia, widows of servicemen.

I repeat and stress that the bulk of what this chapter has discussed are federal rights and privileges and that there are additional rights and privileges derived from state law. The Supreme Judicial Court of Massachusetts, in its opinion in *Hillary Goodridge v. Department of Public Health*, decided November 18, 2003, described these benefits in Massachusetts as follows (citations deleted):

> Without question, civil marriage enhances the "welfare of the community." It is a "social institution of the highest importance." Civil marriage anchors an ordered society by encouraging stable relationships over transient ones. It is central to the way the Commonwealth identifies individuals, provides for the orderly distribution of property, ensures that children and adults are cared for and supported whenever possible from private rather than public funds, and tracks important epidemiological and demographic data.
>
> Marriage also bestows enormous private and social advantages on those who choose to marry. Civil marriage is at once a deeply personal commitment to another human being and a highly public celebration of the ideals of mutuality, companionship, intimacy, fidelity, and family. "It is an association that promotes a way of life, not causes; a harmony in living, not political faiths; a bilateral loyalty, not commercial or social projects." *Griswold v. Connecticut.* Because it fulfills yearnings for security, safe haven, and connection that express our common humanity, civil marriage is an esteemed institution, and the decision whether and whom to marry is among life's momentous acts of self-definition.
>
> Tangible as well as intangible benefits flow from marriage. The marriage license grants valuable property rights to those who meet the entry requirements, and who agree to what might otherwise be a burdensome degree of government regulation of their activities. ("The historical aim of licensure generally is preservation of public health, safety, and welfare by extending the public trust only to those with proven qualifications.") The legislature has conferred on "each party [in a civil marriage] substantial rights concerning the assets of the other which unmarried cohabitants do not have" (rejecting claim for equitable distribution of property where plaintiff cohabited with but did not marry defendant); (government interest in promoting marriage would be "subverted" by recognition of "a right to recover for loss of consortium by a person who

has not accepted the correlative responsibilities of marriage"); (unmarried partners not entitled to rights of separate support or alimony).

The benefits accessible only by way of a marriage license are enormous, touching nearly every aspect of life and death. The department states that "hundreds of statutes" are related to marriage and to marital benefits. With no attempt to be comprehensive, we note that some of the statutory benefits conferred by the legislature on those who enter into civil marriage include, as to property: joint Massachusetts income tax filing; tenancy by the entirety (a form of ownership that provides certain protections against creditors and allows for the automatic descent of property to the surviving spouse without probate); extension of the benefit of the homestead protection (securing up to $300,000 in equity from creditors) to one's spouse and children; automatic rights to inherit the property of a deceased spouse who does not leave a will; the rights of elective share and of dower (which allow surviving spouses certain property rights where the decedent spouse has not made adequate provision for the survivor in a will); entitlement to wages owed to a deceased employee; eligibility to continue certain businesses of a deceased spouse; the right to share the medical policy of one's spouse (defining an insured's "dependent" to include one's spouse) [domestic partners of city employees not included within the term "dependent"]; thirty-nine week continuation of health coverage for the spouse of a person who is laid off or dies; preferential options under the Commonwealth's pension system ["Joint and Last Survivor Allowance"]; preferential benefits in the Commonwealth's medical program MassHealth [A] prohibiting placing a lien on long-term care patient's former home if spouse still lives there; access to veterans' spousal benefits and preferences; financial protections for spouses of certain Commonwealth employees (fire fighters, police officers, prosecutors, among others) killed in the performance of duty; the equitable division of marital property on divorce; temporary and permanent alimony rights; the right to separate support on separation of the parties that does not result in divorce; and the right to bring claims for wrongful death and loss of consortium, and for funeral and burial expenses and punitive damages resulting from tort actions.

Exclusive marital benefits that are not directly tied to property rights include the presumptions of legitimacy and parentage of children born to a married couple; and evidentiary rights, such as the prohibition against spouses testifying against one another about their private conversations, applicable in both civil and criminal cases. Other statutory benefits of a personal nature available only to married individuals include qualification for bereavement or medical leave to care for individuals related by blood or marriage; an automatic "family member" preference to make medical decisions for an incompetent or disabled spouse who does not have a contrary health care proxy; the application of predicable rules of child custody, visitation, support, and removal out-of-State when married parents divorce [temporary custody], [temporary support], [custody and support on judgment of divorce], [removal from Commonwealth], and [shared custody plan]; priority rights to administer the estate of a deceased spouse who dies without a will, and requirement that surviving spouse must consent to the appointment of any other person as administrator [disposition of body], [anatomical gifts]; and the right to interment in the lot or tomb owned by one's deceased spouse.

Where a married couple has children, their children are also directly or indirectly, but no less auspiciously, the recipients of the special legal and economic protections obtained by civil marriage. Notwithstanding the Commonwealth's strong public policy to abolish legal distinctions between marital and nonmarital children in providing the support and care of minors, the fact remains that marital children reap a measure of family stability and economic security based on their parents' legally privileged status that is largely inaccessible, or not as readily accessible, to nonmarital children. Some of these benefits are social, such as the enhanced approval that still attends the status of being a marital child. Others are material, such as the greater ease of access to family-based State and Federal benefits that attend the presumptions of one's parentage.

We see no value in an additional itemization of the benefits of marriage. That they are plentiful and valuable and occasionally vital seems obvious. What is also obvious is that those who are legally deprived of the opportunity to share these benefits are turned into an underclass. They are so victimized not because they have behaved criminally but because they are what they were born to be.

Conclusion:
The Case for Same-Sex Marriage

Donald J. Cantor

If we have done our jobs even passably well, one should now be able to assume that (1) persons do not become possessed of same-sex sexual attraction voluntarily, and they cannot shed such attraction by an exercise of will, it being innate and permanent; (2) same-sex relationships are not inherently less stable, or more unstable, than heterosexual relationships; (3) children reared by same-sex couples or two single gay parents are as likely to develop healthfully as children raised by heterosexual couples or one heterosexual parent; (4) this conclusion is reached not only by prevailing psychological studies but by an experienced child custody evaluator and child psychiatrist who has served the courts in Connecticut for twenty-five years and published in the area of child custody; (5) the history of the law in America concerning adoption by homosexuals of minor children over the past four decades mirrors the conclusions of the psychological and psychiatric commentators referred to here; (6) the inability of same-sex couples to marry deprives them of many important federal and state privileges and benefits; (7) Supreme Court decisions evolving over the past four decades have extended constitutional protection, based on rights of privacy, liberty, and equality, to the point where same-sex marriage seems likely to acquire the same protection; (8) actions by state legislatures during this same period have substantially augmented the growth of feeling that private, consensual, adult sexual decisions should be free of governmental interference; and (9) developments outside the United States evidence, and seem to portend, a continuing and growing acceptance of same-sex marriage.

If these conclusions are accurate, and we assert that they are, then why is there opposition to same-sex marriage? What arguments do the opponents raise? Are they valid, or if not, are they partially valid?

The primary reason advanced to deny same-sex marriage is that it is an attack on heterosexual marriage, the institution historically deemed best suited to the raising of children.

What is required under our law for heterosexuals to marry? First of all, licenses are required. Some states require a medical certificate attesting that the prospective married couple is free from venereal disease. The applicants must be old enough to give consent to marriage, an age that varies from state to state, or if they are not old enough, consent may be required from a parent or guardian. Mental capacity is required and is defined as the ability to give "intelligent assent to the marriage contract." The mental capacity required to make the decision to marry, however, is not defined as being of a particularly high level. A Minnesota court, for instance, once held that a kleptomaniac had sufficient capacity to marry, and an Illinois court held that "the same mental strength necessary to the transaction of business is not necessary to enable the party to contract a marriage."[1] Consanguinity (relation by blood) may be a bar to marriage if the relationship is closer than a particular state allows, and the same applies to affinity (relation through marriage). The parties must give their free consent to the marriage, and normally the marriage must be performed with certain ceremonial requisites. That's it. Comply with these rules, and so long as no one was married to someone else when he or she wed anew, the participants are married. That being so, the following couples are free to marry: (1) a potent man and a barren woman, (2) a fertile woman and an impotent man, (3) an impotent man and a barren woman, (4) a fertile woman and a potent man who unite in their desire never to have children, (5) an older couple who want companionship only from their marriage, and (6) a couple who marry only for social or financial or other pragmatic reasons and have no desire to ever be intimate, physically or otherwise.

All these couples have the same right to be married as those who intend to procreate once married. None of them has violated any aspect of the law of marriage by getting or staying married. Procreation is not now and never has been a prerequisite for marriage.

But, it will be asserted, regardless of the fact that traditional marriage need not result in procreation, it still provides the best setting for the rearing of children and therefore should not be changed.

We agree that a home with two parents provides the best opportunity for children to be raised in the stable, loving atmosphere most conducive to their happy, healthy development. But all children today do not come into being via the vaginal intercourse of a husband and wife, and still more children are not raised by a married heterosexual couple. Gay couples today and gay and lesbian individuals, as well, may acquire children through adoption, artificial insemination, or the use of surrogate mothers. These children have the same need for stability and nurturing and love that children born of heterosexual wedlock have, and there are between six million and fourteen million such children.[2] Why, therefore, should the heterosexual or homosexual children of homosexual parents be denied the benefits of married home life that exist by right to the heterosexual or homosexual children of heterosexual parents?

The claim is made that same-sex marriage would weaken all marriage. Some argue that this is because women domesticate men and thus make marriage work. The appropriate response to this, writes David Brooks, a noted conservative columnist, is to "expect" that gay people will make the commitments required of marriage, not presume that they won't. The conservative position ought to be, he argues, one that *insists* on gay marriage.[3] Surely it follows that if one believes that marriage is a necessary and beneficial social institution, one should want that institution expanded, and especially expanded to include those who fight to be included. One can easily get the impression from the arguments and attitudes of those who disapprove of same-sex marriage that allowing it would somehow threaten or diminish heterosexual marriage. The movement for same-sex marriage is based on admiration of marriage, on a desire to share its promise, not on any wish to lessen it. David Brooks says that today, "marriage is in crisis. Nearly half of all marriages end in divorce," and it is in crisis "because marriage, which relies on a culture of fidelity, is now asked to survive in a culture of contingency."[4] It is the gay community today, more than any other, which, in seeking to join this "culture of fidelity," extols the power and promise of marriage.

Some oppose same-sex marriage because of what they claim it will lead to. They warn us that same-sex marriage will lead to the destruction of the family, polygamy, group marriage, incest, marriage between children and adults, and marriage "between a man and his donkey."[5] They foresee doom, not so much from same-sex marriage itself but from what it will spawn. "What's next?" is their warning and cry of alarm.[6]

How does one respond to these forecasts? Judith Stacey calls them signals of desperation, and indeed they are.[7] But they are more than that. They are debaters' tricks, a way of diverting attention from the issue at hand to issues not actually pending but much easier to attack. I know of no organization favoring same-sex marriage that has on its agenda a subsequent move for group marriage, polygamy, polyandry, or weddings between men and donkeys. I know that the authors of this work do not favor any of these add-ons. But more importantly, I know it's a nonissue, a scare tactic only. How do I know this? I know it because same-sex marriage exists in Massachusetts, Canada, Spain, Belgium, and Holland, and none of these other predicted events have occurred there. Does that mean I claim to have such extensive contacts in all these places that any such social movements in any of them would come promptly and fully to my attention? Not at all. What I do claim, however, is that those who predict that radical social fallout will accompany same-sex marriage are passionate to prove their predictions valid. Therefore, if a movement arose in Massachusetts to legalize polygamy, they would tell us about it. If a movement arose in Belgium for adults marrying children, they would tell us about it. If group marriage was proposed in Holland, they would tell us about it. If in Canada an upsurge in bestiality occurred, within or without the context of marriage, we would hear about it. But we haven't heard of any of these dire events occurring. Because they haven't. Because there is no reason why they should have occurred. Because there is no connection whatsoever between same-sex marriage and these supposed ramifications of it.

There are, of course, other critics of same-sex marriage who allege that heterosexual, "normal" marriages would be damaged by same-sex marriage and need to be protected from it. They are, however, quite vague in describing how and why this damage would occur. Let us hypothesize. Imagine a happily married heterosexual couple named Jones living at 12 Elm Street, Anyville, U.S.A. Residing at 17 Elm Street are Bill and Joe, a gay couple, unmarried. It's June 5, 2005. Since they are not married, they cannot yet have harmed the Joneses' marriage, since the danger that Bill and Joe pose allegedly derives from their being married, and no critic of same-sex marriage known to me has yet suggested that there should be a law barring gay unmarried persons or couples from living near married heterosexuals. Now suppose that on June 10, 2005, Bill and Joe get married, but the Joneses don't know it. Does something automatically endanger the Joneses' marriage simply *because* Bill and Joe are married? Now suppose the Joneses hear of Bill and Joe's marriage. Why does this knowledge endanger the Joneses' marriage? Do critics of same-sex marriage believe that some miasmic reek will exude somehow from 17 Elm

Street and, like a wind-borne virus, contaminate the marriage of the Joneses and other functioning heterosexual marriages within the reek's range? Is it ineffective unless there are a certain number of same-sex marriages? Does it take one such marriage, or a hundred, or a thousand, to send the Joneses to divorce court? Or isn't it true that the Joneses will decide the fate of their marriage by themselves, based on how their relationship progresses over time regardless of the race, ethnicity, religion, or sexual orientation of whoever lives at 17 Elm Street? We vote for the latter.

There is a troubling aspect to this debate over same-sex marriage, generally true of those against it, but occasionally also true of those for it. Too often the debaters seem to reach for the intellectual heights and expose their erudition, treating the issue as a dry exercise in abstract reasoning, ignoring the human cost. There are thousands of people whose quality of life hinges on whether they can marry soon, eventually, or never. I don't criticize objectivity, but I regret the absence of empathy, if not sympathy. When gays were allowed to marry in Massachusetts and when the opportunity for gays to marry seemed to arise in San Francisco and New Paltz, New York, the public outpouring of joy was palpable. Why isn't the happiness a law can provide a proper factor to weigh in judging the aptness of that law? What is the ultimate justification for any law if not the happiness of those it affects?

I struggled with the problem of grasping fully the meaning of the right to marry to same-sex couples. It occurred to me later than it probably should have that I had within easy reach the way to do this, a way that did not require a greater power of projection than I had. All I had to do was imagine how qualitatively my life would have been diminished over the past twenty-eight years had I been unable to marry my wife. And so I suggest to those heterosexuals who have been happily married, and to those who hope in the future to be so, that they measure the value of that experience or dream and consider what life would be like without it. If heterosexual people can understand that "they"—gay people—live with the same needs as "we" do, perhaps their view of same-sex marriage will change.

The desire to make same-sex marriage lawful everywhere not only subtracts nothing from heterosexual marriage but constitutes no attack on anybody's right to hold any religious belief concerning the nature of marriage. But it is an appropriate message to those who oppose same-sex marriage on religious grounds to remind them that American marriage is a status created by civil law and to remind them also that American law is, and should remain, independent of the laws and philosophy of all churches of whatever persuasion. It is also important to realize that, as with the abortion dispute, "religion" is not opposed to same-sex marriage; only some religionists are. Others have taken outspoken positions in favor of same-sex marriage.[8] Some will say that all gays and lesbians do not wish to marry, and they are correct. But all heterosexuals do not wish to marry either, and more importantly, no one pressing for same-sex marriage is suggesting that anyone should *have* to marry. They ask only for the *ability* to marry.

Others say that civil unions should be enough—after all, they give *most* of the benefits of marriage. It's remarkable how easy it is for opponents *with* rights to minimize the value of those rights to others. Let's suppose a statement from Jim Crow to Rosa Parks:

> *Jim Crow*: Rosa, we got it all worked out. You can sit on any seat in any bus in town except that, on the Elm Street line, you have to sit in the back Thursdays between 10:00 p.m. and midnight. How's that? Pretty good, right?

Can anyone imagine Rosa Parks or others in the civil rights movement finding this proposal attractive? Of course not. Because being almost equal is less than equal, and less than equal is wrong, and only equal is acceptable. Civil unions were a stage, an advance, but they cannot be a goal.

The evolution of American sexual law did not specifically intend to result in same-sex marriage. Rather, it had disparate goals, often with different constituencies. There was not a single organized push but rather several distinct ones. Those who fought for abortion rights differed from those who wanted divorce reform, and they differed from those who wanted the freedom to use birth control materials. Many, in turn, differed from those who opposed miscegenation laws and criminalization of adultery and fornication. Only the underlying philosophy was the same: sexual decisions should be made by consenting adults free of governmental involvement to the greatest extent possible. This philosophy meshed perfectly with the aspirations of another movement growing over the same period—that of gays and lesbians seeking equality in all phases of American life. The first and irreplaceable step that any group must take if it is to attain equality is to believe that it is entitled to it. The second step is to assert this belief publicly and consistently, the aim being to impress the rest of society with both the nature of the cause and the justice of it. The homosexual community has done this, and it has happened concurrently with, and sometimes as a part of, the general sexual evolution, so that today the attainment of same-sex marriage throughout America is the combined objective of both philosophies.

But if same-sex marriage is a goal unanticipated by most of those who fought for abortion and other rights, how surprising must it be to the general public to face this issue in its ripened form today? And how threatening must it be to those raised on utterly different religious and philosophical bases to find the assumed nature of marriage as the union of a woman and a man undergoing challenge? It is wholly understandable that there be an instantaneous, protective reaction to this challenge, that the wagons be circled and an angry posture of resistance be adopted. Those who favor same-sex marriage but fail to empathize with this reaction misjudge and are unfair to their opposition. These opponents represent genuine disquiet, not malice. But it does not follow from the comprehension of what motivates this resistance that it therefore deserves to prevail. Fear of change should never be a reason sufficient to perpetuate social deprivations that the desired change would eradicate, and it should never be doubted that the inability to marry causes much practical loss and emotional deprivation to millions of gay and lesbian adults and to millions of their children.

So what does the future hold? The Supreme Court seems on the verge of making same-sex marriage a constitutional right, but this is surely not a certainty. In 1996 Congress passed the Defense of Marriage Act (Title 28, Ch. 115, Section 1728C, U.S. Code), which defined marriage for all federal purposes as being only between "one man and one woman as husband and wife" and declared that no state, territory, possession, or Indian tribe was required to recognize any same-sex marriage of any other state, territory, possession, or Indian tribe. Forty-one states have either passed acts similar to this act or have amended their constitutions so that only traditional heterosexual marriages are lawful. These enactments can retard and complicate the spread and acceptance of same-sex marriage (unless the Supreme Court gives constitutional protection to it, in which event the federal and state acts are all negated), but they cannot stop the tide.

Of infinitely greater long-term importance is the fact that public-opinion data show that heavy majorities of younger Americans readily support same-sex marriage.[9] They are reaching adulthood in a far different social context from the one their parents knew, and an utterly different one than their grandparents experienced. Gays and lesbians are known as people, not hidden and thus mysterious, and thus fearsome because mysterious. And what they seek is known and on the political agenda and, now, law in Massachusetts as well as elsewhere. Young Americans today know gays and know of gays. Their reasoning is of the familiar, not the unknown. Thus they can deal with the issue of same-sex marriage in the way that most people deal with most such questions—by asking simply, "Is it fair?" Also of greater importance over the long term is the fact that, where same-sex marriage has been legalized, it has become commonplace, accepted, not news, approaching trite. "While the United States fiercely debates the issue of allowing same-sex marriage, marriage for gay men and lesbians in the Netherlands has become so commonplace that today, two years after being legalized, it is hardly recognized as different."[10]

Acceptance of same-sex marriage is a rapidly moving social force worldwide. It may be slowed by the so-called Defense of Marriage Acts, but they will not thwart it even if the Supreme Court fails to settle the issue. The more it is shown that Massachusetts and Spain and Canada and Belgium and the Netherlands absorb same-sex marriage into their citizens' lives without noticeable result, the more the age of the population grows to include citizens who are used to gays and lesbians as associates, the more the fear of them will subside, the more their basic sameness to the rest of us will be understood, and the less how they marry will be an issue until, eventually, as in the Netherlands now, same-sex marriages will be nonevents.

That this process is presently and powerfully afoot in the United States was vividly shown in Massachusetts on Wednesday, September 14, 2005. Approximately one year before, the Massachusetts legislature had voted 105 to 92 in favor of an amendment to the Massachusetts Constitution barring same-sex marriage. This proposed amendment, which had to be passed in two consecutive sessions, was this time defeated 157 to 39. In explaining this striking change of legislative attitude, state senator Brian Lees, a Republican who had been a cosponsor of the amendment, said: "Gay marriage has begun, and life has not changed for the citizens of the commonwealth, with the exception of those who can now marry."[11] After about one year of allowing same-sex marriage in Massachusetts, it was evident that the hills of the Berkshires still stood, the Cape Cod dunes had not eroded, the Red Sox were winning, nothing bad had happened; there was not, after all, anything to fear from letting this marital subclass enjoy equality.

There is a problem with the reasoning of "eventually." It can make us oblivious to the casualties that occur daily if we focus on the future. We should never become so academic and philosophical in our thinking that we lose sight of the millions of people today who are denied the full lives that come with marriage and the ability to offer these full lives to their children. They need help now; they should not have to wait.

As we absorb and weigh the evolution in thought over the last forty years in psychology, psychiatry, and law, isn't it clear that same-sex marriage will hurt no one and help many?

Isn't it therefore time that this nation, which has granted more freedom to more diverse people over more time than any other, extend the freedom to marry to same-sex couples?

Isn't it fair to do so?

Isn't it fair to do so now?

Of course it is.

Of course it is.

Notes

1. The U.S. Supreme Court

1. Griswold et al. v. Connecticut, 381 U.S. 379 (1965).
2. *Id.* at 480.
3. *Id.*
4. *Id.* at 482.
5. *Id.* at 486, 487.
6. *Id.* at 486.
7. Loving et ux. v. Virginia, 388 U.S. 1 (1967).
8. *Id.* at 3.
9. *Id.* at 7.
10. *Id.* at 12.
11. Stanley v. Georgia, 394 U.S. 557 (1969).
12. *Id.* at 568.
13. Roe et al. v. Wade, 410 U.S. 113 (1973).
14. *Id.* at 164, 165.
15. *Id.* at 152.
16. Bowers v. Hardwick et al., 478 U.S. 186 (1986).
17. *Id.* at 188 n.1.
18. Lawrence et al. v. Texas, 123B S. Ct. 2472 (2003).
19. *Id.* at 2473.
20. *Id.* at 2484.
21. *Id.* at 2496, 2497.
22. *Id.* at 2497, 2498.

2. The Evolution of State Law toward Sexual Privacy

1. Donald J. Cantor, *Deviation and the Criminal Law*, 55 J. CRIM. L., CRIMINOLOGY & POL. SCI. 441, 447 (1964).
2. ALA. CODE § 13A-12-2 (2004); ARIZ. REV. STAT. § 13-1408 (2004); COLO. REV. STAT. § 18-6-501 (2003); FLA. STAT. ANN. § 798.01 (2004); 720 ILL. COMP. STAT. ANN. 5/11-7 (2004): IDAHO CODE § 18-6601 (2004); KAN. STAT. ANN. § 21-3507 (2003); MD. CODE ANN., CRIM. LAW § 10-501 (2003); MASS. ANN. LAWS. CH. 272, § 14 (2004); MICH. COMP. LAWS § 750.30 (2003); MINN. STAT. § 609.36 (2003); MISS. CODE ANN. § 97-29-1 (2004); N.Y. PENAL LAW § 255.17 (2004). N.C. GEN. STAT. § 14-184 (2004); N.D. CENT. CODE § 12.1-20.09 (2003); OKLA. STAT. TIT. 21, § 872 (2004); R.I. GEN.

LAWS § 11-6-2 (2004); S.C. CODE ANN. § 16-15-70 (2003); UTAH CODE ANN. § 76-7-103 (2003); VA. CODE ANN. § 18.2-365 (2004); W. VA. CODE ANN. § 61-8-3 (2003); WIS. STAT. ANN. § 944.16 (2003).

3. 73 WASHINGTON LAW REVIEW 767, at 769 (1998).

4. IDAHO CODE 16-6-18; ILL. COMP. STAT. ANN. 5/11-8; MASS. ANN. LAWS ch. 272-18; MINN. STAT. ANN. 609-34; MISS. CODE ANN. 97-29-1; N.C. GEN. STAT. 14-184; S.C. CODE ANN. 16-15-60; UTAH CODE ANN. 76-7-104; VA. CODE ANN. 61-8-3.

5. ARIZ. REV. STAT. ANN. 13-1409; FLA. STAT. ANN. 798.02; MICH. COMP. LAWS ANN. 750-335; N.M. STAT. ANN. 30-10-2.

6. George Will, HARTFORD COURANT, January 5, 2005, A7.

7. Lawrence v. Texas, 539 U.S. 558 (2003).

8. Cantor, *supra* note 1, at 445.

9. *Id.*

10. *Id.* at 446.

11. *Id.* at 446–48.

12. The foregoing discussion of divorce law in the 1960s has been adapted from DONALD J. CANTOR, ESCAPE FROM MARRIAGE: HOW TO SOLVE THE PROBLEMS OF DIVORCE 25–30 (New York: William Morrow, 1971).

13. *Id.* at 88, 91.

14. CAL. FAM. CODE § 2310 (2004).

15. KAN. STAT. ANN. 60-1601; NEV. REV. STAT. ANN. 125.010; N.J. STAT. ANN. 2A: 34-2; N.M. STAT. ANN. 40-4-1; OKLA. STAT. ANN. 101.

16. ALA. CODE 25.24.200; ARIZ. REV. STAT. 25-314; CAL. CODE. 2310; COLO. REV. STAT. 14-10-10; CONN. GEN. STAT. ANN. 466-40; DEL. CODE ANN. 1502; FLA. STAT. ANN. 61.052; GA. CODE ANN. 19-5-3; HAW. REV. STAT. ANN. 580-41; KY. REV. STAT. ANN. 403.170; MASS. ANN. LAWS 3, ch. 2081; MICH. COMP. LAWS 552.6; MINN. STAT ANN. 518.06; MO. STAT. ANN. 452.310; MONT. CODE ANN. 40-4-104; NEB. REV. STAT. ANN. 42-361; OR. STAT. ANN. 107.025; R.I. GEN. LAWS 15-5-3.1; WASH. REV. CODE ANN. 26.09.030; WIS. STAT. ANN. 767.12.

17. ILL. COMP. STAT. ANN. 750 5/401; IND. CODE ANN. 31-15-1-2; IOWA CODE 598.17; PENN. STAT. ANN. 3301.

18. IDAHO CODE 32-603; ME. REV. STAT. 902; MISS. CODE ANN. (1972) 93-5-2; N.H. REV. STAT. ANN. 458:7-a; N.D. CENT. CODE 14-05-03; S.D. CODIFIED LAWS 25-4-2; TENN. CODE ANN. 36-4-101; UTAH CODE ANN. 30-3-1; W. VA. CODE ANN. 48-5-201; WY. STAT. ANN. 20-2-104.

19. ARK. CODE ANN. (1987) 9-12-301; LA. STAT. art. 103; MD. CODE ANN. 7-103; N.J. STAT. ANN. 2A:34-2; N.C. GEN. STAT. 50-6; OHIO REV. CODE ANN. 3105.01; S.C. CODE ANN. 20-3-10; VT. STAT. ANN. 551; VA. CODE ANN. 20-191.

20. TEX. CODE ANN. 6.001.

21. JAMES C. BLACK & DONALD J. CANTOR, CHILD CUSTODY 5–6 (New York: Columbia University Press, 1989).

22. *Id.* at 13–14.

4. Gays and Lesbians as Parents and Partners

1. According to the National Center for Health Statistics, the rate of divorce (3.8 per 1,000) is just over one-half the rate of marriage (7.5 per 1,000) with 46 states reporting, in 2003.

5. Same-Sex Parents and Their Children's Development

1. The term "gay" is used here, as in modern parlance, to signify male homosexuals. Female homosexuals are referred to as lesbians.

2. While a strong correlation between adult abuse and childhood victimization is clearly established, the relative roles of genetic and psychosocial factors have not yet been established. That adult abusers are far more likely to have been abused as children is well known, but a solid causal link cannot presently be inferred.

3. We must be careful, however, not to treat our own cultural preferences as self-evident virtues. Some people might characterize tolerance for alternative points of view, for example, as a lack of standards and values. Indeed, opponents of gay marriage often use the same research cited here to argue that gay parents are unfit. Thus, where I have stated that boys raised by lesbian mothers are less aggressive than boys raised by heterosexual parents, opponents of gay marriage have characterized such boys as passive.

6. Homosexuality and Adoption

1. Karla J. Starr, Adoption by Homosexuals: A Look at Differing State Court Opinions, 40 ARIZ. L. REV. 1497 (1998).

2. Joanne Mariner, *Anita Bryant's Anti-Gay Legacy, at* http://www.findlaw.com (Feb. 3, 2004).

3. FLA. STAT. ANN. § 63.042(3).

4. 359 F.3d 804 (11th Cir. 2004).

5. 539 U.S. 558, 123 S. Ct. 2472 (2003).

6. 284 S.E.2d 799 (Va. 1981).

7. *Id.* at 804–5.

8. *Id.* at 805.

9. *Id.* at 806.

10. 255 Cal. App. 2d 523 (1967).

11. 212 N.W.2d 55, 59 (Mich. App. 1973).

12. 404 A.2d 1256, 1260 (N.J. Super. Ct. 1979).

13. 410 N.E.2d 1207, 1216 (Mass. 1980).

14. 418 N.E.2d 286, 293 (Ind. Ct. App. 1981).

15. 669 A.2d 886, 888 (1983).

16. 699 P.2d 875, 879 (Alaska 1985).

17. *In re* J. S. & C., 324 A.2d 90 (1974); *In re* Jane B., 380 N.Y.S.2d 848 (1976); Chaffin

v. Frye, 45 Cal. App. 3d. 39 (1979); S. v. S., 608 S.W.2d 64 (Ky. Ct. App. 1980); Jacobsen v. Jacobsen, 314 N.W.2d (N.D. 1981); Irish v. Irish, 300 N.W.2d (Mo. Ct. App. 1982); J.L.P. (H) v. D.J.P., 643 S.W.2d (Mo. Ct. App. 1982); N.K.M. v. L.E.M., 606 N.W.2d 179 (Mo. Ct. App. 1980); M.J.P. v. J.G.P., 640 P.2d 966 (Okla. 1982); L. v. D., 630 S.W.2d 240 (Mo. Ct. App. 1982); Roberts v. Roberts, 489 N.E.2d 1067 (Ohio Ct. App. 1985); Constant A. v. Paul, C.A., 496 A.2d 1 (Penn. Super. Ct. 1985).

18. 324 S.E.2d 691 (Va. 1985).

19. 727 P.2d 830 (Ariz. Ct. App. 1986).

20. 478 U.S. 186, 106 S. Ct. 2841 (1986) *reh'g denied*, 478 U.S. 1039, 107 S. Ct. 29 (1986).

21. *Id.* at 834.

22. 736 P.2d 967, 970 (Mont. 1987).

23. N.H. Rev. Stat. Ann. § 170-B:4.

24. 530 A.2d 21 (N.H. 1987).

25. *Id.* at 24.

26. *Id.*

27. *Id.*

28. *Id.*

29. *Id.* at 28.

30. *Id.* at 28–29.

31. 552 N.E.2d 884 (Ohio 1990).

32. *Id.* at 888.

33. *Id.* at 889–890.

34. 601 N.Y.S.2d 215 (1993).

35. 609 N.Y.S.2d 209 (1994).

36. 622 N.Y.S.2d (4th Dept. 1994).

37. 628 A.2d 1271 (Vt. 1993).

38. *Id.* at 1272–73.

39. *Id.* at 1274.

40. *Id.* at 1276.

41. *Id.*

42. *619 N.E.2d 315, 319 (Mass. 1993).*

43. *Id.* at 319.

44. 632 A.2d 550 (N.J. Super. 1993).

45. 666 A.2d 535 (1995).

46. 583 N.Y.S.2d 997 (1992).

47. 662 N.Y.2d 835 (1994).

48. *Id.* at 841.

49. 636 N.Y.S.2d 716 (1995).

50. *653 N.E.2d 888, 892 (Ill. App. Ct. 1995).*

51. 715 N.E.2d 674 (Ill. App. Ct. 1999).

52. 662 A.2d 837 (D.C. 1995).

53. *Id.* at 860.

54. *Id.*

55. 785 N.E.2d 267 (Ind. Ct. App. 2003).

56. *Id.* at 270–71.

57. 804 N.E.2d 1253 (Ind. Ct. App. 2004).

58. *Id.* at 1257.

59. *Id.* at 1258.

60. *Id.* at 1259.

61. 44 S.W.3d 41, 56–57 (Tenn. Ct. App. 2000).

62. 806 A.2d 1179, 1184–85 (Del. Fam. Ct. 2001).

63. *Id.* at 1186.

64. 803 A.2d 1195 (Pa. 2002).

65. 516 N.W.2d 678 (Wis. 1994).

66. 931 P.2d 488 (Colo. Ct. App. 1996).

67. Adoption of Luke, 640 N.W.3d 374 (2002).

68. Adoption of Doe, 719 N.E.2d 1071 (1998).

69. 724 A.2d 1035 (1999).

70. 902 S.W.2d 254, 256 (Ark. Ct. App. 1995).

71. 730 So. 2d 1190, 1196 (Ala. 1998).

72. 478 U.S. 186, 106 S. Ct. 2841 (1986) *reh'g denied*, 478 U.S. 1039, 107 S. Ct. 29 (1986).

73. 539 U.S. 558, 123 S. Ct. 2472 (2003).

74. 724 A.2d 1035 (1999).

75. Conn. Gen. Stat. § 45a-724(a)(2) and (3); Conn. Gen. Stat. § 45a-731(5)(6) & (7).

76. Miss. Code Ann. § 93-17-3 (2005).

77. Utah Code Ann. § 78-30-1 (2005).

78. Conn. Gen. Stat. § 45a-726(a).

79. 16 Fla. L. Weekly C52 (Cit. Ct. 1991); *see* Starr, supra note 1, at 1512.

80. No. 87-24926 DA (Fla. Cir. Ct. 1989); *see* Starr, supra note 1, at 1512.

81. 656 So. 2d 902 (Fla., 1995).

82. *Id.* at 903.

83. *Id.* at 904.

84. Ann. M. Reding, *Lofton v. Kearney: Equal Protection Mandates Equal Adoption Rights*, 36 U.C. Davis L. Rev. 1285, 1297.

85. 359 F.3d 804 (11th Cir. 2004).

86. 539 U.S. 558,123 S. Ct. 2472 (2003).

87. *See supra* note 29.

7. The Present Status of the Law of Marriage in the United States and Abroad

1. 388 U.S. 1, 87 S. Ct. 1817 (1967).

2. 191 N.W.2d 185 (Minn. 1971), *appeal dismissed,* 409 U.S. 810, 93 S. Ct. 37 (1972).

3. *Id.* at 186.

4. *Id.* at 187.

5. 67 Misc. 2d 982 (N.Y. Sup. Ct. 1971).

6. *Id.* at 984.

7. 501 S.W.2d 588, 590 (Ky. 1973).

8. *Id.* at 589.

9. *Id.* at 590.

10. 522 P.2d 1187 (Wash. Ct. App. 1974), *review denied*, 84 Wash. 2d 1008 (Wash. 1974).

11. *Id.* at 1192.

12. *Id.* at 1195.

13. 673 F.2d 1036 (9th Cir. 1982).

14. *Id.* at 1040.

15. *Id.* at 1040–41.

16. *Id.* at 1042–43.

17. 476 A.2d 952 (Pa. Super. Ct. 1984).

18. *Id.* at 954.

19. *Id.* at 955.

20. 478 U.S. 186, 106 S. Ct. 2841 (1986) *reh'g denied*, 478 U.S. 1039, 107 S. Ct. 29 (1986).

21. *Id.* at 190–91.

22. 653 A.2d 307 (D.C. 1995).

23. *Id.* at 331.

24. 564 N.Y.S.2d 684 (N.Y. Sup. Ct. 1990), *aff'd*, 592 N.Y.2d 797 (N.Y. App. Div. 1993), *appeal dismissed*, 604 N.Y.S.2d 558 (N.Y. 1993).

25. *Id.* at 685.

26. 852 P.2d 44 (Haw. 1993).

27. 852 P.2d, at 56.

28. *Id.* at 56–57.

29. *Id.* at 57.

30. *Id.* at 61.

31. *Id.* at 61.

32. *Id.* at 63.

33. Baehr v. Miike, No. 91-1394 1996 WL 694235 (Haw. Cir. Ct. Dec. 3, 1996), *aff'd*, 950 P.2d 1234 (Haw. 1997).

34. HAW. CONST. ART I, § 23.

35. HAW. REV. STAT. § 572-1 (2003).

36. 1 U.S.C. § 7.

37. 28 U.S.C. § 1738C.

38. 744 A.2d 864 (1999).

39. *Id.* at 868.

40. *Id.* at 868–69.

41. *Id.* at 876.

42. *Id.* at 884.

43. *Id.* at 881–84.

44. *Id.*

45. *Id.* at 884–85.

46. *Id.* at 883.

47. *Id.* at 886.

48. *Id.*

49. Vt. Stat. Ann. tit. 15 § 1204(a) (2000).

50. Brause v. Bureau of Vital Statistics, No. 3AN-95-6552, 1998 WL 88743*6 (Alaska Super. Ct. Feb. 27, 1998).

51. Ak. Const. art. A, § 25.

52. No. 15-30, 2003 WL 23191114 (N.J. Super. Ct. Law Div. Nov. 5, 2003).

53. No. 49D13-211-PL-1946, 2003 WL 23119998 (Ind. Super. Ct. May 7, 2003), *aff'd*, 821 N.E.2d 15 (Ind. Ct. App. 2005).

54. 802 A.2d 170 (Conn. App. 2002), *cert. granted*, 806 A.2d 1066 (Conn. 2002).

55. *Id.* at 184.

56. 539 U.S. 558, 123 S. Ct. 2472 (2003).

57. *Id.* at 571, 2480.

58. *Id.* at 578, 2484.

59. 798 N.E.2d 941 (Mass. 2003).

60. *Id.* at 950.

61. *Id.* at 949.

62. *Id.* at 951.

63. *Id.* at 948.

64. *Id.*

65. *Id.*

66. *Id.* at 953.

67. *Id.* at 968.

68. *Id.*

69. *Id.* at 961.

70. *Id.* at 964.

71. *Id.* at 965.

72. *Id.* at 983 (Cordy, J. dissenting).

73. 77 P.3d 451 (Ariz. Ct. App. 2003).

74. *Id.* at 456–57.

75. *Id.* at 459–60.

76. *Id.* at 463–64.

77. *Lockyer v. San Francisco* and *Lewis v. Alfaro*.

78. Or. Const. art. XV, § 5a; Mont. Const. art. XIII, § 7.

79. Nev. Const. art. 1, § 7.

80. Mo. Const. art. 1, § 23.

81. Ohio Const. art. 15, § 11.

82. Neb. Const. art. I, § 29.

83. N.D. CONST. art. 11, § 28; UTAH CONST. art. I, § 29.

84. KY. CONST. pt. 2, §233A.

85. GA. CONST. art. I, § IV.

86. MICH. CONST. art. I, § 25.

87. OKLA. CONST. art. II, § 35(c).

88. ARK. CONST., amend. 83.

89. No. 04-2-4964-4, 2004 WL 1738447 (Wash. Super. Ct., Aug. 4, 2004).

90. No. 04-2-614-4, 2004 WL 1985215 (Wash. Super. Ct., Sept. 7, 2004).

91. Hernandez v. Robles, 2005 WL 363778 (N.Y. Sup. Ct., Feb. 4, 2005).

92. 2005 Conn. Pub. Acts 05–10.

93. 172 O.J. No. 2714, Par. 71 (2003).

94. *Id.* at Par. 71.

95. *Id.* at Par.

96. B.C.J. No. 994.

97. *Id.* at Par. 153.

98. *Id.* at Par. 7.

99. 2004 Y.K.S.C. 54.

100. In the Matter of a Reference by the Governor in Council concerning the Proposal for an Act Respecting Certain Aspects of Legal Capacity for Marriage for Civil Purposes, 2004 S.C.C. 79 (2004)

101. *Civil Marriage Act*, S.C. 2005, c. 33.

102. *A White Paper: An Analysis of the Law Regarding Same-Sex Marriage, Civil Unions, and Domestic Partnerships*, 38 FAM. L.Q. 339, at 408–412 (2004).

103. *Id.*

8. The Practical Benefits of Marriage

1. 12 CONN. GEN. STAT. § 45a-437.

2. Letter and enclosure to representative Henry J. Hyde from U.S. General Accounting Office (Jan. 31, 1997) no. B-275860 (Barry R. Bedrick, Associate General Counsel).

3. 42 U.S.C. § 402 (2002).

4. U.S. General Accounting Office, *supra* note 2, enclosure at 3.

Conclusion

1. Flynn v. Troesch, 373 Ill. 275, 292 (1940).

2. Patricia J. Falk, "The Gap between Psychosocial Assumptions and Empirical Research in Lesbian Mother Child Custody Cases," in *Redefining Families: Implications for Children's Development*, ed. Adele Eskeles Gottfried and Allen W. Gottfried (New York: Plenum Press, 1994), 132.

3. David Brooks, "The Power of Marriage," *New York Times*, November 22, 2003, A15.

4. Ibid.

5. Judith Stacey, *The Nation*, July 5, 2004, 25.

6. McKinniss, *Hartford Courant*, February 27, 2005, C1.

7. Stacey, 25.

8. For instance, the following statement by the Reverend Michael Schuenemeyer, minister for Lesbian, Gay, Bisexual, and Transgender Ministries of the United Church of Christ, Wider Church Ministries:

It is time for both church and society to come to terms with the truth that gender is not a defining characteristic for whether a couple is able to live the vocation of marriage, and that same-gender-loving couples are equally able to live the vocation of marriage as are heterosexual couples.

On July 4, 2005, the General Synod of the United Church of Christ (the representative body of the denomination) adopted a resolution supporting marriage equality for all couples without regard to gender, becoming the first mainline Christian denomination in the United States to do so. Many who know this denomination see this action as a natural evolution, consistent with the trajectory of more than thirty years of biblical study, theological reflection, and social policy actions concerning the welcome and full inclusion of lesbian, gay, bisexual, and transgender persons in church and society.

Marriage is about relationships, and the movement toward marriage equality has come in large measure because same-gender-loving relationships have been made increasingly real and visible. Countless UCC General Synod delegates have been transformed by their encounters with the real lives of the real people who are most profoundly affected by policies and legislation that discriminate. Many United Church of Christ members have come to know the integrity of the lives and the loves of lesbian, gay, bisexual, and transgender persons who sit next to them in the pew, serve with them in the mission of the church and as leaders on councils, boards, and committees. So when the time came for delegates to cast their votes on marriage equality, it was clear to an overwhelming number that they could not sit next to and across from their brothers and sisters and vote for discrimination. They voted for equality because they believe it is right, right for the church and right for society.

The voting delegates also recognized that there would be both cost and joy in that decision. Rev. John Thomas, general minister and president of the United Church of Christ, spoke of the cost a few days before the General Synod vote when he announced his support for the marriage equality resolution: "There will be a cost if the General Synod affirms marriage equality. I am well aware of that and in some ways dread it. But there will be a cost if we don't. Of that I am also sure. While it may not be the institution that will bear the cost, it will, I fear, be as it often is, the marginalized and vulnerable among us who will have to bear it. Before that prospect we ought to tremble as well."

What moves us forward in this movement toward equality are those who are willing to make clear who is bearing the cost of marriage discrimination in the United States. The stories of how this form of discrimination affects our families, friends, colleagues, neighbors, and their children make a difference. Through these stories more and more people come to know that marriage discrimination is not only costly and unfair but also unjust and inconsistent with the values of life, liberty, and the pursuit of happiness that we hold dear as a nation and project to the world. These stories help all of us to realize that those of us who are struggling for equality are right to be impatient. Regardless of where you are on the political continuum—conservative, liberal, progressive—there are good, strong, and compelling grounds for supporting marriage equality now.

In the final analysis, neither the church nor the state marries anyone. People marry each other. Any two consenting adults who have made their vows of marriage to each other are as married as any two people on the face of the planet. The state decides which couples it will give the rights, benefits, and responsibilities of civil, legal marriage, and religious bodies decide which couples they will recognize, respect, and bless with the ritual of marriage. The legal standard for the state under the U.S. Constitution is equal protection under the law for every citizen and respect for religious liberty. Each religious body gets to set its own standard. But in this nation, it is time for both church and society to recognize that civil marriage equality is right and discrimination is wrong.

9. "Toward a More Perfect Union," *New York Times Magazine*, May 9, 2004, 57.

10. *Hartford Courant*, reprinted from the *Washington Post*, September 24, 2003, A3.

11. *Hartford Courant*, September 15, 2005, A3.

References

Alderson, K. (2004). A phenomenological investigation of same-sex marriage. *Canadian Journal of Human Sexuality, 13*(2), 107–122.

Allen, G. (1997). The double-edged sword of genetic determinism: Social and political agendas in genetic studies of homosexuality, 1940–1994. In V. Rosario (Ed.), *Science and Homosexualities* (pp. 242–270). New York: Routledge.

Allen, L. S., & Gorski, R. A. (1992). Sexual orientation and the size of the anterior commisure in the human brain. *Proceedings of the National Academy of Sciences of the US, 89*, 7199–7202.

Allen, M., & Burrell, N. (1996). Comparing the impact of homosexual and heterosexual parents on children: Meta-analysis of existing research. *Journal of Homosexuality, 32*(2), 19–35.

American Psychiatric Association. (1952). *Diagnostic and statistical manual of mental disorders* (1st ed.). Washington, DC: Author.

American Psychiatric Association. (1973). *Diagnostic and statistical manual of mental disorders* (2nd ed.). Washington, DC: Author.

American Psychiatric Association. (1980). *Diagnostic and statistical manual of mental disorders* (3rd ed.). Washington, DC: Author.

American Psychiatric Association. (1987). *Diagnostic and statistical manual of mental disorders* (3rd rev. ed.). Washington, DC: Author.

American Psychiatric Association. (1994). *Diagnostic and statistical manual of mental disorders* (4th ed.). Washington, DC: Author.

Anderssen, N., Amlie, C., & Ytteroy, E. A. (2002). Outcomes for children with lesbian or gay parents: A review of studies from 1978 to 2000. *Scandinavian Journal of Psychology, 43*, 335–351.

Aroth, A. N., & Birnbaum, H. J. (1978). Adult sexual orientation and attraction to underage persons. *Archives of Sexual Behavior, 7*(3), 175–181.

Bailey, J. M., Bobrow, D., Wolfe, M., & Mikach, S. (1995). Sexual orientation of adult sons of gay fathers. *Developmental Psychology, 31*(1), 124–129.

Bailey, J. M., & Pillard, R. C. (1991). A genetic study of male sexual orientation. *Archives of General Psychiatry, 48*(12), 1089–1096.

Bailey, J. M., & Pillard, R. C. (1995). Genetics of human sexual orientation. *Annual Review of Sex Research*, 126–150.

Bailey, J. M., Pillard, R. C., Neale, M. C., & Agyei, Y. (1993). Heritable factors influence sexual orientation in women. *Archives of General Psychiatry, 50*(3), 217–223.

Baumrind, D. (1995). Commentary on sexual orientation research and social policy implications. *Developmental Psychology, 31*(1), 130–136.

Bayer, R. (1981). *Homosexuality and American psychiatry: The politics of diagnosis.* New York: Basic Books.

Bearman, P. S., & Brückner, H. (2002). Opposite-sex twins and adolescent same-sex attraction. *American Journal of Sociology, 107,* 1179–1205.

Bene, E. (1965a). On the genesis of female homosexuality. *British Journal of Psychiatry, 111,* 815–821.

Bene, E. (1965b). On the genesis of male homosexuality: An attempt at clarifying the role of the parents. *British Journal of Psychiatry, 111,* 803–813.

Bieber, I. (1967). Sexual deviations II: Homosexuality. In A. M. Freeman & H. I. Kaplan (Eds.), *Comprehensive textbook of psychiatry* (pp. 963–976). Baltimore: Williams and Wilkins.

Bieber, I., Dain, H. J., Dince, P. R., Drellich, M. G., Grand, H. G., Gundlach, R. H., Kremer, M. W., Rifkin, A. H., Wilbur, C. B., & Bieber, T. B. (1962). *Homosexuality: A psychoanalytic study.* New York: Basic Books.

Bigner, J. J., & Jacobsen, R. B. (1989a). The value of children to gay and heterosexual fathers. *Journal of Homosexuality, 18,* 163–171.

Bigner, J. J., & Jacobsen, R. B. (1989b). Parenting behaviors of homosexual and heterosexual fathers. *Journal of Homosexuality, 18,* 173–186.

Bigner, J. J., & Jacobsen, R. B. (1992). Adult responses to child behavior and attitudes towards fathering: Gay and nongay fathers. *Journal of Homosexuality, 23*(3), 99–113.

Black, J. C., & Cantor, D. J. (1989). *Child custody.* New York: Columbia University Press.

Blanchard, R. (1997). Birth order and sibling sex ratio in homosexual versus heterosexual males and females. *Annual Review of Sex Research, 8,* 27–67.

Blumstein, P., & Schwartz, P. (1983). *American couples: Money, work, sex.* New York: William Morrow.

Bos, H., van Balen, F., & van den Boom, D. (2004). Experience of parenthood, couple relationship, social support, and child-rearing goals in planned lesbian mother families. *Journal of Child Psychology and Psychiatry, 45*(4), 755–764.

Bowlby, J. (1969). *Attachment and loss, vol. 1.* New York: Basic Books.

Bowlby, J. (1980). *Attachment and loss, vol. 3.* New York: Basic Books.

Bozett, F. W. (1980). Gay fathers: How and why they disclose their homosexuality to their children. *Family Relations, 29,* 173–179.

Bozett, F. W. (1982). Heterogeneous couples in heterosexual marriages: Gay men and straight women. *Journal of Marital and Family Therapy, 8,* 81–89.

Bozett, F. W. (1987). Children of gay fathers. In F. W. Bozett (Ed.), *Gay and lesbian parents.* New York: Praeger.

Bozett, F. W. (1989). Gay fathers: A review of the literature. In F. W. Bozett (Ed.), *Homosexuality and the family* (pp. 137–162). New York: Harrington Park Press.

Brewaeys, A., Ponjaert, I., Van Hall, E. V., & Golombok, S. (1997). Donor insemination: Child development and family functioning in lesbian mother families. *Human Reproduction, 12*(6), 1349–1359.

Byne, W., Tobet, S., Mattiace, L., Lasco, M. S., Kemether, E., Edgar, M. A., Morgello, S., Buchsbaum, M. S., & Jones, L. B. (2001). The interstitial nuclei of the human anterior hypothalamus: An investigation of variation within sex, sexual orientation, and HIV status. *Hormones and Behavior, 40*, 86–92.

Cameron, P., & Cameron, K. (1996). Homosexual parents. *Adolescence, 31*, 757–776.

Chan, R., Brooks, C., Raboy, B., & Patterson, C. (1998). Division of labor among lesbian and heterosexual parents: Associations with children's adjustment. *Journal of Family Psychology, 12*(3), 402–419.

Chan, R., Raboy, B., & Patterson, C. (1998). Psychosocial adjustment among children conceived via donor insemination by lesbian and heterosexual mothers. *Child Development, 69*, 443–457.

Ciano-Boyce, C., & Shelley-Sireci, L. (2002). Who is mommy tonight: Lesbian parenting issues. *Journal of Homosexuality, 43*(2), 1–13.

Coontz, S. (1992). *The way we never were: American families and the nostalgia trap.* New York: Basic Books.

Coontz, S. (1997). *The way we really are: Coming to terms with America's changing families.* New York: Basic Books.

Crompton, L. (2003). *Homosexuality and civilization.* Cambridge, MA: Belknap Press of Harvard University Press.

DiLapi, E. M. (1989). Lesbian mothers and the motherhood hierarchy. *Journal of Homosexuality, 18*(1–2), 101–121.

Dundas, S., & Kaufman, M. (2000). The Toronto lesbian family study. *Journal of Homosexuality, 40*(2), 65–79.

Dupree, M., Mustanski, B., Bocklandt, S., Nievergelt, C., & Hamer, D. (2004). A candidate gene study of CYP19 (aromatase) and male sexual orientation. *Behavior Genetics, 34*(3), 243–250.

Elizur, Y., & Mintzer, A. (2003). Gay males' intimate relationship quality: The roles of attachment security, gay identity, social support, and income. *Personal Relationships, 10*, 411–435.

Ellis, L., & Ames, M. A. (1987). Neurohormonal functioning and sexual orientation: A theory of homosexuality-heterosexuality. *Psychological Bulletin, 101*(2), 233–258.

Erikson, E. H. (1950). *Childhood and society.* New York: W. W. Norton.

Everett, C. A. (Ed.). (1998). *Child custody: Legal decisions and family outcomes.* New York: Haworth Press.

Falk, P. J. (1994). The gap between psychosocial assumptions and empirical research in lesbian-mother child custody cases. In A. E. Gottfried & A. W. Gottfried (Eds.), *Redefining families: Implications for children's development* (pp. 131–156). New York: Plenum.

Fausto-Sterling, A. (2000). *Sexing the body.* New York: Basic Books.

Fitzgerald, Bridget (1999). Children of lesbian and gay parents: A review of the literature. *Marriage and Family Review, 29*(1), 57–75.

Flaks, D. K., Ficher, I., Masterpasqua, F., & Joseph, G. (1995). Lesbians choosing motherhood: A comparative study of lesbian and heterosexual parents and their children. *Developmental Psychology, 31*(1), 105–114.

Fone, B. (2000). *Homophobia.* New York: Metropolitan Books.

Ford, C. S., & Beach, F. A. (1951). *Patterns of sexual behavior.* New York: Harper and Row.

Freud, S. (1957). Group psychology and the analysis of the ego. In J. Rickman & C. Brenner (Eds.), *A general selection from the works of Sigmund Freud* (pp. 169–209). Garden City, NY: Doubleday Anchor Books. (Original work published 1921)

Freud, S. (1963). The psychogenesis of a case of homosexuality in a woman. In *Sexuality and the psychology of love* (pp. 133–159). New York: Collier Books. (Original work published 1920)

Fulcher, M., Chan, R. W., Raboy, B., & Patterson, C. (2002). Contact with grandparents among children conceived via donor insemination by lesbian and heterosexual mothers. *Parenting: Science and Practice, 2*(1), 61–76.

Gartrell, N., Banks, A., Hamilton, J., Reed, N., Bishop, H., & Rodas, C. (1999). The national lesbian family study: Interviews with mothers of toddlers. *American Journal of Orthopsychiatry, 69,* 362–369.

Gartrell, N., Banks, A., Reed, N., Hamilton, J., Rodas, C., & Deck, A. (2000). The national lesbian family study 3: Interviews with mothers of five-year-olds. *American Journal of Orthopsychiatry, 70*(4), 542–548.

Gartrell, N., Hamilton, J., Banks, A., Mosbacher, D., Reed, N., Sparks, C. H., & Bishop, H. (1996). The national lesbian family study: Interviews with prospective mothers. *American Journal of Orthopsychiatry, 66*(2), 272–281.

Gebhard, P. H., & Johnson, A. B. (1998). *The Kinsey data: Marginal tabulations of the 1938–1963 interviews conducted by the Institute for Sex Research.* Bloomington: Indiana University Press.

Gemelli, R. (1996). *Normal child and adolescent development.* Washington, DC: American Psychiatric Press.

Gershon, T. D., Tschann, J. M., & Jemerin, J. M. (1999). Stigmatization, self-esteem, and coping among the adolescent children of lesbian mothers. *Journal of Adolescent Health, 24,* 437–445.

Golombok, S., Perry, B., Burston, A., Murray, C., Mooney-Somers, J., Stevens, M., & Golding, J. (2003). Children with lesbian parents: A community study. *Developmental Psychology, 39*(1), 20–33.

Golombok, S., Spencer, S., & Rutter, M. (1983). Children in lesbian and single-parent households: Psychosexual and psychiatric appraisal. *Journal of Child Psychology and Psychiatry, 24*(4), 551–572.

Golombok, S., & Tasker, F. (1996). Do parents influence the sexual orientation of their children? Findings from a longitudinal study of lesbian families. *Developmental Psychology, 32*(1), 3–11.

Golombok, S., Tasker, F., & Murray, C. (1997). Children raised in fatherless families from infancy: Family relationships and the socioemotional development of children of lesbian and single heterosexual mothers. *Journal of Child Psychology and Psychiatry, 38*(7), 783–791.

Gonsiorek, J. C. (1991). The empirical basis for the demise of the illness model of homosexuality. In J. C. Gonsiorek & J. D. Weinrich (Eds.), *Homosexuality: Research implications for public policy* (pp. 115–136). Newbury Park, CA: Sage.

Gottman, J. M., Levenson, R. W., Gross, J., Frederickson, B. L., McCoy, K., Rosenthal, L., Ruef, A., & Yoshimoto, D. (2003). Correlates of gay and lesbian couples' relationship satisfaction and relationship dissolution. *Journal of Homosexuality, 45*(1), 23–43.

Gottman, J. M., Levenson, R. W., Swanson, C., Swanson, K., Tyson, R., & Yoshimoto, D. (2003). Observing gay, lesbian and heterosexual couples relationships: Mathematical modeling of conflict interaction. *Journal of Homosexuality, 45*(1), 65–91.

Gottman, J. S. (1989). Children of gay and lesbian parents. *Marriage and Family Review, 14*(3–4), 177–196.

Gottman, J. S. (1990). Children of gay and lesbian parents. In F. W. Bozett & M. B. Sussman (Eds.), *Homosexuality and family relations*. New York: Harrington Park Press.

Green, G. D., & Bozett, F. W. (1991). Lesbian mothers and gay fathers. In J. C. Gonsiorek & J. D. Weinrich (Eds.), *Homosexuality: Research implications for public policy* (pp. 197–214). Newbury Park, CA: Sage Publications.

Green, R. (1978). Sexual Identity of 37 children raised by homosexual or transsexual parents. *American Journal of Psychiatry, 135*(6), 692–697.

Green, R. (1982). The best interest of the child with a lesbian mother. *Bulletin of the American Academy of Psychiatry and the Law, 10*, 7–15.

Green, R., Mandel, J. B., Hotvedt, M. E., Gray, J., & Smith, L. (1986). Lesbian mothers and their children: A comparison with solo parent heterosexual mothers and their children. *Archives of Sexual Behavior, 15*(2), 167–185.

Green, R., & Young, R. (2001). Hand preference, sexual preference, and transexualism. *Archives of Sexual Behavior, 30*(6), 565–574.

Groth, A. N., & Birnbaum, H. J. (1978). Adult sexual orientation and attraction to underage persons. *Archives of Sexual Behavior, 7*(3), 175–181.

Haack-Moller, A., & Mohl, H. (1984). Born af lesbiske modre [Children of Lesbian Mothers]. *Dansk Psykolog, 38*, 316–318.

Haldeman, D. (1991). Sexual orientation conversion therapy for gay men and lesbians: A scientific examination. In J. C. Gonsiorek & J. D. Weinrich (Eds.), *Homosexuality: Research implications for public policy* (pp. 149–160). Newbury Park, CA: Sage.

Hall, J. A. Y., & Kimura, D. (1995). Sexual orientation and performance on sexually dimorphic motor tasks. *Archives of Sexual Behavior, 24*(4), 395–408.

Hall, M. (1978). Lesbian families: Cultural and clinical issues. *Social Work, 23,* 380–385.

Hamer, D. H., & Copeland, P. (1994). *The science of desire.* New York: Simon and Schuster.

Hamer, D. H., Hu, S., Magnuson, V. L., Hu, N., & Pattatucci, A. (1993). A linkage between DNA markers on the X chromosome and male sexual orientation. *Science, 261*(5119), 321–327.

Harris, M. B., & Turner, P. H. (1986). Gay and lesbian parents. *Journal of Homosexuality, 12*(2), 101–113.

Herek, G. (1998). Bad science in the service of stigma: A critique of the Cameron group's survey studies. In G. Herek (Ed.), *Stigma and sexual orientation.* Thousand Oaks, CA: Sage Publications.

Hershberger, S. (1997). A twin registry study of male and female sexual orientation. *Journal of Sex Research, 34*(2), 212–222.

Hoeffer, B. (1981). Children's acquisition of sex-role behavior in lesbian-mother families. *American Journal of Orthopsychiatry, 51*(3), 536–545.

Hooker, E. (1957). The adjustment of the male overt homosexual. *Journal of Projective Techniques, 21*(1), 18–31.

Hotvedt, M. E., & Mandel, J. B. (1982). Children of lesbian mothers. In W. Paul, J. D. Weinrich, J. C. Gonsiorek, & M. E. Hotvedt (Eds.), *Homosexuality: Social, psychological, and biological issues* (pp. 275–285). Beverly Hills, CA: Sage.

Hu, S., Pattatucci, A. M., Patterson, C., Li, L., Fulker, D. W., Cherny, S. S., Kruglyak, L., & Hamer, D. H. (1995). Linkage between sexual orientation and chromosome Xq28 in males but not in females. *Nature Genetics, 11,* 248–256.

Huggins, S. L. (1989). A comparative study of self-esteem of adolescent children of divorced lesbian mothers and divorced heterosexual mothers. *Journal of Homosexuality, 18,* 123–135.

Javaid, G. (1993). The children of homosexual and heterosexual single mothers. *Child Psychiatry and Human Development, 23*(4), 235–248.

Julien, D., Chartrand, E., & Begin, J. (1999). Social networks, structural interdependence, and conjugal adjustment in heterosexual, gay, and lesbian couples. *Journal of Marriage and the Family, 61,* 516–530.

Julien, D., Chartrand, E., Simard, M., Bouthillier, D., & Begin, J. (2003). Conflict, social support, and relationship quality: An observational study of heterosexual, gay male, and lesbian couples' communication. *Journal of Family Psychology, 17*(3), 419–428.

Kallmann, F. (1952). Comparative twin study on the genetic aspects of male homosexuality. *Journal of Nervous and Mental Disease, 115,* 283–298.

Kendler, K. S., Thornton, L. M., Gilman, S. E., & Kessler, R. C. (2000). Sexual orientation in a US national sample of twin and non-twin sibling pairs. *American Journal of Psychiatry, 157,* 1843–1846.

Kinsey, A. (1948). *Sexual behavior in the human male.* Philadelphia: W. B. Saunders.

Kinsey, A. (1953). *Sexual behavior in the human female.* Philadelphia: W. B. Saunders.

Kirkpatrick, M., Smith, C., & Roy, R. (1981). Lesbian mothers and their children: A comparative survey. *American Journal of Orthopsychiatry, 51*(3), 545–551.

Kotelchuck, M. (1972). *The nature of the child's tie to his father.* Unpublished doctoral dissertation, Harvard University.

Kraft, P. (1983). Recent developments: Lesbian child custody. *Harvard Women's Law Journal, 6,* 183–192.

Kurdek, L. (1991). Correlates of relationship satisfaction in cohabiting gay and lesbian couples: Integration of contextual, investment, and problem-solving models. *Journal of Personality and Social Psychology, 61*(6), 910–922.

Kurdek, L. (1992). Assumptions versus standards: The validity of two relationship cognitions in heterosexual and homosexual couples. *Journal of Family Psychology, 6*(2), 164–170.

Kurdek, L. (1994a). Areas of conflict for gay, lesbian, and heterosexual couples: What couples argue about influences relationship satisfaction. *Journal of Marriage and the Family, 56*(4), 923–934.

Kurdek, L. (1994b). Conflict resolution styles of gay, lesbian, heterosexual nonparent, and heterosexual parent couples. *Journal of Marriage and the Family, 56*(3), 705–722.

Kurdek, L. (1994c). The nature and correlates of relationship quality in gay, lesbian, and heterosexual cohabiting couples. In B. Greene & G. Herek (Eds.), *Lesbian and gay psychology: Theory, research, and clinical applications.* London: Sage Publications.

Kurdek, L. (1998). Relationship outcomes and their predictors: Longitudinal evidence from heterosexual married, gay cohabiting, and lesbian cohabiting couples. *Journal of Marriage and the Family, 60*(3), 553–568.

Kurdek, L. (2003). Differences between gay and lesbian cohabiting couples. *Journal of Social and Personal Relationships, 20*(4), 411–436.

Kurdek, L. (2004). Are gay and lesbian cohabiting couples *really* different from heterosexual married couples? *Journal of Marriage and the Family, 66,* 880–900.

Kurdek, L., & Schmitt, P. (1986a). Early development of relationship quality in heterosexual married, heterosexual cohabiting, gay, and lesbian couples. *Developmental Psychology, 22*(3), 305–309.

Kurdek, L., & Schmitt, P. (1986b). Relationship quality of partners in heterosexual married, heterosexual cohabiting, and gay and lesbian relationships. *Journal of Personality and Social Psychology, 51*(4), 711–720.

Kweskin, S. L., & Cook, A. S. (1982). Heterosexual and homosexual mothers self-described sex-role behavior and ideal sex-role behavior in children. *Sex Roles, 8,* 967–975.

Lalumiere, M. L., Blanchard, R., & Zucker, K. J. (2000). Sexual orientation and handedness in men and women: A meta-analysis. *Psychological Bulletin, 126*(4), 575.

Lamb, M. E. (1976). *The role of the father in child development.* New York: John Wiley and Sons.

LeVay, S. (1991). A difference in hypothalamic structure between heterosexual and homosexual men. *Science, 253*(5023), 1034–1037.

LeVay, S. (1996). *Queer science.* Cambridge, MA: MIT Press.

Lewis, K. G. (1980). Children of lesbians: Their point of view. *Social Work, 25,* 198–203.

Lyons, T. A. (1983). Lesbian mothers' custody fears. *Women and Therapy, 2,* 231–240.

MacCallum, F., & Golombok, S. (2004). Children raised in fatherless families from infancy: A follow-up of children of lesbian and single heterosexual mothers at early adolescence. *Journal of Child Psychology and Psychiatry, 45*(8), 1407–1419.

Mackey, R., Diemer, M., & O'Brien, B. (2000). Psychological intimacy in the lasting relationships of heterosexual and same-gender couples. *Sex Roles, 43*(3–4), 201–227.

Mackey, R., Diemer, M., & O'Brien, B. (2004). Relational factors in understanding satisfaction in the lasting relationships of same-sex and heterosexual couples. *Journal of Homosexuality, 47*(1), 111–136.

Mahler, M. S. (1968). *On human symbiosis and the vicissitudes of individuation: Infantile psychosis, vol. 1.* New York: International Universities Press.

McCormick, C. M., & Witelson, S. F. (1994). Functional cerebral asymmetry and sexual orientation in men and women. *Behavioral Neuroscience, 108*(3), 525–532.

McNeill, K. F., Rienzi, B. M., & Kposowa, A. (1998). Families and parenting: A comparison of lesbian and heterosexual mothers. *Psychological Reports, 82,* 59–62.

Metz, M., Rosser, B. R., & Strapko, N. (1994). Differences in conflict-resolution styles among heterosexual, gay, and lesbian couples. *Journal of Sex Research, 31*(4), 293–308.

Meyer-Bahlburg, H. F. L., Ehrhardt, A. A., Rosen, L. R., Gruen, R. S., Veridiano, N. P., Vann, F. H., & Neuwalder, H. F. (1995). Prenatal estrogens and the development of homosexual orientation. *Developmental Psychology, 31*(1), 12–21.

Meyer-Bahlburg, H. F. L., Gruen, R. S., New, M. I., & Bell, J. I. (1996). Gender change from female to male in classical congenital adrenal hyperplasia. *Hormones and Behavior, 30*(4), 319–332.

Miller, B. (1979). Gay fathers and their children. *Family Coordinator, 28*(4), 544–552.

Miller, B. (1995). *Out of the past.* New York: Vintage Books.

Miller, J. A., Jacobsen, R. B, & Bigner, J. J. (1981). The child's home environment for lesbian vs. heterosexual mothers: A neglected area of research. *Journal of Homosexuality, 7*(1), 49–56.

Moses, A. E., & Hawkins, R. O. (1982). *Counseling lesbian women and gay men: A life-issues approach.* St. Louis: C. V. Mosby.

Mucklow, B. M., & Phelan, G. K. (1979). Lesbian and traditional mothers' responses to adult response to child behavior and self-concept. *Psychological Reports, 44,* 880–882.

Mustanski, B., Bailey, J., & Kaspar, S. (2002). Dermatoglyphics, handedness, sex, and sexual orientation. *Archives of Sexual Behavior, 31*(1), 113–122.

Mustanski, B., Chivers, M., & Bailey, J. (2002). A critical review of recent biological research on human sexual orientation. *Annual Review of Sex Research, 13,* 89–140.

Nicolosi, J. (1995). The importance of the father-son relationship. In R. M. Baird & M. K. Baird (Eds.), *Homosexuality: Debating the issues.* Amherst, NY: Prometheus Books.

Nungesser, L. G. (1980). Theoretical bases for research on the acquisition of social sex-roles by children of lesbian mothers. *Journal of Homosexuality, 5*(3), 177–187.

O'Connell, A. (1993). Voices from the heart: The developmental impact of a mother's lesbianism on her adolescent children. *Smith College Studies in Social Work, 63*(3), 281–299.

Orlebeke, J. F., Boomsma, D. I., Gooren, L. J., Verschoor, A. M., & van den Bree, M. J. (1992). Elevated sinistrality in transsexuals. *Neuropsychology, 6*(4), 351–355.

Ostrow, D. (1977). *Gay and straight parents: What about the children?* Unpublished bachelor's thesis, Hampshire College, Amherst, MA.

Pagelow, M. D. (1980). Heterosexual and lesbian single mothers: A comparison of problems, coping and solutions. *Journal of Homosexuality, 5,* 198–204.

Parks, C. (1998). Lesbian parenthood: A review of the literature. *American Journal of Orthopsychiatry, 68*(3), 376–389.

Pattatucci, A. (1998). Biopsychosocial interactions and the development of sexual orientation. In C. Patterson & A. D'Augelli (Eds.), *Lesbian, gay, and bisexual identities in families: Psychological perspectives* (pp. 19–39). New York: Oxford University Press.

Pattatucci, A., & Hamer, D. (1995). Development and familiality of sexual orientation in females. *Behavior Genetics, 25,* 407–420.

Pattatucci, A., Patterson, C., Benjamin, J., & Hamer, D. (1998). A crossover interaction between sex, sexual orientation, and handedness. *Laterality: Asymmetries of body, brain, & cognition, 3*(4), 331–342.

Patterson, C. (1992). Children of lesbian and gay parents. *Child Development, 63,* 1025–1042.

Patterson, C. (1994). Children of the lesbian baby boom: Behavioral adjustment, self-concepts and sex-role identity. In I. B. Greene & G. M. Herek (Eds.), *Contemporary perspectives on lesbian and gay psychology: Theory, research and applications* (pp. 156–175). London: Sage Publications.

Patterson, C. (1995a). Families of the lesbian baby boom: Parents' division of labor and children's adjustment. *Developmental Psychology, 31*(1), 115–123.

Patterson, C. (1995b). Lesbian mothers, gay fathers, and their children. In A. R. D'Augelli & C. J. Patterson (Eds.), *Lesbian, gay and bisexual identities across the lifespan* (pp. 262–290). New York: Oxford University Press.

Patterson, C. (1996). Lesbian mothers and their children: Findings from the Bay Area Families Study. In J. Laird & R. Green (Eds.), *Lesbians and gays in couples and families: A handbook for therapists.* San Francisco: Jossey-Bass.

Patterson, C. (1998). The family lives of children born to lesbian mothers. In C. Patterson & A. D'Augelli (Eds.), *Lesbian, gay, and bisexual identities in families: Psychological perspectives.* New York: Oxford University Press.

Patterson, C., Fulcher, M., & Wainwright, J. (1987). Children of lesbian and gay parents. *Child Development, 63,* 188.

Patterson, C., Hurt, S., & Mason, C. (1998). Families of the lesbian baby boom: Children's contact with grandparents and other adults. *American Journal of Orthopsychiatry, 68*(3), 390–399.

Paul, J. P. (1986). *Growing up with a gay, lesbian, or bisexual parent: An exploratory study of experiences and perceptions.* Unpublished doctoral dissertation, University of California at Berkeley.

Pennington, S. B. (1987). Children of lesbian mothers. In F. W. Bozett (Ed.), *Gay and lesbian parents* (pp. 58–74). New York: Praeger.

Peplau, L., & Cochran, S. (1990). A relational perspective on homosexuality. In D. McWhirter, S. Sanders, & J. Reinisch (Eds.), *Homosexuality/heterosexuality: Concepts of sexual orientation.* New York: Oxford University Press.

Perry, B., Burston, A., Stevens, M., Golding, J., Steele, H., & Golombok, S. (2004). Children's play narratives: What they tell us about lesbian-mother families. *American Journal of Orthopsychiatry, 74*(4), 467–479.

Pillard, R. C. (1991). Masculinity and femininity in homosexuality: "Inversion" revisited. In J. C. Gonsiorek & J. D. Weinrich (Eds.), *Homosexuality: Research implications for public policy* (pp. 32–43). Newbury Park, CA: Sage.

Pine, F., & Furer, M. (1963). Studies of the separation-individuation phase. In *The psychoanalytic study of the child.* New York: International Universities Press.

Rahman, Q., & Wilson, G. D. (2003). Born gay? The psychobiology of human sexual orientation. *Personality and Individual Differences, 34*(8), 1337–1382.

Rand, C., Graham, D. L. R., & Rawlings, E. I. (1982). Psychological health and factors the court seeks to control in lesbian mother custody trials. *Journal of Homosexuality, 8,* 27–39.

Rees, R. L. (1979). *A comparison of children of lesbian and single heterosexual mothers on three measures of socialization.* Unpublished doctoral dissertation, California School of Professional Psychology, Berkeley.

Rice, G., Anderson, C., Risch, N., & Ebers, G. (1999). Male homosexuality: Absence of linkage to microsatellite markers at Xq28. *Science, 284,* 665–667.

Richardson, D. (1981). Lesbian mothers. In J. Hart & D. Richardson (Eds.), *The theory and practice of homosexuality*. London: Routledge and Kegan Paul.

Riddle, D., & Arguelles, M. (1981). Children of gay parents: Homophobia's victims. In I. R. Stuart & L. E. Abt (Eds.), *Children of separation and divorce: Management and treatment* (pp. 174–197). New York: Van Nostrand Reinhold.

Riley, M. (1975). The avowed lesbian mother and her right to child custody: A constitutional challenge that can no longer be denied. *San Diego Law Review, 12,* 799–864.

Rist, D. Y. (1995). Are homosexuals born that way? In R. M. Baird & M. K. Baird (Eds.), *Homosexuality: Debating the issues* (pp. 71–79). Amherst, NY: Prometheus Books.

Schulenberg, J. (1985). *Gay parenting: A complete guide for gay men and lesbians with children*. New York: Anchor Books.

Schwartz, J. (1985). *An exploration of personality traits in daughters of lesbian mothers*. Unpublished doctoral dissertation, California School of Professional Psychology, San Diego, CA.

Siegelman, M. (1972). Adjustment of homosexual and heterosexual women. *American Journal of Psychiatry, 120,* 477–481.

Siegenthaler, A. L., & Bigner, J. J. (2000). The value of children to lesbian and nonlesbian mothers. *Journal of Homosexuality, 39*(2), 73–91.

Solomon, S., Rothblum, E., & Balsam, K. (2004). Pioneers in partnership: Lesbian and gay male couples in civil unions compared with those not in civil unions and married heterosexual siblings. *Journal of Family Psychology, 18*(2), 275–286.

Spiro, M. (1958). *Children of the Kibbutz*. Cambridge, MA: Harvard University Press.

Spitzer, R. L. (2003). Can some gay men and lesbians change their sexual orientation? 200 participants reporting a change from homosexual to heterosexual orientation. *Archives of Sexual Behavior, 32*(5), 403–418.

Stacey, J. (1996). *In the name of the family: Rethinking family values in a postmodern age*. Boston: Beacon Press.

Stacey, J., & Biblarz, T. (2001). (How) Does the sexual orientation of parents matter? *American Sociological Review, 66,* 159–183.

Steckel, A. (1985). *Separation-individuation in children of lesbian and heterosexual couples*. Unpublished doctoral dissertation, Wright Institute Graduate School, Berkeley, CA.

Steckel, A. (1987). Psychosocial development of children of lesbian mothers. In F. W. Bozett (Ed.), *Gay and lesbian parents* (pp. 75–85). New York: Praeger.

Susoeff, S. (1985). Assessing children's best interests when a parent is gay or lesbian: Toward a rational custody standard. *UCLA Law Review, 32,* 852–903.

Swaab, D. F., & Hofman, M. A. (1990). An enlarged suprachiasmatic nucleus in homosexual men. *Brain Research, 537,* 141–148.

Tasker, F., & Golombok, S. (1995). Adults raised as children in lesbian families. *American Journal of Orthopsychiatry, 65*(2), 203–215.

Tasker, F., & Golombok, S. (1997a). *Growing up in a lesbian family: Effects on child development.* New York: Guilford Press.

Tasker, F., & Golombok, S. (1997b). Young people's attitudes toward living in a lesbian family: A longitudinal study of children raised by post-divorce lesbian mothers. In C. Everett (Ed.), *Child custody: Legal decisions and family outcomes.* New York: Haworth Press.

Terry, J. (1997). The seductive power of science in the making of deviant subjectivity. In V. Rosario (Ed.), *Science and homosexualities* (pp. 271–295). New York: Routledge.

Thompson, N., McCandless, B., & Strickland, B. (1971). Personal adjustment of male and female homosexuals and heterosexuals. *Journal of Abnormal Psychology, 78,* 237–240.

Turner, P. H., Scadden, L., & Harris, M. B. (1990). Parenting in gay and lesbian families. *Journal of Gay and Lesbian Psychotherapy, 1*(3), 55–66.

Vanfraussen, K., Ponjaert-Kristoffersen, I., & Brewaeys, A. (2003). Family functioning in lesbian families created by donor insemination. *American Journal of Orthopsychiatry, 73*(1), 78–90.

Wainright, J., Russell, S., & Patterson, C. (2004). Psychosocial adjustment, school outcomes, and romantic relationships of adolescents with same-sex parents. *Child Development, 75*(6), 1886–1898.

The Wolfenden Report (1963). New York: Stein and Day.

Zucker, K. J., Bradley, S. J., Oliver, G., Blake, J., Fleming, S., & Hood, J. (1996). Psychosexual development of women with congenital adrenal hyperplasia. *Hormones and Behavior, 30*(4), 300–318.

Index

limbic region, 42
linguistic function, 41
Lofton v. Secretary of Department of Children and Family Services (2004), 102, 112–13
Lombroso, Cesar, 28
loss of consortium, 136, 146–47
Louisiana, 128
Loving, Richard, 3
Loving v. Virginia (1965), 3–5, 6, 115, 117, 118, 124, 126, 130, 131

MacCallum, F., 53, 56, 68, 96, 98
Mackey, R., 76–77
Mandel, J. B., 52, 86–87, 89, 97, 98
marital breakdown, 19
Marmor, Judd, 36
Maryland, 11
Massachusetts: homosexual adoption in, 103, 107; same-sex marriage in, 77, 125–28, 133, 135, 153, 156
Mason, C., 60, 61
Masterpasqua, F., 65–66
masturbation, 13
Matter of Adoption of Child by JMG (1993), 107
Matter of Estate of Cooper (1990), 120, 130
McCormick, C. M., 41
McNeill, K. F., 66
medical leave, 143, 148
Medicare, 141
Menninger, Karl, 36
Metz, M., 76
Michigan: cohabitation prohibited in, 12; foster care in, 103; same-sex marriage prohibited in, 128, 129–30
Middle Ages, 25–26
military service, 82, 139, 141–42
Miller, B., 50, 71, 93–94
Miller, J. A., 59–60
Minnesota: adultery statute in, 12; same-sex marriage prohibited in, 115–16
Minnesota Multiphasic Personality Inventory (MMPI), 33
Mississippi: adultery statute in, 12; homo-

sexual adoption limited in, 111; same-sex marriage prohibited in, 128
Missouri, 128, 129
molestation, 50, 71, 92, 93–94
monozygotic twins, 43
Montana: homosexual adoption in, 104; same-sex marriage prohibited in, 128, 129
Montesquieu, Charles de Secondat, Baron de, 26
Mooney-Somers, J., 65
moral development, 90, 93
Morrison v. Sadler (2003), 125
mortgages, 144
motor skills, 41
MP v. SP (1979), 103
Mucklow, B. M., 60
Murray, C., 49–50, 52, 65, 68
Mustanski, B., 41, 42
mutuality, 72

Nadler v. Superior Court (1967), 103
names, of children, 60, 61
National Housing Act, 144
National Service Life Insurance, 141
natural resources law, 139, 145
Neale, M. C., 71
Nebraska: homosexual adoption in, 110; same-sex marriage prohibited in, 128, 129
Nebraska Psychological Association, 78
Netherlands, 25, 55, 69, 77, 133, 156
neuroanatomy, 39–41, 42, 45
neuropsychology, 40
Nevada, 128, 129
New Hampshire, 104–5, 111, 113
New Jersey: child custody in, 103; homosexual adoption in, 107–8; same-sex marriage prohibited in, 125
New Mexico: cohabitation prohibited in, 12; divorce law in, 19
New Paltz (N.Y.), 153
New York: anti-sodomy statute in, 13–14; divorce law in, 19; homosexual adoption in, 106, 107–8; inheritance rights denied in, 120; same-sex marriage pre-

toddlerhood, 83

toys, 51, 52

transsexuals, 41, 42, 97, 99

Turner, P. H., 99

twins, 43

Tyson, R., 76

Ulrichs, Karl, 27

United Church of Christ, 167n8

universal latency fear, 99

unjust enrichment, 138

Utah: homosexual adoption limited in, 111; same-sex marriage prohibited in, 128, 129

Value of Children scale, 67, 72

Vanfraussen, K., 55, 63–64

Van Hall, E. V., 55–56, 63

verbal skills, 40

Vermont: civil unions in, 77, 123–24, 131, 133; homosexual adoption in, 106–7

veterans' benefits, 139, 141–42, 145, 147

Virginia: antimiscegenation statute in, 3, 4, 115; anti-sodomy statute in, 13; homosexual adoption in, 102–3

visitation rights, 137–38, 148

wage garnishment, 144–45

Wainwright, J., 50, 56–57, 86, 96

Washington state: homosexual adoption in, 103; same-sex marriage prohibited in, 118; state DOMA held unconstitutional in, 130

West Virginia, 11–12

wills, 136, 142, 147, 148

Wilson, David, 135–36

Wisconsin, 110

Witelson, S. F., 41

Wolfenden, John, 38

women's movement, 20

working parents, 61, 62, 92

wrongful death, 147

Xq28 chromosome, 44

Yoshimoto, D., 76

Yukon Territory, 132

zones of privacy, 2

Zucker, K. J., 41

About the Authors

Donald J. Cantor is a partner in the Hartford, Connecticut, law firm of Hyman & Cantor P.C. Attorney Cantor earned his LL.B. at Harvard; he is the author of *Escape from Marriage* (1971) and coauthor with James C. Black of *Child Custody* (1989), and has contributed articles to the *Atlantic Monthly*, the *Humanist*, and the *Journal of Criminal Law, Criminology, and Police Science*. He is listed in *Who's Who in Connecticut, Who's Who in the East, Who's Who in American Law, Who's Who in America, Best Lawyers in America*, and *Who's Who in the World*.

Elizabeth Cantor is a licensed clinical psychologist who lives and works in Rhode Island. She received her A.B. in art history from Brown University in 1983, her CAGS in school psychology from Gallaudet University in 1987, and her Ph.D. in child clinical psychology from the University of Denver in 1996.

James C. Black is an eminent child and adolescent psychiatrist with Clinical Associates of Greater Hartford and is associate clinical professor of psychiatry at the University of Connecticut. He earned his M.D. at Loyola University's Stritch School of Medicine in 1959 and is the coauthor with Donald J. Cantor of *Child Custody* (1989).

Campbell D. Barrett, a partner in the Hartford, Connecticut, law firm of Budlong & Barrett, LLC, focuses his practice primarily on matrimonial and appellate matters. In 2002 Attorney Barrett was recognized as one of Connecticut's top thirty "New Leaders of Law" by the *Connecticut Law Tribune*, and he was the 2005 recipient of the Judge Maxwell Heiman Memorial Award by the Hartford County Bar Association. Attorney Barrett is a graduate of American University's Washington College of Law in Washington, D.C., and of Trinity College in Hartford.